Travel Writing in an Age of Global Quarantine

# Travel Writing in an Age of Global Quarantine

*Edited by*

*Gary F. Fisher and David Robinson*

Anthem Press
An imprint of Wimbledon Publishing Company
www.anthempress.com

This edition first published in UK and USA 2022
by ANTHEM PRESS
75–76 Blackfriars Road, London SE1 8HA, UK
or PO Box 9779, London SW19 7ZG, UK
and
244 Madison Ave #116, New York, NY 10016, USA

First published in the UK and USA by Anthem Press in 2021

© 2022 Gary F. Fisher and David Robinson editorial matter and selection;
individual chapters © individual contributors

The moral right of the authors has been asserted.

All rights reserved. Without limiting the rights under copyright reserved above,
no part of this publication may be reproduced, stored or introduced into
a retrieval system, or transmitted, in any form or by any means
(electronic, mechanical, photocopying, recording or otherwise),
without the prior written permission of both the copyright
owner and the above publisher of this book.

*British Library Cataloguing-in-Publication Data*
A catalogue record for this book is available from the British Library.

Library of Congress Control Number: 2021941960

ISBN-13: 978-1-83998-533-1 (Pbk)
ISBN-10: 1-83998-533-X (Pbk)

Cover image: bpk / Nationalgalerie, SMB / Jörg P. Anders

This title is also available as an e-book.

# CONTENTS

*Foreword* vii
*Acknowledgements* ix

| | Introduction | 1 |
| | *David Robinson and Gary F. Fisher* | |
| Chapter One | 'Off- Stage, A War': Wuhan, 1938 | 11 |
| | *Jonathan Chatwin* | |
| Chapter Two | Frederic Lees in Varese Ligure, 1911 | 21 |
| | *Ross Balzaretti* | |
| Chapter Three | 'A Rude People Subjected to No Restraint': In Tanimbar with Anna Keith Forbes, Henry Forbes and So'u Melatunan | 39 |
| | *Will Buckingham* | |
| Chapter Four | Sent to Coventry: A Journey Home? | 51 |
| | *David Civil* | |
| Chapter Five | Bedouin Is a Place: Freya Stark's Travel with Nomads | 65 |
| | *EmmaLucy Cole* | |
| Chapter Six | With Wilkie in the West: Reading Wilkie Collins's *Rambles beyond Railways* from a Cornish Perspective | 81 |
| | *Tim Hannigan* | |
| Chapter Seven | Picturing Rome: Walking the Eternal City with the Last Victorian | 93 |
| | *Tory Hayward* | |
| Chapter Eight | *Su e zo per i ponti*; or, How History Does Not Help | 107 |
| | *David Laven* | |
| Chapter Nine | A Town Called Entropy: Boom and Bust in Arnold Bennett's Potteries | 119 |
| | *Gary F. Fisher* | |
| Chapter Ten | Travelling towards Transculturalism? Statues, Remembrance and Mourning in Bloemfontein, South Africa | 135 |
| | *Kate Law* | |

## CONTENTS

| | | |
|---|---|---|
| Chapter Eleven | Recollections of the King's House<br>*David Robinson* | 147 |
| Chapter Twelve | Occupying Her Time: Ginette Eboué, France, 1940–42<br>*Sarah Frank* | 161 |
| | Epilogue<br>*David Robinson and Gary F. Fisher* | 173 |

*List of Contributors*     175
*Works Cited*     179

# FOREWORD

There is a condition called aphantasia where missed connections in the brain do not allow humans to visualise images in the mind's eye. Etymologically phantasia means imagination, channelled to Modern English from the Greek word phainomai: to appear. The prefix 'a' – not or without – added here feels especially cruel to me. My father suffered from this disorder. Once, just after the 9/11 terrorist attacks in 2001, he had a dream where I was captured in a white van and disappeared. He didn't dream. I was a loudmouth, an activist. His dream held truth. We both knew it, but what set him off was the veracity of the image in his mind because it was new to him. 'Picture a dragon,' my father said. And I easily conjured Smaug from the animated *Hobbit* and told him as much. 'I can't do that,' he said. 'Even if I try, I can't.' I didn't think to ask him then if it had always been this way, and I cannot ask now because he died soon after, but I've been terrified of losing my mental theatre ever since. I spent most of my childhood deeply invested in my fantasy life, one so necessary to my everyday existence that I'd set aside time as a boy to follow my designs either in my bedroom, or I'd choose to face the back of the couch when my mother wanted me near, the grey dark, a perfect atmosphere to drift through phantasia. I grew up in a poor, urban centre where water veins and abandoned houses were my hundred-acre wood, and so movies often served as catalysts. The movie *Stand by Me*, perhaps more than any other correlative in my early life, created the beginnings of fantasy travel. There were so many elements that appealed to my sense of self, but chief among them was the rag-tag friendships and the attempt to suspend a fracturing of the gang through adventure. It is dark to say, but I wanted adventure to begin with a lie told to my parents that ended with finding a dead body. I saw through those boys' experience – Chambers, LaChance, Tessio, Duchamp – how important fear, near-death, the breakdown of self-esteem and the admittance of thresholds and boundaries were to the adventure itself. Perspective.

And so, it makes sense that the first time I travelled alone, at 14, my friend and I lied to our parents and said the one was sleeping at the other's just as the boys in *Stand by Me* had done. We took a greyhound bus to Philadelphia from Memphis, which was scheduled to be 24 hours, but ended up being 30 or more. A friend had been moved by his parents to a suburb of Philly. He'd said we could stay with him, and my parents said I couldn't go. But what about perspective, what about friendship, what about dead bodies or train bridges or leeches – what would I miss if I followed the safer path of obedience and care? It was a beautiful trip: we chased a man who had ripped my friend's backpack from his shoulder and stopped the thief with the help of a schizophrenic homeless man; we were not allowed to sleep at the friends' house, after all, and he set us up under a bridge on the outskirts of his high school; we cared for him as he used our visit to get high, and then, after two nights, we slept our way back home on the greyhound. And it worked; I'd learned that I could survive without a bed, and I'd learned that the man everyone avoided at the terminal could be the one prone to heroism. I learned that my desire for travel wasn't simply a fantasy. It suited me.

In the years since, I've seen most of the world either as tourist or touring musician, sometimes as a scholar, and I've come to realise the writer is always somewhat isolated even when international/transcontinental travel was easily accomplished before the Covid pandemic. As writers, we watch, listen, smell, taste, touch the world and all with the goal of transferring those senses onto the page once we are alone again. This same attention to detail is what allows the mind to become memory and reignite the deep past as if it happened recently. We learn to craft imagination into a practice of intellectual engagement that is sharpened on doubt, curiosity, frustration, roadblocks, distraction and, most necessary of all, evidence and authenticity – authentic: that miraculous accident honed by experiences that can raise us to the sky and weigh us towards the grave. With education and time, the mind becomes a whet stone and a blade. With each project, the edge dulls and we whet the blade, and it dulls, and we sharpen. This exhilaration and exhaustion – so much like breathing – is our soundtrack. One that I depend on as much as I once depended on the darkened crevices of my mother's couch to show me the way to experience.

I am at a beach on the North Carolina coast. Today is my 40th birthday. The Covid-19 pandemic that caused so much isolation, so much death, so much loss and, paradoxically, freedom to be still, freedom to exist adjacent to late-stage capitalism *and with the knowledge* that everyone else the world over was doing the same – this pandemic – is in a new phase with so many people vaccinated, myself included. I've spent the morning with my dog and wife, feeling the warm breeze through the subdued sun, on top of a blanket, on top of millennia of battered stone, bone, shell, trash and salt. The ocean has always been a way of being among a timeless, selfless phantasia. And yet 'I appear' as a second self – phainomai – hand in hand with this moment and the images of bone as flesh, of stone whole again, of shell as a scurrying thing, of trash as the modern condition.

What draws me to the essay as an art form is what Samuel Johnson called loose sally of the mind, or tunnelling, as Virginia Woolf thought of her own process. Or: travels in isolation, as we might think of it here in this anthology. Through the conceit drawn up by editors Robinson and Fisher, the minds of complex and varied writers are captured through inward-facing gazes and outward efforts to make sense of our messy human nature. I've found kindred spirits in the writers who make up this anthology. I'm sure you will, as well.

M. Randal O'Wain

# ACKNOWLEDGEMENTS

This volume would not have been possible were it not for the help of numerous friends, colleagues and supporters.

It first stands to thank the contributors themselves. Coming from a wide variety of disciplines, backgrounds and professions, each of them has brought something special and unique to this volume, both in terms of their chapters and in terms of the conversations and advice given to us as editors along the way.

It must also be acknowledged that surrounding each and every contributor is a support network of family members, loved ones, colleagues and friends who have toiled unseen – doing everything from reading drafts and discussing ideas to offering moral support over a pint. Unorthodox by design, this project has pushed many contributors out of their comfort zone. These support networks have not only allowed us to push ourselves in this manner but also ensured we have a comfort zone to return to.

In particular, David would like to thank his wife, Carol, and his son and daughter, Alex and Beth, for their support and unblinking faith in the importance of the project. There are moments of crisis in any creative project such as this, and without their love and succour, it may never have been completed. Equally important to the project was the four-legged solace provided by a certain Working Cocker Spaniel, Jack and the regular Saturday-morning hangover phone calls with David's colleague and good friend, David Civil (also a contributor to this volume). Finally, the project would not have started, let alone been completed, had Tim Hannigan not been so encouraging in his belief in the idea, and had he not, unselfishly, provided advice and material from his own forthcoming publications, from which the editors drew.

Gary would also like to take the time to his wife, Lois, and his recently born son, Gregory. Lois has, as always, proved herself invaluable in reading countless drafts and redrafts, offering a critical eye and wise counsel on how best to proceed. Gregory has not yet learned to read, so has been unable to help in this manner. Nonetheless, he has been a source of constant motivation and emotional support throughout the production of this volume, even if he was not aware of it. Finally, it remains to thank Dylan Mansfield for first introducing Gary to the works of Arnold Bennett and providing the initial spark of inspiration from which Gary's chapter grew.

We must also take care to remember the unfortunate global circumstances in which the production of this volume has occurred. Compared to many, we have had it easy. The global quarantines have provided us with a unique opportunity to explore new ideas and approaches to travel writing and historical memory as a whole. For many, this global pandemic has occasioned the loss of loved ones, the suffering of sickness and the risking of personal safety. It is our hope that, while reading this book, you will spare a thought not just for those whose families have been affected by the virus but also the countless medical professionals, carers, teachers, service personnel, shop assistants, engineers, data analysts, cleaners, agricultural labourers, production operatives, refuse collectors, hauliers and many, many more who have tirelessly worked throughout this pandemic to ensure that our most vulnerable are kept safe, that our pantries have remained stocked and that we have a society to which we might one day return.

# INTRODUCTION

## David Robinson and Gary F. Fisher

Second travellers do not simply imitate the experiences made by previous authors […] because they return to previous texts and to paths already travelled, the journeying subject may discover not only the first traveller, but perhaps also him or herself.[1]

As we write, the 2020 Covid-19 outbreak continues to pose an unprecedented challenge to the travel writing community, but in our isolation from places, spaces and landscapes, we can still turn to historical travel accounts to remind us of the locations we have previously visited. Although, currently, 'a way of life driven by unceasing mobility is shuddering to a stop' and 'our lives are going to be more physically constrained', as John Gray notes, 'an advantage of quarantine is that it can be used to think afresh'.[2] *Travel Writing in an Age of Global Quarantine* is a collection of chapters by authors from a variety of backgrounds. We have gathered an ensemble cast of distinguished and widely published travel writers, novelists and academics. Each contributor travels vicariously, writing about a place they have visited, with reference to an historical account of the same place.

*Travel Writing in an Age of Global Quarantine* is something of a double entendre. We have asked contributors to 'travel' while subjected to epidemiologically mandated isolation. Yet, these travels are anything but isolated, as they are conducted in the company of an historical companion. Whether it be living with Freya Stark and the Bedouin in the Sinai Peninsula, riding with Dorothy Wordsworth in her nineteenth-century 'travelling car' through the Scottish Highlands or hiking Liguria with Frederic Lees in 1913, our personal memory and understanding of space and place is influenced by our historical predecessors. Our current enforced stasis offers us a unique opportunity to explore this process. Hopefully, the recent vaccines will free us once again, and for the future reader, this book will serve to explain what it felt like not to be able to move, to travel. This is how we explored and imagined the places we had been before.

Prior to early 2020, Wuhan was not a place that loomed large in the European imaginary. It is now, perhaps, the most famous place in the world. Strangely, this is the third time that Wuhan has risen from obscurity to worldwide prominence, as Jonathan Chatwin discusses in the opening chapter of this volume. The first time was in 1911, when the revolution that ended the Qing Dynasty began there; then in 1938, when it became the very temporary capital of China; and once more in 2020. Jonathan explores the idea of what it means for a place to suddenly and briefly transcend the parochial identity it has for those who live there to become a place rich with association and importance for the rest of the world.

As change is forced upon us, at least for the immediate future, so we also have the chance to reflect. *Travel Writing in an Age of Global Quarantine* presents opportunities to differently approach a text as a scholar. We break with the traditional academic 'rules' by inserting ourselves into the narrative and foregrounding the personal, subjective elements of literary scholarship. Each contributor critiques an historical description of a place about which, simultaneously, they write a personal account. Is this a problematic loss of essential academic 'distance' from the place about which we write, or does our involvement enhance our understanding of the historical account and of the place itself? The volume presents a twist to the 'in the footsteps of' subgenre of travel writing or what Maria Lindgren Leavenworth calls the 'second journey'. Through such revisiting,

> it is possible for the traveller to begin to redefine his or her relationship to the world, thereby relaying experiences which, although not necessarily surpassing those of the earlier traveller, at least provide the reader with a different and alternative version.[3]

Often, a traveller approaches a destination for the first time, influenced by not just historical accounts of the place but by academic and literary accounts of those accounts. This is what one of our contributors, Tory Hayward, describes as 'travel Inception', a reference to the Christopher Nolan movie, in which the protagonists invade each other's dreams and subconscious. The characters are never sure which world they inhabit, and Nolan asks them and the viewer to question the nature of reality and authenticity. As she describes, before ever visiting there, Tory had configured an image of Rome through a combination of her familiarity with Augustus Hare's account, first published in 1871, and contemporary academic analysis of Hare. Tory's personal account of Rome adds yet another layer, and she considers how they combine and intersect in her understanding of the city. Do they make for a more authentic account of historical and contemporary Rome, or do they send Tory and her readers down just another rabbit hole to an imagined world? Is authenticity ever possible, or is this simply an academic conceit?

Certainly, we challenge the conventional view of maintaining 'academic distance' from the place subject to scrutiny. As John Urry points out, 'People gaze upon the world through a particular filter of ideas, skills, desires, and expectations, framed by social class, gender, nationality, age, and education.'[4] Indeed. Why, then, should a different case apply to the analysing scholar of a place or a text? As another of our contributors, Tim Hannigan, notes, travellers and those who critique their accounts assign *meaning* to the people and places observed. It seems problematic, therefore, for a scholar to make that critique, into which the personal and subjective cannot help but intrude, without acknowledging and considering their own relationship with place and text.[5]

Although this book falls within the 'in their footsteps' subgenre of travel writing, we mean it to be a radical intervention. We do not think there are any directly comparable texts. In his *Footnotes: A Journey Round Britain in the Company of Great Writers* (2019), Peter Fiennes travels with his historical writers but for a different purpose, to consider the connections between them and Britain over a period of 800 years. The individual authors of Eland Publishing's series, Through Writers' Eyes, collect other travellers' writings about a particular place but do not 'accompany' them there to the same extent as we do. Saidiya Hartman's *Lose Your Mother: A Journey along the Atlantic Slave Route* (2007) is a single-authored monograph, rather than a collection of essays, and is much more biographical, although the sense of relationship between the past and the present relates to our themes. Antoinette Burton's *How Empire Shaped Us* is similar only in the sense that it asks historians to think about how their own lives and contexts have shaped their historical research. Scholars such as these have long argued that travellers' representations of societies and geographies are constituted through a dialogue with other, past travel writings alongside their projections of desire for difference and similarity onto those unfamiliar societies. Unlike previous texts, though, this volume shows *how* that process takes place.[6]

It is usual for a collection such as this to be neatly divided into sections which represent particular themes. We have resisted this temptation, partly because we believe the chapters defy such easy categorisation. In a sense, that *is* the theme of the book, or one of them. The idea is to reveal the subjectivities at the heart of travel and its description. Unsurprising, then, to find that each writer, past and present, has travelled their own path. This does not mean there are not commonalities. The key one, perhaps, is the way in which different interpretations and configurations of space and place, past and present, intersect and shift to fulfil the fantasies and preconceptions, the emotional, cultural and political needs of the traveller, but also of the travellee. As both Tim Hannigan and David Civil find, such tropes are not restricted to the visitor, which problematises the assumed authority of the native resident to claim they 'know' a place because they are 'from' it, that it is 'theirs'. Travel writer Philip Marsden posits a fundamental difference between traditional 'academic' writing and travel writing, in that travel narratives do not, or ought not anyway, begin by assuming a scholarly authoritative understanding of the places they describe. Indeed, quite the reverse, as Marsden points out,

> I love that thing that travel writing does, and in a way nature writing does too, of taking the reader on – I know it sounds trite – a voyage of discovery. It's all about the process of finding out about the world, of uncovering connections. The writer is learning about something and is filled with the thrill and urgency of that discovery. You just tell that story, and that can be a wonderful thing for a reader to share. This is a fundamental difference between academic writing and travel writing. In a travel narrative, you don't start off as an expert saying, 'This is how it is.' You're saying, 'This is what I found.'[7]

Of course, that assertion can be immediately challenged. The *idea* of a place is, often, much more present in the traveller's mind than the place they find – something Augustus Hare recognised in the introduction to his 1871 travel guide, *Walks in Rome*. Hare speaks about the unique experience of visiting a city which you already know before you set foot in it. When travellers come to Rome, they come to see things they are familiar with: the Coliseum, St. Peter's Basilica, the Pantheon, the Trevi fountain. As Hare wrote on the opening page of his introduction, travellers arrive to see sights they have known 'for long years before they come to gaze upon the reality'.[8]

Long before Hare, in 1729, Danie Defoe pointed out the authority of the travel account for the armchair traveller who could 'if he has not travell'd [...] make a tour of the world in books [...] he may go round the globe with Dampier and Rogers, and kno' a thousand times more doing it than all those illiterate sailors'.[9] Defoe refers, here, to an account of a privateer voyage, by Woodes Rogers, who funded and led, along with another captain, William Dampier, a plundering mission against Spanish shipping. Is Defoe presuming the scholarly authority of an account written from, for example, a position of leadership over the first-hand experiences of the ordinary sailor? Or from Roger's higher social or economic standing? Or his more extensive education? An 'illiterate' sailor would be unable to write their own account and, even if they were capable, would not likely have the resources or connections to see it published. To a large degree, the authority of Roger's account stems from it being the only account available. Very likely, the perspectives of Rogers and those of his sailors were different, and the lower social, economic and educational standing of the sailor in no way invalidates the authenticity of their experiences. But only one of those voices is available and is presumed, by Defoe, to carry more authority and authenticity for the non-travelling reader, than a first-hand experience of a sailor, even if the latter were to be heard.

On his return, Rogers was sued by his crew for withholding their share of the considerable return to investors. To recover his fortunes, in 1712, Rogers published *A Cruising Voyage Round the World*, which sold well, largely due to public interest in his rescue of Alexander Selkirk, the inspiration for Defoe's *Robinson Crusoe*. The degree to which Roger's 'scholarly authority' is problematised by his economic motivation to write an account which appealed to the public imagination is not considered by Defoe and certainly not foregrounded by Rogers himself. As it transpired, unfortunately for Rogers, the book's high volume of sales were still not sufficient to recover his fortunes, and Rogers was made bankrupt. Ironically, Rogers now, theoretically anyway, occupied a lower economic and social standing than his 'illiterate' sailors, although this seems not to have diminished his 'scholarly authority' in the mind of Defoe.

In his chapter exploring the ambiguities and assumptions of colonial and postcolonial travel writing, Will Buckingham considers similar pressing questions about the limits of such writing, about whose stories get told and about whose journeys are considered worthy of being included in the privileged sphere of the travel narrative. Will uncovers a world where head-hunters are as likely to come from Aberdeenshire in Scotland as they are from Alusi Krawain in Tanimbar, and where the journeys of European adventurers among the 'savage' peoples of southeast Maluku find their parallels in the brave journeys of Tanimbarese travellers through the 'primitive' world of the colonial Dutch East Indies.

More recently than Defoe and Hare, Edward Said described the travel account as 'about as "natural" a kind of text, as logical in their composition and in their use, as any book one can think of'. Said noted the 'human tendency to fall back on a text' which tells the traveller 'that a country *is* like this' when faced with alterity in a new location.[10] Crucially, Said goes on to say that 'such texts can *create* not only knowledge but also the very reality they appear to describe'.[11] The context in which Said made this observation was one where eighteenth- and nineteenth-century European travellers to colonial territories arrived with a sense of certainty about their comparative personal and national cultural, civic and political 'superiority'. Often, those travellers went on to write their own accounts which confirmed what they already 'knew' from previous reading, in a way which justified and authorised the colonial intervention of the 'civilising mission'. This may not be quite the case for the modern travel writer or scholar of travel, but nor can they claim their critiques to be free of the baggage of the markers of their own identity.

The very good point we think Marsden makes, though, and the one this book tries to demonstrate is that, as a matter of form, the first-person narrative has the ability to expose the research process: to allow the reader to see when and how a scholarly transformation takes place; to give the scholar the opportunity to openly foreground their own subjectivity and say 'this is the personal journey that led me to my conclusions'; to problematise the unchallenged authority of the scholar. *Travel Writing in an Age of Global Quarantine* challenges that idea of scholarly authority by embracing the subjective nature of research and the first-person element. We address a problematic distance between travel writing practice and travel writing scholarship, in which the latter talks *about* the former without ever really talking *to* it. Defining travel writing as a genre has often proved more difficult than it might seem, but Peter Hulme has suggested that it is ethically necessary for the writer to have visited the place described.[12] Hulme asserts that 'travel writing is certainly literature, but it is never fiction'.[13] This seems obvious, but it is a theme to which we will return in a second. In the meantime, we ask the reader to consider the idea that if visiting the place described is necessary for the writer to claim they have produced a travel account, might it also be necessary, or at least advantageous and valuable, for the writer of a scholarly *critique* of that account to have done the same? These are themes touched on by Tim Hannigan in his visit to Cornwall, in the 'company' of nineteenth-century novelist Wilkie Collins. Tim explores the interaction between travellee and traveller's text – something seldom considered by travel writing scholarship, where the travellee sometimes ends up as a sort of mute victim requiring a righteous academic to step in on their behalf. Tim considers the possibility of being on the receiving end of the traveller's gaze as a not – or not entirely – negative or denigrating dynamic

Approaching the subject of what constitutes travel writing from another angle, slightly in opposition to Peter Hulme, Michael Kort has pointed out that, given its reliance on various techniques taken from fictional writing, reliance on memory, selective material, reconstructed dialogue and so forth, there are many ways in which travel writing *is* indistinguishable from fictional travel accounts.[14] Germain de Stael's 1807 *Corrine* was one of the most well-known and influential fictional accounts of Italy, although based on the actual travel experiences of its author. Robert Casillo notes that *Corinne* was 'paradigmatic' for a nineteenth-century British 'understanding' of Italy.[15] As de Stael's reviewer, Francis Jeffrey, suggested in the *Edinburgh Review*, 'it is Great Britain and Italy, the extremes of civilised Europe, that are personified and contrasted in the hero and heroine of this romantic tale'.[16] Twenty years later, *The Oriental Herald and Colonial Review* went a step further in pointing out the weakness of some travel accounts of India. Factual accounts, or 'a dry enumeration of customs' as they put it, were 'irksome, both to writers and readers'. Perhaps, they argued, 'tales, novels, romances, plays, &c., are the best medium through which a knowledge of the East can be conveyed to Europeans'.[17] To consider the similarities and differences between fiction and 'factual' travel accounts, we have included Gary F. Fisher's account of contemporary Stoke-on-Trent, in which he reflects on Arnold Bennett's depiction of the town in his early twentieth-century novels. Like de Stael's *Corrine*, Bennett's fictional representations were based on his actual experiences.

Our purpose is not to try and define travel writing but to make readers aware of the many interconnections between different writing genres.[18] The reader is invited to compare the subtle similarities and differences between creative writing that has travel or observation of place as a motif and that which sets out to record the factual experiences of a traveller. Tim Youngs notes that travel writing of the latter variety not only draws on characteristics of other types of writing, it is neither literal nor objective but culturally mediated by the traveller's prior experience – that travel writing is *ideological*. Consequently, the travel account, like other types of writing, configures its own 'narrators, characters, plots and dialogue' which emerge from the cultural experiences of the writer.[19] Again, we attempt not to define the genre but to problematise the idea of the authority of the travel account, with its conceit of authenticity from having 'been there and seen it myself'. This is meant in no way to diminish the importance or significance of travel writing. The notion that a travel account exposes more about the writer's home culture than it does about the place observed is, perhaps, overstated, particularly as that idea assumes the traveller to have come from a homologous and monolithic culture. It is reasonable, though, to say that the traveller's observations do reveal much about the traveller. This is one of the reasons why travel writing is such a valuable window onto, as Carl Thompson puts it, a 'broad range of cultural, political and historical debates'.[20]

In another fictional work based on the author's actual travel experiences, Joseph Conrad's *Heart of Darkness*, the main protagonist, Marlow, talks about his youthful 'passion for maps' and his desire to, one day, visit the 'many blank spaces on the earth'. As an adult, he notes that the biggest blank space, or Africa, was no longer quite as empty but 'had got filled [...] with rivers and lakes and names'.[21] Of course, those geographical features had been there all along, just as Tim Youngs points out that those blank spaces were not 'blanks to those who lived there'.[22]

There is a kind of treble meaning to Marlow's (Conrad's) blank spaces. They are, firstly, blank because of a lack of information about them, but they are also, secondly, assumed to be culturally blank until the West has had sight of them; like some kind of quantum mechanical existence, it is not, apparently, until the West has observed, categorised, related, written about and intervened in those spaces that they have cultural existence. Up until then, despite their own millennia-long histories, such spaces are presumed to exist only in some state of potential and possibility. The third meaning is the assumption that a geographical 'blank space' is also a philosophical tabula rasa onto which the West was authorised, almost morally obligated, to paint their own versions of modernity with all the accompanying paraphernalia of 'civilisation': bodies of armed men; occupation; systems for trade and economic exploitation; the imposition of civic, legal and political control; imported religious conversion; the provision of 'native education'; permanent settlement building.

In one sense, travel – movement in geographical space – has been implied as the conduit through which 'European civilisation' arrives. There is some irony in the fact, then, that it is only when the European stops travelling, becomes immobile and constructs permanence, in the form of ports, forts, settlements and cities, that the blank space becomes a place, in Western eyes, of potential civilisation and modernity. When people are nomadic or live in semi-permanent surroundings, their movement through space is a marker of their apparent premodernity. And yet, in a further irony, their constant physical mobility stands in contrast to the way in which European observers have historically configured their cultural immobility, their rootedness in the past. Further still, as Geoffrey Nash describes, many nineteenth- and early twentieth-century European travellers sought the apparently timeless Arabian deserts in 'an urge to escape' the very 'Western modernity' that was often extolled to justify Western intervention![23] All of this calls into question what we even mean by 'place'. Are Marlow's blank spaces still places, or the absence of place? To what degree have (do) travellers configured an absence of what they understand to be place as an absence of civilisation and modernity?

These are some of the questions readers may wish to consider as they join EmmaLucy Cole and the Bedouin of the Middle East. Emma travels alongside Freya Stark in the early twentieth century, living and moving among Bedouin communities across the Middle East. She explores Stark's belief that travel can reconnect that which has become alienated and delves into the apparent dichotomy of travellers and travellees being both nomadic and geographically and culturally 'placed'. EmmaLucy and Freya Stark also share a proximity to Dartmoor. Looking out at the south-west countryside, writing in pandemic isolation, EmmaLucy compares themes of 'home' and 'place' which resonate throughout both of their experiences of travel with the Bedouin. Stark travelled at a time when the Middle East was moving out of a long period of colonialist control. For many, their freedom of movement was about to be significantly restricted and ownership of land disputed, and hundreds of Bedouin tribes found that quite suddenly their millennia-old routes and seasonal camps were no longer accessible. Larger tribes, such as Tarrabin in the 1970s, were forced to settle in breezeblock houses on the edge of the Red Sea and run tourist camps to survive. Yet, even the youngest members of the tribe, born long after the resettling took place, refer to themselves in ways which suggest that where they are from goes far beyond geography. It is as if to be 'Bedouin' is to be *a place* in itself.

The focus of postcolonial scholars who consider travel writing has often been on the ways in which travellers drew on their encounters with difference to construct a discourse of racial inferiority and superiority – one which authorised and justified colonial intervention and domination. While such accounts have been shown to configure an inferior 'East', so they also construct the corollary, or Western 'superiority'.[24] Mary Louise Pratt, for example, reverses the Eurocentric gaze to look *back* at Europe from the 'imperial frontier', to highlight how 'Europe's aggressive colonial and imperial ventures' acted 'as models, inspirations, and testing grounds for modes of social discipline' in the very *creation* of the *idea* of the West.[25] While not denying the value of such approaches and, in particular, Pratt's seminal work in this area, we do consider Mary Campbell's comment that a traditional laser focus on the colonial 'other' risks initiating 'critical discussion of modern travel writing in a crude form: the West vs. the Rest'.[26]

In his discussion of Glencoe in the Scottish Highlands, David Robinson discusses how, in her 1803 account of the Highlands, Dorothy Wordsworth configures the place and people in ways that anticipate and rehearse later travellers' accounts of Britain's imperial territories.

Dorothy's descriptions of Highland domestic scenes also map onto ideas about the ways in which English middle-class domesticity was advanced, throughout the nineteenth century, as the basis of British civic and political stability at home and 'superiority' abroad. Such observations question traditional understandings of 'metropole' and 'colony', or 'centre' and 'periphery', and an East–West binary of uncivilised/civilised. As David comes to realise, though, in his own written experience of Glencoe, he is guilty of projecting his own fantasies and desires on to the Scottish landscape, even as he critiques Dorothy Wordsworth's interpretation of the Highlands.

Our contributors provide new angles on a number of well-known historical writers while also introducing a diverse array of largely forgotten literary travellers. As well as thinking about new ways of approaching texts and travel, we also hope that the general reader will be variously fascinated, moved, amused, but always sufficiently absorbed to pursue our historical travellers for themselves, to explore further from their freely accessible accounts. Simultaneously, we demonstrate to readers the extent to which the modern Western understanding of the world has been shaped by the accounts of travellers, at the exact point, ironically, when our mobility juddered to a halt.

A multidisciplinary approach encourages, for example, the benefits of considering travel accounts within their historical context and as historical sources. Ross Balzaretti does exactly this, in his visit to Varesi Liguria with Frederick Lees, and finds the late nineteenth-century traveller a still reliable source, even 150 years later. At the time of writing, in the aftermath of the tragic death of George Floyd at the hands of American police, the debate rages about heritage, its 'erasure' and what constitutes 'history'. Kate Law's chapter, then, has a very contemporary feel, as she takes us around her previous home town of Bloemfontein in the company of Emily Hobhouse, who reported on the Boer War from there. Kate considers the role of the past and how Afrikaner suffering (in the context of the Boer War) continues to dominate the heritage landscape at the expense of (more relevant) understandings of the legacies of apartheid.

Another historian, David Civil, considers J. B. Priestley's 1933 journey to Coventry, David's own home town, to explore changing understandings of social class in interwar Britain. His chapter explores how travel accounts embed certain assumptions about class and space. In particular, he is interested in Priestley's emphasis on 'new men', arguing that Priestley's account was part of a broader cultural project to remake the relations between intellectualism, skill and technique. This repudiated the cultural elitism associated with gentlemanly intellectuals and embraced a more earthy technical orientation. More to David's surprise, though, was his dawning realisation of the fallacy – his own assumed authority to describe and 'know' Coventry, as a son of the city. Through his engagement with the historical text of a visitor, he is forced to concede that, perhaps, Coventry is not the place he thought it was; or rather, he has invented Coventry as somewhere that suits what he wanted it to be.

In recent years, travel writing has emerged as an ever more interesting and relevant genre. As tragic and difficult as the current global pandemic is, this project is a positive opportunity to think creatively in a unique set of circumstances. Ultimately, the reader will be drawn to the realisation that travellers and their accounts have augmented the very globalisation which has so recently reduced humanity to being, once again, a strictly local species. We believe there is much to learn and to enjoy in reducing the distance between reading historical travel accounts as entertaining and informative diversions and as an academic discipline. For these reasons, we strongly believe that the time is right for such a collection.

## Notes

1. M. L. Leavenworth, *The Second Journey: Travelling in Literary Footsteps* (Umeå: Umeå Press, 2010), 192.
2. J. Gray, 'Why This Crisis Is a Turning Point in History', *New Statesman*, 1 April 2020, https://www.newstatesman.com/international/2020/04/why-crisis-turning-point-history.
3. Leavenworth, *The Second Journey*, 192. See also M. L. Leavenworth, 'Footsteps', in *The Routledge Research Companion to Travel Writing*, ed. A. Pettinger and T. Youngs (Abingdon: Routledge, 2019), 86–98.
4. J. Urry, *The Tourist Gaze 3.0* (London: Sage, 2011), 1–2.
5. The editors would like to record their gratitude to Tim Hannigan for the many discussions which substantially led to the framing of this anthology.
6. The editors' thanks go to Dr Onni Gust for their conversational time and insights in this regard.
7. T. Hannigan, *The Travel Writing Tribe: Journeys in Search of a Genre* (London: Hurst, 2021), 9.
8. A. J. C. Hare, *Walks in Rome* (New York: British Library, 2011), 1.
9. D. Defoe, *The Compleat English Gentleman* (London: D. Nutt, 1890), 225. Defoe refers, here, to Woodes Rogers and William Dampier. The former was a Bristolian shipping magnate who funded and led a two-ship privateering expedition against the Spanish between 1708 and 1711. Rogers captained the *Duke*, while Dampier took charge of *Duchess*. Among various adventures and battles, Dampier and Rogers captured several Spanish ships and rescued Alexander Selkirk, the inspiration for Defoe's 1719 *Robinson Crusoe*, from Juan Fernandez Island in 1809. However, in other ways, the expedition was less successful financially as detailed above and, additionally, as Rogers was wounded and his brother killed.
10. E. Said, *Orientalism* (New York: Vintage Books, 1979), 93, original emphasis.
11. Ibid., 94.
12. T. Youngs, *The Cambridge Introduction to Travel Writing* (Cambridge: Cambridge University Press, 2013), 4.
13. Ibid., 5.
14. Ibid.
15. A.-G.-L. d. Staël, *Corinne, or Italy* (London: M. Peltier, 1807). For the impact of *Corinne* in Britain, see R. Casillo, *The Empire of Stereotypes: Germain de Staël and the Idea of Italy* (New York: Palgrave Macmillan, 2006), 3–4. Also D. Laven, 'The British Idea of Italy in the Age of Turner', in *J. M. W. Turner: Sketchbooks, Drawings and Watercolours*, ed. D. B. Brown (London: Tate Research Publication, September 2015), https://www.tate.org.uk/art/research-publications/jmw-turner/david-laven-the-british-idea-of-italy-in-the-age-of-turner-r1176439, footnote 15.
16. F. Jeffrey, 'Corinne, ou L'Italie', *Edinburgh Review* 11 (October 1807): 183–94 (183).
17. 'Review: The Zenana', *Oriental Herald and Journal of General Literature* 13 (1827): 499–510 (499).
18. For more information on definitions and discussions of travel writing, see, for example, Tim Youngs, who states that travel writing is a 'mixed form, composed of different genres and discourses, and produced at a variety of historical moments': T. Youngs and C. Forsdick, *Travel Writing* (Oxford: Routledge, 2012), 1. Charles Forsdick describes travel literature as 'a literary form situated somewhere between scientific observation and fiction': 'French Representations of Niagra: From Hennepin to Butor', in *American Travel and Empire*, ed. S. Castillo and

D. Seed (Liverpool: Liverpool University Press, 2009), 56–77 (58). Michael Kowaleski calls travel writing 'dauntingly heterogeneous', borrowing from 'the memoir, journalism, letters, guidebooks, confessional narrative, and, most important, fiction': 'Introduction: The Modern Literature of Travel', in *Temperamental Journeys: Essays on the Modern Literature of Travel*, ed. M. Koweleski (Athens: University of Georgia Press, 1992), 1–16 (7). Borm suggests that travel writing is 'not a genre, but a collective term for a variety of texts both predominantly fictional and non-fictional whose main theme is travel': 'Defining Travel: On the Travel Book, Travel Writing and Terminology', in *Perspectives on Travel Writing*, eds G. Hooper and T. Youngs (London: Routledge, 2004), 13–26 (13). For a comprehensive review of what constitutes travel writing, see the chapter 'Defining the Genre', in *Travel Writing*, ed. C. Thompson (Abingdon: Routledge, 2011), 9–33. For an historical overview of travel writing, see the chapter 'Narrating Self and Other: An Historical Overview', in *Travel Writing: The Self and the World*, ed. C. Blanton (New York: Routledge, 2002), 1–29.

19 T. Youngs, *The Cambridge Introduction to Travel Writing* (Cambridge: Cambridge University Press, 2013), 2–3.
20 Thompson, *Travel Writing*, 2.
21 J. Conrad, *Heart of Darkness* (New York: Dover, 1990), 5.
22 T. Youngs, *Travel Writing in the Nineteenth Century: Filling in the Blank Spaces* (London: Anthem Press, 2006), 2.
23 G. Nash, 'Politics, Aesthetics and Quest in British Travel Writing on the Middle East', in *Travel Writing in the Nineteenth* Century, ed. T. Youngs (London: Anthem Press, 2006), 55–70 (57).
24 This is, of course, a central contention of Edward Said's *Orientalism*, a founding text of postcolonial scholarship. Lauded and criticised in equal measure, the influence of *Orientalism* 'can hardly be disputed': R. Young, *Postcolonialism: An Historical Introduction* (Oxford: Wiley-Blackwell, 2001), 384. It is not our intention to enter into this debate, but for a full range of views, see L. Nochlin, 'The Imaginary Orient', *Art in America* (May 1983): 118–31, 187–91; 'The MESA Debate: The Scholars, the Media, and the Middle East', *Journal of Palestinian Studies* 16 (1987): 85–104; I. Warraq, *Defending the West: A Critique of Edward Said's Orientalism* (Amherst: Prometheus Books, 2007); A. J. Caschetta, 'Review: Defending the West: A Critique of Edward Said's Orientalism', *Middle East Quarterly* 16 (2009): 77–79. M. Kramer, *Ivory Towers on Sand: The Failure of Middle Eastern Studies in America* (Washington: Washington Institute for Near East Policy, 2001); F. Halliday, 'Orientalism and Its Critics', *British Journal of Middle Eastern Studies* 20, 2 (1993): 145–63; A. Ahmad, *In Theory: Classes, Nations, Literatures* (London: Verso, 1992); C. A. Breckinridge and P. v. d. Veer, *Orientalism and the Postcolonial Predicament: Perspectives on South East Asia* (Philadelphia: University of Pennsylvania Press, 1993); V. Chaturvedi, *Mapping Subaltern Studies and the Postcolonial* (London: Verso, 2000); R. Inden, *Imagining India* (Oxford: Oxford University Press, 1990); D. Varisco, *Reading Orientalism: Said and the Unsaid* (Seattle: University of Washington Press, 2007); A. J. Caschetta, 'Review: Reading Orientalism: Said and the Unsaid', *Middle East Quarterly* 7 (2010): 78–80.
25 M. L. Pratt, *Imperial Eyes: Travel Writing and Transculturation* (Abingdon: Routledge, 2008), 35–36. In her analysis of three classic English novels, Gayatri Spivak says something similar, that 'one cannot read nineteenth-century British literature without remembering that imperialism, understood as Britain's social mission, was a crucial part of the cultural representation of England to the English': 'Three Women's Texts and a Critique of Imperialism', in *'Race,' Writing, and Difference*, ed. H. L. Gates (Chicago: University of Chicago Press, 1985), 262–81 (262).
26 M. B. Campbell, 'Travel Writing and Its Theory', in *The Cambridge Companion to Travel Writing*, eds P. Hulme and T. Youngs (Cambridge: Cambridge University Press, 2002), 261–78 (264).

# Chapter One

# 'OFF-STAGE, A WAR': WUHAN, 1938

## Jonathan Chatwin

War alters the character and life of a city as effectively as the silting of a harbour or a profound climactic change. A year ago [...] Hankow was hardly more than a name on the map, somewhere halfway up the Yangtze. Six months later it has become, like Barcelona, one of the most interesting cities in the world.[1]

Two rivers meet at Wuhan. The city sprawls around the junction where the tributary Han joins the Yangtze, before that great river's breadth bends itself around the top half of a circle to push eastward to Shanghai and the coast. On the north-western bank of the Yangtze sit two of the three old cities which make up the modern city of Wuhan – split themselves by the winding waters of the Han, and taking their names, in part, from it: Hanyang and Hankou. On the opposite bank of the Yangtze is Wuchang: the third, and most politically important, of Wuhan's tri-cities, which donates its first syllable to the city's portmanteau name.

Wuhan's position at the confluence of these two rivers meant that even the British colonial forces, when they arrived in 1858, could not fail to recognise its potential importance as a trading port, despite some initial misgivings. In December of that year, the British paddle steamer *HMS Furious* anchored off Hankou, as part of the first foreign fleet ever to have ascended the 636 miles of the Yangtze from the coast; those aboard were here to cast an appraising eye over a port to which they had just secured trading rights at the end of what would turn out to be the first phase of the Second Opium War.

On this first occasion when the Western gaze was directed towards Wuhan, those examining the cities were distinctly unimpressed: the site, wrote Laurence Oliphant, private secretary to Lord Elgin, was 'eminently disappointing. We had heard so much of the congeries of cities that are situated at the junction of the Han and the Yang-tse [...] that we had formed grander expectations, and anticipated a nobler reward after all our anxieties and exertions.'[2] They would change their minds, though: a few years later in 1861, the war having concluded in Britain's favour after Lord Elgin's forces torched the Summer Palace in Beijing, the British government forced a punitive treaty on China and leased a concession area at Hankou from which to trade. The city thus began a new life as a centre of international commerce deep in the heartland of China. It would become one of the great trading cities of the world; the British concession would be joined later in the nineteenth century by those of France, Germany, Russia and Japan. Along the river front at Hankou emerged a foreign streetscape, with banks, consulates and company offices in the European style: an architectural echo of the famous Shanghai Bund six hundred miles downriver.

When W. H. Auden and Christopher Isherwood arrived in Wuhan in 1938, it was to the European enclave of Hankou – or *Hankow* as it was then transliterated – that they retreated. On 8 March 1938, with the river 'a terrible race of yellow waves and tearing snow',[3] they took a ferry across the river from Wuchang – it was not until almost two decades later that a bridge was built across the Yangtze's breadth – and felt that they 'would rather be in Hankow at this moment than anywhere else on earth'.[4] They took up lodgings in the British Consulate compound: right on the Hankou Bund, just next to the Russian concession, pitching their camp-beds – bought in Guangzhou on their way north and complete with integrated mosquito nets – in a large, empty, first-floor room.

In 1938 the attention of the Western world was once again trained on Wuhan. The year before, in northern China, a war which would come to be known by many different names, depending on where you were from – the Second Sino-Japanese war, the War of Resistance against Japanese Aggression, the Second World War – began following a skirmish at the Marco Polo Bridge, just outside Beijing.

From there, the Japanese had swept southwards, taking Shanghai after a protracted battle, before moving up the Yangtze to Nanjing where the Japanese army committed the atrocities that became collectively known as the 'Rape of Nanjing', killing tens of thousands of civilians and engaging in the mass rape of Chinese women.

Nanjing was the national capital at the time, having been relocated from Beijing in 1928 by the Nationalist Party that, under 'Generalissimo' Chiang Kai-shek, ruled China. Temporarily setting aside their differences, the warring Nationalists and Communists, themselves established in the town of Yan'an in northern China, had come together in an uneasy alliance known as the 'United Front' to fight the Japanese. On the approach of the Japanese Army, the Nationalists had fled their capital at Nanjing, with military command retreating upriver to Wuhan in late 1937 and the national government heading even further up the Yangtze to Chongqing in Sichuan province.

For 10 months of 1938, Wuhan became China's de facto capital,[5] with Chiang Kai-shek establishing his headquarters in Wuchang. The fierce fighting to the north and east had also pushed hundreds of thousands of refugees onto road and river towards Wuhan. Those who had made the journey included prominent artists and intellectuals such as Lao She, Mao Dun and Guo Moruo. 'The uncertainty in Wuhan created a remarkable, and perhaps unique, oasis of freedom in modern China,' writes the historian Rana Mitter.[6]

By the end of October 1938, however, Wuhan had fallen and the Nationalists had fully relocated another five hundred miles up the Yangtze to the city of Chongqing in Sichuan province. Still, the 10 months of fierce military resistance around Wuhan were of enormous significance to the course of the war both in China and the rest of the world. Ultimately dissuaded from pursuing the Nationalists into Sichuan, deep in the belly of the country, the war settled into a new phase which saw a scrappy stalemate establish itself. The war in China was not 'won' in any real sense; the end of the conflict came with Japanese surrender in September 1945. Yet, China had held down hundreds of thousands of Japanese troops during the war and suffered millions of casualties: it is estimated that over 14 million Chinese people lost their lives during the conflict. Had the Nationalist government surrendered under the intense pressure of Wuhan, 1938, the Japanese forces would likely have taken control of the whole of China and been free to turn their attentions elsewhere.

I spent much of late 2019 thinking, reading and writing about Wuhan. The previous summer, I had travelled to the city as part of a three-thousand-mile journey retracing the route of a trip made in 1992 by Chinese leader Deng Xiaoping: his so-called 'Southern Tour' which reignited China's economic ambitions. His first stop, after an overnight journey by private train from Beijing, was the city of Wuhan, though it was no more than a brief hiatus on a voyage to China's far southern provinces.

Auden had stayed in the British Consulate; I rented a room at a cheap hotel on a side street further upriver.

I arrived one July morning into the city's high-speed railway station, outside of Wuchang. Even though it was almost midday, the mist had not yet lifted off the Yangtze, and my taxi sped across the suspension bridge connecting Wuchang to Hankou in a thick haze; the cityscape occluded by the rising river.

I had little fixed purpose in Wuhan. Deng Xiaoping had spent under an hour on the platform here, so I had few leads to follow up on that front. I spent my first days walking concentric rings around the old city of Hankou, peeking through fences at repurposed colonial buildings and consulting my old 1930s map of the city. As I found my routes repeating, I took subway trains under the Yangtze and Han, emerging up escalators into broiling sunshine and trying to track down some of Wuhan's past in Hanyang and Wuchang.

Wuhan is known in China as the 'Thoroughfare of Nine Provinces', and trade and transport in Central China had been focused on its three cities since long before the British arrived in the nineteenth century. In the era of the Qing dynasty, Hankou was, according to poet Zha Shenxing (1650–1727), the 'greatest of markets, crossroads of land and river trade'.[7] As the historian Chris Courtney notes, 'When the scholar-official Fan Chengda visited the Wuhan area in the twelfth century, he found thriving market cities, home to tens of thousands of households and rows of shops "as thick as teeth in a comb".'[8] It is a place, writes Stephen R. Mackinnon, that 'dominated the economic and political life of the central Yangzi region for well over a millennium'.[9]

In its more recent history, the city played a crucial role in one of the most dramatic and consequential events of China's recent past – the ending of imperial rule in 1911. On 9 October that year, an explosion was reported in the Russian concession at Hankou. A bomb built by anti-Qing revolutionaries had been accidentally detonated, and in the ensuing investigation, police discovered a document listing those involved in the plotting. The rebels quickly came to a realisation: after all their months of planning, it was now or never; they could either act or be arrested. Mutinies were quickly launched in Hanyang and Wuchang, and from there, the anti-Qing uprising escalated, gathering irreversible momentum as it spread from province to province. In February 1912, the last emperor of the Qing dynasty, Puyi, abdicated.

Behind a vast shadeless square in Wuchang, an imposing new museum, built in 2011 and resembling a rusting spaceship, tells the story of Wuhan's role in the uprising. As one display in the museum put it, the emperor's abdication marked the 'termination of monarchy despotism for more than 2,000 years in China and the birth of the Republic of China'.

The city has been central in the national narrative at numerous other points over the course of the past century: in 1966, for example, when Mao Zedong arrived in Wuhan to take a legendary swim in the Yangtze. At 11 a.m. on 16 July, a typically sweltering summer's day, Mao entered the fast-flowing waters of the Yangtze from a motor launch and coasted with the current of the river for an hour and five minutes. Hagiography tells us that he managed 15 kilometres in that time (though his personal best seems to have been set a few years earlier in 1961, when he achieved 12 kilometres in just 40 minutes). On the banks, crowds had gathered, waving red flags and chanting slogans. Two hundred young swimmers joined him in the water and sang a song: 'We are the communist successor generation.'[10] Today, on the riverbank, bronze letters spell out the date of this symbolic event: 66.7.16.

His swim was a demonstration of vigour; a statement of physical action which reflected his ultimate decision – reached definitively in Wuhan – that now was the time to push forward with sweeping change in the country, to root out the bourgeois elements whom, he felt, still lingered in Chinese society. Upon his subsequent return to Beijing, he would officially launch the Cultural Revolution: the campaign which completely upended Chinese life for the next decade.

Even these details are, of course, merely the most prominent facts cribbed from the long history of this place, none of which have much to do with the quotidian experience of living here, and give but scant indication of the city's long, rich past: a past not unknowable or mysterious, but which sits in straightforward contradiction to the idea that there is but one way to know a place like Wuhan.

In my evenings in Hankou, I wandered the promenade, watching the traffic on the Yangtze. The river had burst its banks, and out in the murky water, lampposts and willow trees stood half-submerged. Late July in Wuhan is a time of intense heat – Wuhan is famously one of China's 'furnaces' – and the bank was busy with locals taking a paddle or a swim in the river. The squat, solid colonial buildings of the old Bund behind the waterfront walk – at least those that remain – are today mocked by the ranks of reaching glass-and-steel office towers and apartment blocks on the opposite bank of Wuchang, their nightly neon light shows spilling across the river in oil-slick iridescence. This is a city of 11 million people, and upstream and downstream along the curved Yangtze, it stretches as far as the eye can see.

On my last evening, I clambered down the levee and took off my sandals to stand in the shallows of the Yangtze. The water was murky but surprisingly cool. Night had fallen, and most of the swimmers had returned to shore. Out past the lampposts and willow trees and the neon-lit tourist boats, in the middle channel of the broad Yangtze, I could just see the dark outlines of the barges which still haul cargo up and down this great river.

Having spent another month travelling through China's south and east, I returned to England and set to work typing up notes. My intention was to write a book chapter exploring some of the modern history of Wuhan pertinent to the power struggles of

Communist Party politics in the 1960s and 1970s, and I embarked upon a broad reading around the subject. I had flicked through Auden and Isherwood's *Journey to a War* before my journey, and in the autumn, I sat down to read it properly. There is a relative paucity of writing in English on Wuhan – most literary visitors to China have their heads turned by Beijing and Shanghai – and *Journey to a War* had the virtue of not being a purely journalistic or academic account of the place.

Travel writers often like to freight their journeys with meaning beyond the actual, physical act of moving across land and sea. Nothing lends an account of a journey gravitas like rendering it in poetry, and in its opening section, *Journey to a War* deploys a sonnet sequence titled 'London to Hong Kong' to relate Auden and Isherwood's outward route. A relatively conventional 'Travel Diary' of their rest of the trip, written up by Isherwood from their combined notes and articles, follows, before the volume concludes with more poetry, in a sequence titled 'In Time of War': another, far more abstract, set of sonnets, followed by a verse commentary. For the 1973 revised edition, which was the version I had, Auden had trimmed down the 'In Time of War' sonnets. In the foreword, Auden observes that he had also found, on returning to it, the verse commentary to be too preachy; 'I have always believed, however, that, among the many functions of the poet, preaching is one' – perhaps an unsurprising statement for a poet descended from a line of Anglican priests.

Auden and Isherwood had no particular expertise which qualified them for the job of correspondents in late 1930s China. The book had been commissioned by Faber and Faber in London, and Random House in New York, in the summer of 1937. As they write in the foreword:

> This was our first journey to any place east of Suez. We spoke no Chinese, and possessed no special knowledge of Far Eastern affairs. It is hardly necessary, therefore, to point out that we cannot vouch for the accuracy of many statements made in this book.

Auden had written an earlier travel book, *Letters from Iceland* (1937), in collaboration with fellow poet Louis Macneice. In 1937, Auden had also travelled to Spain, as the Civil War raged there; his visit, though, was brief and he spent much of his time there 'waiting for action that never came, dispirited by the drift and bungle of events';[11] he would write his famous poem, 'Spain 1937', about the conflict, though later distanced himself from it.

As related in Auden's opening poetic sequence, the pair had travelled by ship to Hong Kong via Suez, but their journey proper had begun on 28 February 1938 with a boat journey up the Pearl River Delta to the trading city of Guangzhou, or Canton; the scenery, Isherwood wrote, reminded them of the Severn Valley. On arrival, they got visiting cards printed with the Chinese names they have been given in Hong Kong: *An Dung* for Auden; *Y Hsiao Wu* for Isherwood. A three-night rail journey took them across the Hunan province to Wuhan. Onboard, they read Anthony Trollope and Walter Scott and worried about air raids.

Auden commented in a letter that looking for the war in China was like a novel by Kafka; certainly, given how much ground they ended up covering in Central and Eastern China, it is remarkable how little of the war they actually managed to encounter and describe. Their journey would take them from Wuhan north to Zhengzhou and then east towards the front line, encountering a little distant fighting, before they retraced their steps to the city of Xi'an. From there, they had planned to travel west by lorry to Chengdu, capital of Sichuan province – an ambitious journey of over 450 miles – and then on to Chongqing and back down the Yangtze to Wuhan. The cost of hiring a truck being too prohibitive, however, they returned from Xi'an to Wuhan and then travelled down river to Shanghai.

A perpetual, and well-founded, sense of insecurity haunts the prose account of their travels. At a press conference during their first days in Wuhan, Auden and Isherwood feel the eyes of the old China hands on them, prompting them to hastily explain that they are not proper journalists, having rather come to China to write a book. Later, they meet Peter Fleming, writer, journalist and brother of Ian, who had published two volumes on his travels in China already in the 1930s – *One's Company* (1934) and *News from Tartary* (1936) – and who heightened Auden and Isherwood's sense of being out of their depth.

> [Fleming] took exhaustive notes and made us feel ashamed of our laziness. Also, he knew enough Chinese to understand roughly what was being said. He protested, most impressively, when the translation failed to tally with the original.[12]

Wuhan acted as the axis for their travels and is the most vividly conveyed of their destinations. Over the course of nine days before their 'journey to a war' begins in earnest, they do the rounds of officials and advisors and even manage an encounter with the Generalissimo himself, having crossed the river to Wuchang for a visit with his wife, Soong Mei-ling. The litany of those they met testifies to Wuhan's international significance in 1938: there is William Henry Donald, Australian ex-journalist and advisor to Chiang; Agnes Smedley, American writer and communist fellow traveller (one of only a handful of foreigners to end up buried in China's national cemetery); Logan H. Roots, American bishop; and Alexander von Falkenhausen, German general and military advisor to Chiang, whom they encounter the day after Nazi troops invade Austria: the news prompts Auden and Isherwood to question 'What does China matter to us in comparison with this?'[13] During the first press conference Auden and Isherwood attend, Hungarian photographer Robert Capa and Dutch film-maker John Fernhout arrive: both, like Auden, were graduates of the Spanish Civil War.

Wuhan had become the new front line against fascism, and the sense of this place and time as momentous is implicit in *Journey to a War*. For both Auden and Isherwood, the conflict in China is metaphoric of much grander dualities: between good and evil; between fascism and freedom, in a 'world that has no localized events'.[14]

Rarely, however, do either address the specifics of the war for those who actually live there. Isherwood's breezy prose account of their journeying is characterised by an amused detachment which renders the Chinese people they encounter as performative figures, unreal in the same way as the characters of the Chinese opera they attend in Wuhan. Auden's poetic contributions, likewise, seem broadly uninterested in individual experience, but instead trace the human will to power and origins of conflict in a long sonnet sequence which begins with Creation and the expulsion of Adam and Eve from the Garden of Eden. Those they meet on their travels are missionaries, Western doctors and the occasional Chinese official. Their closest encounters with ordinary Chinese people come through their interactions with Chiang, their servant-interpreter, whom they engage for wages of 40 dollars a month and who is the subject of disparaging commentary throughout the prose account.

On returning to Wuhan after their first journey north to try to track down some actual fighting, they find the weather transformed: fine and hot, and perfect for Japanese air raids. They spend almost another fortnight there: more parties and visits to the diverse assortment of important personages who have made their way to the city, including renowned mob boss Du Yuesheng, better known as 'Big-Eared Du', chief of Shanghai's infamous 'Green Gang'. On their last day in the city, 29 April, the Japanese launch an air raid; the speculation is that this is partly in honour of the birthday of their emperor. Auden and Isherwood put on their sunglasses and lie down on the consulate lawn to watch the show. Though the aerial battle is apparently 'won' by the Chinese fighters, Isherwood records later that five hundred civilians had been killed in the raid.

By March 2020, everyone knew Wuhan. There is, of course, more than one way to know a place, and it was notoriety that the city had achieved: signifier and signified having been coupled with remarkable rapidity in the world's mind. This was no longer a city of 11 million individuals living at the confluence of the Han and Yangtze; it was no longer the richly storied 'Thoroughfare of Nine Provinces'; it was no longer even the place I had briefly known the previous summer. It had become two syllables with one meaning.

By April, I had given up on trying to write about the city. A general lockdown lassitude had set in, but alongside it had grown a conviction of the essential pointlessness of my work. The complexities of place and time I found compelling in my work on Wuhan, and China more generally, could never compete against the attractive simplicity of the media coverage that spring – a simplicity which fuelled a widespread outrage about China. Wuhan was suddenly a place of callous, unsanitary people, eating unrecognisable food and stacking wild animals in cages. Wet markets – the fresh food markets I had routinely visited each day to buy meat and vegetables during my years living in China – became sites of unspeakable horror in the world's imagination.

And *Journey to a War* became something of a vector for my feelings of frustration about all of this. These feelings were not inspired by Auden and Isherwood's foundational lack of knowledge about the place: such is the nature, very often, of travel writing, and the outsider's account, when treated as such, is not without a certain value. Rather it was the duo's striking lack of interest towards the experience of those Chinese people living through, rather than journeying to, a war that came to trouble me.

In Auden's poetic contributions to the volume, the Chinese experience is slotted into a sweeping series of images storyboarding nothing less than the history of human development. Though utilising a superficially conventional form, the 20 sonnets from 'In Time of War' are fragmentary and allusive, resisting clear interpretation and, in particular, any attempt to map their oblique references onto Auden's direct experience in China.[15] It is in Sonnets XII and XIII that the war comes most obviously into focus, though, in the sequence's most famous lines, Auden again seeks to place the Chinese experience into a broader ethical and global context:

> And maps can really point to places
> Where live is evil now.
> Nanking. Dachau.[16]

Sonnet XII tells of an unnamed dead Chinese soldier 'abandoned by his general and his lice':

> No vital knowledge perished in that skull;
> His jokes were stale; like wartime, he was dull [17]

Auden's soldier is not only nameless but is stripped of personality and intellect. His death is framed as essentially part of a mass necessity of sacrifice. From Auden's poem 'Spain, 1937', George Orwell singled out the poet's use of the phrase 'necessary murder', commenting in an essay that 'Mr Auden's brand of amoralism is only possible, if you are the kind of person who is always somewhere else when the trigger is pulled'.[18] Orwell's assessment is brutal, yet the emotional coldness he identifies as a flaw of Auden's resonates in the reading of 'In Time of War'.

Auden and Isherwood were, of course, neither the first nor the last Western writers to depersonalise the Chinese people in this way. However, in its portrayal of the country at a time of great suffering, *Journey to a War* came to encapsulate something bothersome to me, presaging attitudes that swirled within the currents of media coverage of Wuhan, 2020.

From the earliest weeks of global news coverage, Wuhan tended not to be presented as constituted of individuals struggling on the frontline against a mysterious new disease – fearful, afraid and uncertain – but rather as a faceless, homogenous 'city of 11 million in Hubei province' which was implicitly part of the causality of the emergence of this new disease. As Auden and Isherwood had seen the Chinese people as nameless figures in a global fight against fascism, so writers and journalists in America and Europe tended to be interested in the suffering of the people of Wuhan only in as much as it could tell them something meaningful about the potential for their own future suffering, back at home.

In her book *Wuhan Diary*, writer Fang Fang relays the true panic and anxiety that gripped the city in early 2020, particularly before national attention was focused on addressing the crisis. She writes of the days around the Lunar New Year, when Chinese families ordinarily come together to celebrate: 'Instead the world froze over; countless people became infected with the coronavirus, and they ended up traipsing all over the city in the wind and rain searching in vain for treatment.'[19] She writes poignantly of those families struggling to get treatment for ill relatives in the early weeks of the epidemic, turned away from hospitals that were already full. In her entry from 30 January, she observes that 'although the people of Wuhan tend to be naturally optimistic, and things around the city are becoming increasingly orderly, the reality here inside the city is growing grimmer by the day'.[20] The state's estimate that around four thousand people died in Wuhan likely represents a dramatic underreporting of the true figures.

In the months subsequent to Wuhan's 76-day lockdown, however, the story of the city and its people has been co-opted by the Chinese Communist Party into another simplified narrative. As one article in the government-mouthpiece *Global Times* put it: 'Step by step, China has managed to bring the risk of the deadly virus under control on its soil, and one virus-attacked city after another has returned to normalcy after efforts made from top down.'[21] The 'victory' over Covid-19 has become a testament to the sacrifices of the people and, most importantly for Chinese leader Xi Jinping, an example both nationally and internationally of the party's apparent competence.

In a solemn ceremony in Beijing in September, President Xi awarded medals to a carefully selected group of doctors and local officials from Wuhan. Notably absent from the list of those honoured was Li Wenliang, the young ophthalmologist from the city who had been censured by authorities for warning about coronavirus in late December 2019. Li died in early February from the virus, aged 33. In his speech, Xi pointedly criticised those who, in his words, twisted facts or scapegoated others, praising the party and the 'heroes' of Wuhan as victors in a 'people's war'.

## Notes

1. W. H. Auden, '"Hankow", W H Auden's Early Drafts for *Journey to a War*', Add MS 61838, Western Manuscripts, British Library.
2. L. Oliphant, *Narrative of the Earl of Elgin's Mission to China and Japan in the Years 1857, '58, '59*, vol. 2 (Edinburgh: William Blackwood and Sons, 1859), 396.
3. W. H. Auden and C. Isherwood, *Journey to a War* (London: Faber and Faber, 1973), 38.
4. Ibid., 39.
5. Nor is 1938 the only time Wuhan has served as a capital city: in late 1926, the left wing of the Nationalist Party established a short-lived government there: for a time, it looked as though the city may become China's national capital.
6. R. Mitter, *China's War with Japan, 1937–1945: The Struggle for Survival* (London: Penguin, 2013), Kindle edition, location 2689.
7. Quoted in W. T. Rowe, *Hankow: Commerce and Society in a Chinese City, 1796–1889* (Stanford: Stanford University Press, 1984).
8. C. Courtney, *The Nature of Disaster in China: The 1931 Yangzi River Flood* (Cambridge: Cambridge University Press, 2018), 30.
9. S. R. MacKinnon, *Wuhan, 1938: War, Refugees, and the Making of Modern China* (Berkeley: University of California Press, 2008), 5.
10. A. V. Pantsov and S. I. Levine, *Mao: The Real Story* (New York: Simon and Schuster, 2012), Kindle edition, location 1480–5.
11. R. Davenport-Hines, *Auden* (London: Vintage, 2003), Kindle edition, location 3543.
12. Auden and Isherwood, *Journey to a War*, 200. Auden and Isherwood should, perhaps, have been less concerned about living up to Fleming's example. In the front matter to Fleming's book *One's Company*, an account of his 1933 travels, the author includes a warning to the reader, explaining that the book was written by a 26-year-old who had spent about seven months in China and did not speak Chinese.
13. Auden and Isherwood, *Journey to a War*, 49.
14. Ibid., 263.
15. As with 'Spain, 1937', Auden would end up revising these poems substantially: the original, longer sonnet sequence is substantially trimmed down.
16. Auden and Isherwood, *Journey to a War*, 253.

17 Ibid., 263.
18 G. Orwell, *Inside the Whale, a Selection of Essays also Containing 'Charles Dickens' and 'Boys' Weeklies'* (London: Victor Gollancz, 1940), https://www.orwellfoundation.com/the-orwell-foundation/orwell/essays-and-other-works/inside-the-whale/.
19 Fang Fang, *Wuhan Diary: Dispatches from a Quarantined City*, trans. M. Berry (London: HarperCollins, 2020), 17.
20 Ibid., 65. The book was adapted from posts on Chinese microblogging site Weibo and became the target of widespread online vitriol in China, much of it state-sponsored; the campaign particularly intensified after it was revealed that the book was to be translated into English.
21 Zhao Yusha and Liu Caiyu, 'China's Commendation of Role Models Who Fought Covid-19 Signals the Country's Phased Victory in Virus Battle: Chief Epidemiologist', *Global Times*, 6 September 2020, https://www.globaltimes.cn/content/1200067.shtml.

# Chapter Two

# FREDERIC LEES IN VARESE LIGURE, 1911

## Ross Balzaretti

I first visited Varese Ligure in January 1995.[1] It was very cold. There was thick ice along the roadsides. The hotel I stayed at, the ancient Albergo Amici founded in 1760 and run by the Marcone family ever since,[2] was freezing, as the heating had broken down just before we arrived. We were the only guests and we huddled with the family around the single wood-burning stove in the reception area. It was hard to be impressed, and I really did not want to go back if I am honest, certainly not at that time of year.[3] I travelled there with Charles Watkins from the School of Geography, University of Nottingham. We soon developed a new course for final-year undergraduates, called 'The Landscape History of Liguria', centred on an annual week-long field trip to Varese.[4] The first field trip was 24–31 March 1995. As it turned out, I have been returning almost every year since with between 10 and 30 final-year university students in tow, usually in March/April, but last year for the first time in September.[5] I have also been there in August for summer holidays. I will not be going in 2020, as the Covid-19 pandemic caused the cancellation of the module, as well as all overseas field work at my university (University of Nottingham, UK). For this year at least, I have become a Victorian cliché, the 'fireside traveller' who features elsewhere in my teaching portfolio.[6] Instead I shall have to visit from a suitable social distance (roughly 1670 km) looking again at Varese through the eyes of Frederic Lees, a rather eccentric traveller, who made a single visit to Varese in 1911 during a three-month walking tour of Liguria.[7] He was 39 years old.

Varese Ligure is a small town, the capital of the Upper Vara Valley in the far east of the Liguria region. The northern part of the town's jurisdiction (Ital.: *comune*) borders the region of Emilia Romagna at the Pass of Cento Croci (1055 m a.s.l.). The earliest historical evidence for the town is a brief mention of the *plebs de Varia* ('Vara parish') in a register of the archbishops of Genoa dated 1031 AD.[8] It is likely that the earliest nucleated settlements in this area were hamlets sited around 400–500 m a.s.l. on hillside slopes, places such as Cassego, Scioverana and Zanega, perhaps evidenced in the ninth century, earlier than in the town.[9] The history of the area is pretty dark until the fourteenth century when the noble Fieschi family built a small round town (Ital.: *borgo rotondo*) and encouraged settlers to come there from the Ligurian coast.[10] This was accompanied by the construction of a new parish church with the curious dedication to the Madonna of Mantua and later a castle built by rivals to the Fieschi during skirmishes to gain control of the area which was of strategic importance in connecting this part of Liguria with the region of Parma to the north-east.[11] When much of the extended Fieschi family was wiped out by the Genoese state after an attempted coup in 1547 (the famous Fieschi conspiracy dramatised by Schiller in 1783),[12] Varese passed into the control of Genoa.[13] At that point, a local priest, Antonio Cesena, and a member of the local gentry wrote the first known history of the town,[14] a fascinating mixture of book-learning, direct observation and gossip. Genoese aristocrats soon built new palaces in Varese for their summer *villeggiatura*[15] and two churches for the use of new communities of Augustinian monks (Santa Croce, 1563, demolished) and nuns (San Filippo Neri).[16] The nuns remained in Varese until a few years ago. Continuing investment in Varese by wealthy Genoese and others over many centuries has resulted in a fine historic townscape which attracts summer tourists.[17] Throughout its history, the town has been supported by local agriculture as well as trade. It has been a market centre for the immediate locality and beyond, a 'zone of transit' as it has been called.[18] During the nineteenth and early twentieth centuries, the town, like most of Italy, suffered poverty and, as a consequence, depopulation as families emigrated in search of a better life, mostly to California and Argentina.[19] Further migration to rapidly developing coastal resorts, such as Rapallo after the Second World War, began a further period of decline for Varese, which has only recently begun to be modestly reversed. Varese's local politicians took advantage of EU funding in the 1990s to convert a significant proportion of its agricultural production to organic and to develop eco-friendly ways of generating electricity. The Vara Valley as a whole is now marketed as 'the organic valley' (Ital.: *la valle del biologico*), and this has led to a small revival in local tourism.[20] It has also not been universally well received.[21]

### Frederic Lees

British visitors to Varese may not be as common as Italian, German and French ones, but 'we' have been going there for at least a century. The earliest account of the town in English I have found is a short chapter by Frederic Lees in his *Wanderings on the Italian Riviera. The Record of a Leisurely Tour in Liguria*, published in London and New York in 1912 by Isaac Pitman's (of shorthand fame). I forget how I came across the reference, but I do remember that I bought my copy in 1997 from a seller in Australia, its original route there unknown and unknowable as there are no names of previous owners in it and no annotations which might provide the necessary clues. Like many books, it is a traveller in its own right, having been to Varese many times over the years and, although versions are now available in electronic form and in cheap reprints, I could not part with it.

When I bought my copy, I did not know that Varese figured in the book. I knew nothing about Frederic Lees, who remained mysterious in the age before online library catalogues. It was likely, though, that his *Wanderings* – a common enough title for travelogues from the mid-1800s – were typical of the period.[22] By 1912 there was a huge market in English for travel writing, and it was hard to write anything original or new.[23] Once I read the book and realised, to my amazement, that Lees had visited Varese, of course I wanted to find out about the author. This has not been easy because, despite being a prolific writer, Lees has left little biographical residue. His father Frederic Arnold Lees (1847–1921) and paternal grandfather Frederic Richard Lees (1851–1897) were well-known literary men, and their lives are better documented. Frederic Arnold was a medical doctor and surgeon who specialised in digestive illnesses and published in the *British Medical Journal*.[24] He married his first wife Mary Esther Bannister in Leeds in March 1872. It is almost certain that our author Frederic is the same person as George Frederick W. Lees, whose birth was registered in December 1872 at Hartlepool, where Frederic Arnold was practising at that time. Mary Esther died in 1906, and Frederic Arnold married for a second time in June 1907. Besides his medical career, he was also a well-known botanist who published *The Flora of West Yorkshire* in 1888.[25] Frederic Richard was a prominent public advocate for teetotalism in the north of England.[26] Our Frederic published a biography of his grandfather in 1904, with an appreciation by Frederic Arnold.[27] His bibliography of Frederic Richard's work on temperance runs to 16 pages of books and papers published between 1837 and 1896.[28] David M. Fahey, in his *Oxford Dictionary of National Biography* entry for F. R. Lees, states that our Frederic was 'perhaps his son [Frederic Arnold's] or a son of one of F. R. Lees' half-brothers'. This is in fact not the case as in *Wanderings* he clearly states that Frederic Arnold was his Father, with a capital F.[29] Frederic seems to have been close to him as in that book he also refers to the many letters and botanical specimens which he sent back to Leeds while he was travelling in Liguria. Their whereabouts are currently unknown.[30]

A further snippet of biographical information is provided by the frontispiece to Frederic's book about his grandfather. This reproduces a pencil sketch of the subject in 1892 taken 'from life by Miss Edith Fithian (Mrs Frederic Lees)'. Edith Sarah Fithian (b. 1871) had trained at Herkomer's Art School in Bushey, Hertfordshire, in 1889.[31] She exhibited at the Royal Academy Summer Exhibition in 1894.[32] She and Frederic married in 1898. Whether she accompanied her husband on his travels is unknown, but as she contributed the occasional illustration to some of his books, including *Wanderings* as we shall see, it is certainly possible.[33]

When he published his Ligurian book, Lees was already a very productive author in various genres, encompassing journalism and art history as well as travel. He published some classic essays, including 'Can Old Age Be Cured?' (answer 'yes' by eating yoghurt)[34]; 'How I Lived in Paris without Money. The Story of a Modern Bohemian',[35] illustrated with wonderfully quirky photographs of him as a 'down and out' harassing society ladies in cafes two decades before George Orwell's famous book; and many journalistic pieces for middle-class tourists with a focus on France.[36] *A Summer in Touraine*, illustrated by Maxwell Armfield, was published in 1909 by Methuen and very successful with the public.[37] He translated many French novels and art books into English, perhaps tapping into the spirit of the Entente Cordiale, signed in 1904. He published at least 27 books (as evidenced by the British Library Catalogue), and there must be many more articles in the popular magazines of his day. His *Wanderings* was his first, and I think only, published foray into Italian culture. Lees continued writing until the late 1930s but, despite considerable searching, I have as yet been unable to establish when he died.

## Lees in Liguria

Further biographical information is to be found in *Wanderings* itself. It has to be read fully and carefully to find it, and even so some mysteries remain. The book was published in 1912 in Britain, and in 1913 in the United States. The introduction is dated February 1912 when Lees was 'once more in his native land' of grey sky and cold wind.[38] It is addressed to 'J.K. Antiquary. Member of the Società Ligure di Storia Patria, San Remo'.[39] Lees states that he spent 14 months in Liguria 'wandering along the shores and up the green valleys of your native province, or else basking in the sunshine in your incomparable gardens', but he does not often say exactly when. He implies that he went to Italy for his health and that it was a new country and language for him. He met J. K. in the latter's antique shop in San Remo 'in search of books to increase my knowledge of the history of Liguria'.[40] The two became friends and went on their three-month walking tour in search of curios (J. K.) and the picturesque (Lees). Until that point, Lees's knowledge of Ligurian history derived entirely from books; after his walking tour, he had added 'living knowledge' by discovering the landscape and its monuments.[41] He stressed the importance of doing this when writing history, a view I share.[42] I have spent twice as long as Lees in Liguria but spread out over many years rather than all at one go. Annual visits to the same place mean that I have learnt far more about one part of this region – the Vara Valley – than he did, but like him, my understanding has been transformed by walking the land. I should add that I have visited much less of Liguria than him. I know Genoa well and several places on the Riviera di Levante, but I hardly know the western part of the region in the flesh. In some respects, I too am just another of the fireside travellers he numbered among his readers when I step outside of my eastern Ligurian comfort zone.[43]

For a historian it is important to date as precisely as possible when Lees visited the many villages he writes about. He tends to vagueness in this regard. For example, he says he went to Torriglia in late March, but does not say in which year.[44] Exact dating is important because it helps us judge how accurate Lees's impressions may be, perhaps by cross-referencing with local weather records. This is particularly important to the information he records about plants he encountered, which was one of his many subjects (local history, architecture and art, literature, the people he met, food and wine, hunting, picturesque views, topography, geology and gardens). His interest in plants was fuelled by needing to send specimens and notes back to his botanist father in Leeds with whom he was in active correspondence.[45] Successful identification of plants in the field depends greatly on the time of year they are observed. In winter, most of the trees would not be easily identifiable in the absence of their leaves, and other plants, especially deciduous flowering ones, could be impossible to identify. In the very cold interior valleys, local people would be more likely to be inside their homes, and strangers would be less likely to meet anyone on the road. At some seasons, 'views' can be entirely obscured because Liguria is one of the wettest regions of Italy. This can even happen in summer when high up. Summer can also be variable, especially in temperature. Traditionally city dwellers left the coast for the valley to escape the summer heat and associated disease (Ital.: *villegiatura*), and Lees comments on the intense heat in several chapters.[46] As it

**Figure 2.1:** Map in Frederic Lees, *Wanderings on the Italian Riviera*, 1912.

happens in 1911, Italy, like the rest of Europe, experienced one of the hottest summers known up to that time.[47]

Lees certainly seems to have experienced the weather at different seasons because he was in Liguria for 14 months in total. Four of these months were spent living in Genoa.[48] Three of these months comprised his road trip, which began in September. A map at the back of the book plots the whole tour, and seen visually, it is remarkable that they covered so much ground in that time (Figure 2.1). He walked with his friend from Ventimiglia in the far west of the region to La Spezia in the far east where they separated. The Antiquary went back to his business in San Remo by train. Lees went on to Viareggio to view the beach where Percy Shelley's body had been cremated. Just before that, they had taken a detour inland from Sestri Ligure, a well-known resort on the coast, with the intention of proceeding to Borgotaro in neighbouring Emilia via the Velva pass and then to La Spezia via the Taro and Magra valleys.[49] This took them through Varese Ligure probably in November or December. In September, their tour had commenced on the road from Ventimiglia to the Nervia valley, when the oleanders which had made that valley famous were still in bloom.[50] Then, the road was hot and dusty.[51] Varese a couple of months on was certainly not that. References to other months appear in a few chapters. At the hotel in Pigna, probably in October, they read the visitors' book and found comments about all the wonderful wildflowers in bloom on 29 March 1909. At Ospedaletti, Lees described the thriving flower industry and the 'special flower-trains at various times during the day between October and June', which in December took flowers to London, Berlin and St. Petersburg.[52] The pair was at Albenga on a sunny October afternoon, inspecting the cathedral library when they saw 'suspended from canes stretching between two pieces of furniture, were dozens of bunches of grapes, drying for winter use'.[53]

The trip must have involved some very serious walking with 'knapsack on back and stick in hand'.[54] Lees notes that they usually used mule tracks in preference to carriage roads. Such tracks are always more direct but often very steep, and the gradient is more suited, unsurprisingly, to mules than to people: 'long and tiring', as he put it on the road to Toriano.⁵⁵ At the present time, many of these paths are in disrepair and impassable, making it impossible to replicate Lees's tour today. Walking tourism was quite common at the time Lees was writing, and his book tapped into an existing and expanding market.⁵⁶ Hilaire Belloc (1870–1953) had walked from France to Rome on pilgrimage in 1901 and published his famous book *The Path to Rome* the following year. G. M. Trevelyan (1876–1962), the renowned historian of nineteenth-century Italy and, like Belloc, a contemporary of Lees, published a passionate essay simply called 'Walking' in 1913 and stated there that 'I have two doctors, my left leg and my right'.⁵⁷ And ever since, the traveller who goes on foot has been regarded as the most 'genuine' type of that breed, and walking has been subject to reams of academic analysis.⁵⁸ In fact, most travellers then, as now, travelled by train and some by car and bicycle, and the Touring Club Italiano, founded in 1894, provided detailed transport advice in its guide to Liguria, first published in 1916 in an edition of 200,000 copies.⁵⁹ The walkers were keen to react against these signs of modernity and made every effort to go off the beaten track. Lees was typically dismissive of signs of industry, especially on the road from Savona to Genoa which he advised should be passed over as quickly as possible as 'the coast has been spoiled by manufactories' especially at San Pier d'Arena, 'the Manchester of Italy'.⁶⁰ Lees did not stop in this western suburb of Genoa which is now post-industrial. As some readers may know, it is home to football's Sampdoria, a club with a history going back to the 1890s which Lees ignored as well, probably because he had never heard of it.

## Lees as a Photographer

During the current pandemic, photographs have been an important way to remind ourselves of places we have been to and places we may want to go to when that is possible again. Yet, if a rapid internet search from home can provide images of imagined places in seconds, it cannot replace the multisensory real thing. Our virtual visual saturation has also robbed us of the delight of travelling without having seen our destinations before we set off. This is one of the major cultural changes of modernity as art historians know well but many historians still tend to underplay. Before photographs took hold of our imaginations during the nineteenth century, we should remember that it was indeed possible to visit places one had never seen. Travellers were pleased, impressed, irritated, distressed, shocked and horrified by what they saw in ways no longer possible when so little of our travelling experience is new. In contrast, their experience of travel was perhaps richer than ours, at least for those who could afford to travel. It was, on the other hand, harder for them to take the experience of travel back home because travellers themselves had, again unless they were wealthy, to draw, paint and write in order to memorialise their trips abroad.⁶¹ It can reasonably be argued that these amateur skills declined once tourists could buy commercial photographs from local dealers, and became rarer still once new types of camera pre-loaded with film made taking one's own snaps possible from the 1880s. Technological change also facilitated the production of postcards at the same time with effects similar to our own experience of travel with the mobile phone: imagery became ephemeral. That is not to say that photographs are not an important part of travel history but rather the opposite. For many people, photographs are all that is left as travel itself fades into the past. Indeed, there is a case to be made that illustrating a written account of travel with photographs is a significant statement to make precisely because photographs do not replace our lived experience of travel but are an intrinsic part of it.

This must have been the case for Frederic Lees as he decided to include 60 of his own photographs in his Ligurian book, including two of Varese Ligure. Despite not being in a formal photographic archive and little known to local historians, these images are an important record of Ligurian life at this time. Photographs taken by amateurs like Lees have increasingly caught the attention of cultural historians in recent years, who have suggested that their value as evidence is high and their meaning always complex.[62] Lees most likely took what he termed 'photographic illustrations' using a portable camera, perhaps the Kodak Brownie box camera which became available at this time.[63] He was tapping into a current trend because, by 1912, photographs were rapidly gaining ground as the preferred means of illustrating travel books. They had not quite replaced conventional engravings as those could be reproduced in colour and so were still favoured by many authors, their publishers and readers. Several books about Liguria fall into this category, including William Scott's *The Riviera* (1907) and Walter Tyndale's *An Artist in the Riviera* (1914).[64] Frederic's wife Edith painted one such picture of 'The Via Palma and San Siro, San Remo', which was reproduced in colour as the frontispiece to her husband's book.[65] It is a highly skilled sketch of a well-known tourist location, very similar in style to Tyndale's 'Vicolo della Providenza' in the same town.[66] It is a pity no other pictures by Edith were included in the book, as she was clearly an artist of quality.

The photographs in *Wanderings* fall into several distinct categories.[67] The majority are of the countryside, picturesque landscapes, views of villages especially hilltop villages, castles (often ruined) and churches. There are fewer but still a good number of shots of towns and their streets, houses and palaces, bridges, gates and sculptures. There are a few coastal images of harbours and fishing villages. There are also classic tourist shots of sites with English literary associations (Dickens and Shelley) and of local lace workers.[68] There are almost none of people. It is annoying that Frederic never comments in the text about taking his photographs or why he chose the shots he did, although he does discuss the subjects of the images, sometimes in detail.

His photographs of Varese show two sites frequently reproduced in more recent guides. The first, simply titled 'Varese Ligure' (Figure 2.2), is a landscape showing a bridge over a river complete with drying washing, another of the many clichés of Victorian travel literature.[69] This might seem a typical tourist snap of little interest given that many similar Ligurian towns have similar bridges similarly photographed. However, as an aficionado of Varese, I see it as a rather more interesting image especially if scanned and enlarged which reveals its surprising amount of detail. On the surface, the scene itself seems similar today with the same buildings, mostly sixteenth- and seventeenth-century palaces in the main town lining the river to the right and the smaller, older houses of Grecino to the left. The left and right banks are linked by the impressive stone bridge built in 1515 which is around 15 metres above the riverbed. Interestingly, the river is rather dry, especially if Lees was visiting in late autumn/early winter which can be very wet in these parts. This could have been the result of the previous very hot summer.

**Figure 2.2:** 'Varese Ligure', photographed by Frederic Lees in 1911.

However, as the river is also much less embanked than it is now with stone walls on the Grecino side which are not in Lees's photograph, perhaps it really was significantly wider and therefore shallower than it is now. The land around the town has also changed, perhaps even more so. The state of the steep terraced hillsides, for which this part of Italy is famous,[70] is surprisingly clear once one zooms in. In the background, there are two houses visible on a slope which is entirely terraced. In November 1911, which is when I think Lees took this image, the terraces were clear of trees, either being cultivated or grazed. Today, they are completely invisible, overgrown entirely with trees and shrubs. This is also the case above Grecino where there are far fewer trees than today, and those that there are appear to have been shredded, a technique used to provide leaf fodder for cattle and sheep. These changes have not necessarily happened slowly since the 1910s because regeneration by plants can take hold quite quickly once land stops being routinely managed, as our own photographic evidence from 25 years of local fieldwork has very clearly demonstrated.[71] Land management is closely tied to other economic change, and in the case of Varese, depopulation and emigration played a big role in the neglect of the land.

This surprisingly complex image teaches the useful lesson that landscapes which visitors may think 'timeless' – and in Lees's terms 'picturesque' – are usually nothing of the sort.[72] Comparing dated photographs of the same view across time is therefore an important method through which to assess landscape change. Lees probably did not understand this as his text plays up the lack of change: 'there is also a very old and picturesque bridge across the Vara' is all he says and, unfortunately, this is a slip of the pen as the river is the Vara's tributary, the Crovana!

The other photograph, *Early Christian Art at Varese Ligure* (Figure 2.3), shows in close-up a stone relief which has been placed on the town side of the bridge. Lees thought this relief was 'perhaps, the oldest thing in Varese'.[73] This could be true although there are several other sculptures and inscriptions which might be as old, but it is definitely not as old as Lees thought as it is not 'very early Christian' art. Lees noted that this

*Early Christian art at Varese Ligure*

**Figure 2.3:** 'Early Christian art at Varese Ligure', photographed by Frederic Lees in 1911.

bas-relief crudely represented five human figures. In the centre, Mary and Christ as a child. Mary has a crown, and the Holy Ghost represented as a dove is flying towards her. The Crucifixion is on the right, and on the left next to Mary, Lees saw Saint Joseph, although it is more likely to be the solider Longinus who pierced the side of Jesus on the Cross.[74] Lees was 'at a loss to say who is indicated by the remaining figure, with what appears to be a scythe suspended over his head, – unless this symbol represents Death?' The latter is the risen Christ carrying a *vexilla* (banner) to signify his triumph over death.[75] The relief is still in situ today in the same position Lees described, although this is not likely to be its original site as the stone is probably somewhat older than the bridge. It is in a rather more eroded condition than in 1911 and is now covered by wisteria, making photography almost impossible. Over the years I have photographed it a fair bit, and the one on the cover of my *Dark Age Liguria* shows it in 2012.

## Lees in Varese

Lees and J. K. approached Varese from Sestri Ligure on the coast and took the Velva pass (Colle di Velva, 545 m a.s.l.) which connects the Graveglia and Vara valleys. They would then descend to Torza in Val di Vara. These two valleys have markedly different characters. In the Graveglia you can still see the sea from as far inland as Castiglione Chiavarese, a few kilometres from Moneglia on the coast, and the vegetation is noticeably more Mediterranean, with many productive olive groves and significant wine production now classified as Portofino DOP. In Varese, olives do not reliably fruit as it is too wet and too cold in the winter months and the local wine can be sharp albeit in a good way.[76] It is no surprise therefore that Lees saw it as 'a rather deserted district' while implying that was precisely why he and his friend went there, to be 'off the beaten track'. His description of the route up – one I have done many times by car, once or twice by bus but never on foot – is made interesting for me by what Lees found worthy of comment. He notes the mountain scenery, of course, which is extremely beautiful on a clear day but also the geological and mineralogical interest of the area, appealing no doubt to rock collectors back home who were surely impressed by his reference to 'the rare mineral called datolite'. This was first discovered in Norway in 1806 but is not as rare as Lees thought. It is now popular with spiritual healers. Noting the copper mines at Libiola and Bargone, he tells us that these 'produced in 1903, 7621 tons of copper, valued at nearly £13,000' and that there was a smelting works at Bargonasco (run by the Società Ligure Ramifera founded in 1904).[77] Manganese was also mined, used at that time in making steel to protect it against rust. It is frustrating that, as with most things Lees writes in this book, we are left to guess where he got this information from, but there is little reason to doubt these points about mining in the face of other evidence. In some places he advised that 'there is no special inducement to linger', telling readers to press on through Castiglione Chiavarese, Missano and Velva to the prize of Varese. Nowadays there is certainly reason to stop at each of these villages: Castiglione has one of the best butchers in the region, making prized local salami; excellent olive oil and wines are produced by Azienda Agricola Pino Gino at Missano;[78] and there is a small but worthwhile museum at Velva.

Lees was, as if you could forget, on foot and he wanted to reach his bed for the night in Varese. This part of the journey was made much easier by the construction of a tunnel (Madonna della Guardia, 2,126 m, opened in 1981) on the SP523 which connects Missano and Torza, greatly shortening the journey from the coast by at least an hour or two, in a car or by bus. Walkers though, even today, would still have to go up to Velva by the old route and walk down into Torza. Before this tunnel was completed, Varese had seen several decades of depopulation, and times were tough as older local residents will tell you.[79] Its opening helped to revive the town, or even to save it (it was never connected to the railway network). Now it is once more a 'summer resort' as Lees noted, much cooler than the coast in July and August, popular with older people in search of peace and quiet.

Lees began his account of Varese in the centre of the town with some medieval history telling us (correctly) that throughout that period Varese was the property of the Fieschi family. He then begins his tour of the town with the castle built by a rival named Piccinino in the fifteenth century. Lees reported that its two towers were ruined, and in fact, it was this, coupled with a genuinely picturesque tree growing from the roof, that helped to draw early twentieth-century Italian tourists to the town. This is demonstrated by the survival of postcards of the castle written and posted between 1901 and 1913, which do indeed document its ruinous state.[80] This was still the case in the 1950s when it was even more covered with greenery (Figure 2.4). The castle was restored between 1961 and 1965, and the tree was removed, so that the images are all that remain. It is now used to host occasional exhibitions.

Lees thought (wrongly) that castle was at the centre of the circular planned settlement (*borgo rotondo*) which the Fieschi funded to bring new residents to Varese from the coast. It is in fact to one side, protecting the residents from the north. Much of this *borgo* survives as a series of medieval houses with characteristic arches (*portici*) on the ground floor.

**Figure 2.4:** Varese Ligure, Castello dei Fieschi, postcard c. 1957.

These were also the subject of tourist postcards at the time Lees was writing and still attract tourists today. It was this point in his narrative that he turned to the bridge and bas-relief which he photographed (as discussed earlier). He then commences a longer section about the Augustinian nunnery which is opposite the castle. This is a fine baroque structure and dedicated to Saint Philip Neri. What Lees has to say can be quoted in full as it is one of the most engaging parts of the whole book:

> Ignorant of the strict regulations which govern the lives of the inmates of this monastery, I sought to inspect that part of the establishment where, for the benefit of the poor of the district, these holy women carry on a very interesting industry: that of drying mushrooms and making confectionery. But I found that this was impossible; no human being, save a priest to hear confessions and a doctor to give medical advice, ever puts his or her foot across the threshold of those sacred precincts. You can enter a little vestibule and talk with one of the nuns who stands behind a revolving apparatus with shelves, but look on her face you cannot; you can step into an adjoining waiting-room and sample the confectionery, which will be brought to you by an attendant, who herself has never seen any of the sisters of this convent; and if you are satisfied with their wares, you can give your order and shortly receive, at the above-named revolving counter, a neatly made up parcel of sweetmeats, made of almond paste and fashioned in the form of fruit, flowers, and fishes, each with its appropriate colouring. Similarly, you can purchase samples of the dried fungi which the nuns of San Filippo Neri export to all parts of the world.[81]

This passage is completely true, for these Augustinians were an enclosed order who did make sweets (*sciuette*) and dry mushrooms (*porcini*) until a few decades ago.[82] Within recent memory it was possible to ask for advice in the very way Lees describes. All this came to an end when, a few years ago, the nuns left suddenly much to the dismay of local residents. Lees could not get access to the nuns, which is not surprising given that they were a closed order and he found difficulty in obtaining any information about the convent. In fact, its history is well evidenced in local archives, which he presumably was not shown. He did though, as I have done, look down upon 'their beautiful and extensive garden', but here I can outtrump Lees. In March 1998, my colleagues Charles Watkins, Susanne Seymour and Setsu Tachibana (reputedly the first Japanese person to visit Varese) and I were lucky to be admitted to this very garden behind the residential parts of the complex and discovered that, while we could see in, the nuns could also see out perfectly well! They were very curious to see us from a suitable distance. Perhaps Lees was therefore correct when he noted that the nuns 'live very happy and healthy lives' despite being unable to leave their building until death, when their coffins were removed through a back gate to the nearby graveyard.

Lees completed his Varese sojourn at the Colle di Centro Croci on his way to Borgotaro in the next valley. In the past, this high pass was the only route from Parma to the Mediterranean, making it of great strategic and commercial importance. He explained that the old Parma customs house was now a comfortable inn with summer accommodation; the area is usually impassable with snow in winter. Now that inn is derelict, but a number of tourists perhaps were increasingly getting attracted to the 'Alta Via dei Monti Liguri', a well-maintained high path for serious walkers which passes through this area. Lees ended with a local tradition: 'a band of robbers, disguised as monks, used to attack and murder the muleteers, or other travellers, and from the large number of crosses which were raised on the mountain to the memory of these victims it ultimately took its name'.[83] A comparison with Antonio Cesena's sixteenth-century history is revealing about the power of tradition to linger in a place down the centuries:

> No greater danger remains on this journey than at the horrible, wild and dark place of Cento Croci [...] in this place besides those who died at the hands of assassins, who were many, there died an infinite number of people, suffocated by great snow falls, by storms, cold and bad weather [...] for each dead body found one placed a cross, so that the number of crosses was such that one spoke of the hundred crosses.[84]

Cesena also reported a tale about a wicked monk. Somehow the two stories became entwined and ended up in Lees's book three and a half centuries later.[85]

## Conclusions

It is perhaps inevitable that brief visits to any place will only scratch its surface, and in our different ways, both Lees and I have experienced Varese briefly. The eye of the outsider can see what local do not, at least sometimes. Short immersive experiences can be memorable whether a day or two spent in Varese or annual week-long field trips spread out over a quarter of a century. Reading about travel is not quite the same, but even so I have certainly enjoyed revisiting Lees's fine book during 'lockdown'. It is of course only one travel book among very many just as Lees was only one traveller among the 900,000 who had visited Italy in 1911, the year of the much-celebrated 50th anniversary of the Unification of Italy.[86] The Italian Riviera was saturated with tourists well before that – Italians as well as British and Germans,[87] and with guides to instruct them how to experience it.[88] Lees as a professional writer surely knew that few of those sightseers ventured inland and that a book about places like Varese might sell because of its novelty. His book does indeed provide a good guide to Liguria even today, but it is also much more than a mere guide. It tells us a great deal about historical change to Ligurian landscapes, about the impact of modernity and not least about the process of travelling itself. Travel writing is a slippery genre and often dismissed as a variety of fiction. It can be that, but it does not have to be. Diego Moreno, Italy's foremost historical ecologist, has demonstrated throughout his long career how human practices create 'landscape', and that reading the land realistically (Ital.: *decifrazione realistica*) is our best chance of understanding why it has changed.[89] This reading technique can also be applied to travel books, appreciating their literary conventions while verifying their statements against the current landscape and what other sources tell us about its history. From my home in Nottingham, I have tried to read Lees like this. I hope he would have approved.

## Notes

1. To be precise, 5–9 January. In my diary I simply put 'Varese' in capitals.
2. Albergo Ristorante Amici, 'Albergo Ristorante Amici, Varese Ligure', accessed 16 October 2020, http://www.albergoamici.it/. The Marcone family and their staff have provided us and generations of students with superb hospitality. Heartfelt thanks to them all.
3. In addition to Charles, his course has been co-taught with Professor Diego Moreno (University of Genoa) and Don Sandro Lagomarsini (director of the Museo Contadino in Cassego, one of his parishes). I have learnt so much in many years of stimulating work and companionship.
4. R. Balzaretti and C. Watkins, 'The Landscape History of Liguria Field Courses of the University of Nottingham', in *La natura della montagna. Scritti in ricordo di Giuseppina Poggi*, ed. R. Cevasco (Genoa: Oltre Edizioni, 2013), 204–10; C. Watkins and R. Balzaretti, 'Experiences of Historical Ecology in Val di Vara', in *Dal documento al terreno. Storia e archeologia dei sistemi agro-silvo-pastorali. Attualità di una proposta storica*, ed. D. Moreno (Genoa: Genova University Press, 2019), 305–9.
5. The 2014 trip resulted in an excellent video produced by Myles Grover: 'Geography Field Trip to Varese Ligure 2014', YouTube, accessed 16 October 2020, https://www.youtube.com/watch?v=8exQqr-xPms.
6. The final-year module 'Victorians in Italy: Travelling South in the Nineteenth Century'. I have been humbled by the wonderful insights into travel history provided by my students over the years, including two who are contributors to this volume.
7. F. Lees, *Wanderings on the Italian Riviera. The Record of a Leisurely Tour in Liguria* (London: Isaac Pitman and Sons, 1912).
8. R. Balzaretti, *Dark Age Liguria. Regional Identity and Local Power, c. 400–1020* (London: Bloomsbury, 2013), 5–6; P. Tomaini, *Varese Ligure. Insigne borgo ed antica pieve* (Città di Castello: A. c. grafiche, 1978), 134.
9. Tomaini, *Varese Ligure*, 209.
10. Ibid., 19–20; R. Balzaretti, 'Fieschi', in *Medieval Italy: An Encyclopedia*, vol. 1, ed. C. Kleinhenz (New York: Routledge, 2004), 336–7.
11. Tomaini, *Varese Ligure*, 23–24.
12. It was staged by the New Diorama Theatre, London, 5 January–23 February 2013, a wonderful production which I was fortunate to see.
13. Tomaini, *Varese Ligure*, 38–40.
14. This circulated in manuscript among local families until it was first printed in 1982. A more recent edition is A. Cesena, *Relatione dell'origine et successi della terra di Varese descritta dal rev. prete*

*Antonio Cesena l'anno 1558*, ed. S. Lagomarsini (La Spezia: Accademia Lunigianese di Scienze 'Giovanni Capellini', 1993).
15 Now via Garibaldi. Some of these houses are well preserved but not generally open to the public.
16 S. Lagomarsini, 'Arte religiosa e iconografia in Val di Vara', in *Arte e devozione in Val di Vara*, ed. M. Ratti (Genoa: Sagep Editrice, 1989), 21–32.
17 G. Bagioli, *Guida d'Italia. Liguria* (Milan: Touring Club Italiano, 1982), 614–16.
18 O. Raggio, 'Social Relations and Control of Resources in an Area of Transit: Eastern Liguria, Sixteenth to Seventeenth Centuries', in *Domestic Strategies: Work and Family in France and Italy 1600–1800*, ed. S. Woolf (Cambridge: Cambridge University Press, 1991), 20–42.
19 P. d. Nevi, *Viaggio senza ritorno. Documenti, volti e testimonianze d'emigrazione in Val Di Vara* (Val di Vara: Centro Studi Val di Vara, 1989).
20 Biodistretto Val di Vara, 'Biodistretto Val di Vara, Valle del Biologico', accessed 16 October 2020, https://www.biodistrettovaldivara.it/. For a discussion of these developments, see R. Raiteri, *Trasformazioni dell'ambiente costruito. La diffusione della sostenibilità* (Rome: Gangemi editore, 2003), 49–76.
21 S. Lagomarsini, 'Urban Exploitation of Common Rights: Two Models of Land Use in the Val di Vara', in *Ligurian Landscapes*, ed. R. Balzaretti, M. Pearce and C. Watkins (London: Accordia, 2004), 179–88.
22 As I argued in 'Wanderings: A Male Space in the History of Travel?', a paper given at Victorian Masculinities (University of Nottingham, 16 January 2014), a conference organised by the Midlands Interdisciplinary Victorian Studies Seminar. I am grateful to the participants for helpful comments on that occasion.
23 J. Pemble, *The Mediterranean Passion: Victorians and Edwardians in the South* (Oxford: Oxford University Press, 1988) and J. Buzard, *The Beaten Track: European Tourism, Literature and the Ways to Culture* (Oxford: Clarendon Press, 1993) are still the best analyses of this complex genre at that point in time. For travellers to Liguria, R. Balzaretti, 'Victorian Travellers, Apennine Landscapes and the Development of Cultural Heritage in Eastern Liguria, c.1875–1914', *History* 96, 4 (2011): 436–58.
24 He also published F. Arnold, *A Practical Guide to Health, and to the Home Treatment of the Common Ailments of Life, etc.* (London: Kempster, 1874).
25 F. A. Lees, *The Flora of West Yorkshire, with a Sketch of the Climatology and Lithology in Connection Therewith* (London: Lovell Reeve, 1888), 843. It was reviewed (mostly positively) by W. B. H. in *Nature* 38, 972 (1888): 147–48. His papers are deposited at Leeds Local Studies Library, and his other books can be found in the Brotherton Library, University of Leeds. His herbarium is at Cartwright Hall in Bradford. A useful biography by Mark Lawley is available via the British Bryological Society, accessed 16 October 2020, http://britishbryologicalsociety.org.uk/.
26 D. M. Fahey, 'Lees Frederic Richard', *Oxford Dictionary of National Biography* (Oxford University Press, 2004), https://doi.org/10.1093/ref:odnb/39154.
27 F. Lees, *Dr. Frederic Richard Lees. A Biography* (London: H. J. Osborn, 1904).
28 Ibid., 293–308.
29 Ibid., 319.
30 Ibid., 319–35. Due to the Covid-19 pandemic, I have been unable to consult the archival material in Leeds Local Studies Library or the collections at Cartwright Hall in Bradford to see if any of this material has survived.
31 G. Longman, *The Herkomer Art School 1883–1900* (Bushey: Bushey Museum and Art Gallery, 1976), https://busheymuseum.org/bushey-artists/.
32 *The Royal Academy Summer Exhibition: A Chronicle, 1769–2018* (London: William Clowes and Sons, 1894), https://chronicle250.com/1894#catalogue=~.%20Edith%20Fithian.
33 Other images by her can be found on the internet, e.g. E. Fithian, '1897 Vintage Illustration by Edith Fithian of the Actress Sarah Bernhardt in La Dame Aux Camelias', *Alamy*, accessed

16 October 2020, https://www.alamy.com/1897-vintage-illustration-by-edith-fithian-of-the-actress-sarah-bernhardt-in-la-dame-aux-camelias-image240663466.html; a portrait of Sarah Bernhardt published in 1897 in *The Lady's Realm*, a weekly magazine.
34 *Pall Mall Gazette* 35 (June 1905): 6–7.
35 *The Strand Magazine* 42 (July–December 1911): 323–30.
36 'The Holiday Maker in Paris. Sights to See in the French Capital', *Pall Mall Gazette* 48 (September 1911): 397–402, and many articles in *The World Wide Magazine* between 1900 and 1911.
37 F. Lees, *A Summer in Touraine* (London: Methuen, 1909). It has 12 colour plates by Armfield and 87 other illustrations. It had reached its third edition by 1924.
38 Lees, *Wanderings*, v–x.
39 I have so far been unable to identify J. K. The Historical Society was founded in 1857 and based in the Albaro district of Genoa at the time Lees was writing: *Società Ligure di Storia Patria*, accessed 18 October 2020, https://www.storiapatriagenova.it/Default.aspx.
40 Lees, *Wanderings*, viii, 34–61 (chapter on San Remo).
41 The 'Antiquary' was a great walker who 'year after year' and 'ever on foot' knew every yard of Liguria (Lees, *Wanderings*, 2).
42 This hands-on attitude can be traced back at least to W. G. Hoskins, *The Making of the English Landscape* (London: Hodder and Stoughton, 1955) and the many books of the late Oliver Rackham, who visited Varese with us in March 1996.
43 Lees, *Wanderings*, x.
44 Ibid., 242.
45 Ibid., 319.
46 E.g., ibid. 241 describing Torriglia, at this time a favourite inland summer resort for the Genoese.
47 L. Pozzi and D. R. Fariñas, 'The Heat-Wave of 1911. A Largely Ignored Trend Reversal in the Italian and Spanish Transition?', *Annales de démographie historique* 2, 120 (2010): 147–78.
48 Lees, *Wanderings*, 239. I have lived in Genoa for a total of three weeks.
49 Ibid., 292–94.
50 Ibid., 2. Also noted by C. Casey, *Riviera Nature Notes*, ed. R. Cassy (Oxford: Signal Books, 2003), 123–26.
51 Lees, *Wanderings*, 15.
52 Ibid., 44.
53 Ibid., 132–33.
54 Ibid., 144.
55 Ibid., 147.
56 As exemplified later by the 'Kitbag Travel Books' series published by Harrap in the 1920s: B. Lynch, *The Italian Riviera. Its Scenery, Customs and Food with Notes upon the Maritime Alps* (London: George G. Harrap, 1927).
57 G. M. Trevelyan, 'Walking', in *Clio, a Muse, and Other Essays Literary and Pedestrian* (London: Longmans, Green, 1913).
58 J. A. Amato, *On Foot. A History of Walking* (New York: New York University Press, 2004).
59 *Ligúria, Toscana settentrionale, Emília. Guida d'Italia* (Milan: Touring Club Italiano, 1916), 13–20.
60 Lees, *Wanderings*, 207, as was the 'industrialism' in the Bisagno valley (242).
61 Many examples of pre-photographic amateur sketching can be found in R. Balzaretti, P. Piana, D. Moreno and C. Watkins, 'Topographical Art and Landscape History: Elizabeth Fanshawe (1779–1856) in Early Nineteenth-Century Liguria', *Landscape History* 33, 2 (2012): 65–81; P. Piana, C. Watkins and R. Balzaretti, '"Saved from the Sordid Axe": Representation and Understanding of Pine Trees by English Visitors to Italy in the Eighteenth and Nineteenth Century', *Landscape History* 37, 2 (2016): 35–56; P. Piana, C. Watkins and R. Balzaretti, 'Art and Landscape History: British Artists in Nineteenth-Century Val d'Aosta (NW Italy)', *Landscape*

*History* 39, 2 (2018): 91–108; P. Piana, C. Watkins and R. Balzaretti, 'Transport, Modernity and Rural Landscapes in Nineteenth Century Liguria', *Rural History* 29, 2 (2018): 167–93; P. Piana, C. Watkins and R. Balzaretti, 'The Palm Landscapes of the Italian Riviera', *Landscapes* 19, 1 (2018): 43–65.

62 E. Harvey and M. Umbach, 'Introduction: Photography and Twentieth-Century German History', *Central European History* 48, 3 (2015): 290–91; B. Levine and K. M. Jensen, *Around the World: The Grand Tour in Photo Albums* (Princeton: Princeton Architectural Press, 2007), 47–57, examines an album of photographs of Italy made by a young American couple in 1905.

63 E. S. Lothrop, 'The Brownie Camera', *History of Photography* 2, 1 (1978): 1–10.

64 W. Scott, *The Riviera* (London: A. and C. Black, 1907); W. Tyndale, *An Artist in the Riviera* (London: Hutchinson, 1914). Less literary guidebooks were also illustrated with 'original photographs', such as W. T. Beeby and E. Reynolds-Ball, *The Levantine Riviera. A Practical Guide to all the Winter Resorts from GENOA to PISA* (London: Reynolds-Ball's Guides, 1908), 20 photographs including the English Church at Rapallo (70), most taken by Beeby himself. It is a book likely known to Lees.

65 Lees, *Wanderings*, opposite title page.

66 Tyndale, *Artist in the Riviera*, opposite 212.

67 Lees, *Wanderings*, xiii–xv.

68 My own (several thousand) photographs of Varese and the Val di Vara taken between 1995 and 2019 fall into similar categories.

69 Lees, *Wanderings*, opposite 294.

70 C. Watkins, 'The Management History and Conservation of Terraces in the Val di Vara, Liguria', in *Ligurian Landscapes. Studies in Archaeology, Geography and History in Memory of Edoardo Grendi*, ed. R. Balzaretti, M. Pearce and C. Watkins (London: Accordia, 2004), 141–54.

71 R. Balzaretti, R. Hearn and C. Watkins, 'The Cultural and Land Use Implications of the Reappearance of the Wild Boar in North West Italy: A Case Study of the Val di Vara', *Journal of Rural Studies* 36 (2014): 52–63, considers one of the significant consequences of such changes in land management.

72 D. Moreno, 'Escaping from "Landscape". The Historical and Environmental Identification of Local Land-Management Practices in the Post-Medieval Ligurian Mountains', in *Ligurian Landscapes*, ed. R. Balzaretti, M. Pearce and C. Watkins (London: Accordia, 2004), 129–40; A. T. Grove and O. Rackham, *The Nature of Mediterranean Europe. An Ecological History* (New Haven: Yale University Press, 2001); Balzaretti, *Dark Age Liguria*, 13–34.

73 Lees, *Wanderings*, 295.

74 Lagomarsini, 'Arte religiosa', 21–32. The relief is illustrated on 28, figure 21.

75 Ibid., 24.

76 There has been a considerable revival in local wine production in recent years, notably La Casetta in Salino. This and the Pino Gino wines can be tasted at the Albergo Amici in Varese.

77 M. McCullagh and M. Pearce, 'Surveying the Prehistoric Copper Mine at Libiola (Sestri Levante – GE), Italy', in *Ligurian Landscapes*, ed. R. Balzaretti, M. Pearce and C. Watkins (London: Accordia, 2004), 83–95 (83), point out that Frederic Brown, owner of the castle at Paraggi whose father had been British consul in Genoa, was a shareholder in this company. As a result of the US 'bank panic' of 1907, the value of copper fell by 40 per cent.

78 Azienda Agricola Pino Gino, accessed 18 October 2020, http://www.pinogino.it/. Several groups of our students have researched viticulture here over the years due to the kindness of Antonella Pino.

79 We have learnt so much from talking to and formally interviewing local residents that it would be impossible to thank everyone individually here, but I cannot omit Gabriella Figone and her brother Raffaelle of the Bar Colomba who have done so much for us.

80 eBay Italia, accessed 18 October 2020, https://www.ebay.it/sch/i.html?_from=R40&_trksid=p2380057.m570.l1313&_nkw=Varese+Ligure+Castello&_sacat=0.

81  Lees, *Wanderings*, 295–96.
82  *Sciuette* are no longer made, but some have been preserved at the Albergo Amici and in the Museo Contadino in Cassego which match Lees's description. *Porcini* both fresh in season and dried all year round can be found in abundance in Varese. They have a justified reputation as being of the very highest quality and feature prominently in the local cooking.
83  Lees, *Wanderings*, 297–98.
84  Lagomarsini, *Relatione*, 7.
85  For Cesena, see R. Balzaretti, 'The History of the Countryside in Sixteenth-Century Varese Ligure', in *Ligurian Landscapes*, ed. R. Balzaretti, M. Pearce and C. Watkins (London: Accordia, 2004), 123–38.
86  R. J. B. Bosworth, *Italy and the Wider World: 1860–1960* (London: Taylor and Francis, 1996), 163.
87  Balzaretti, 'Victorian Travellers', 445–46.
88  Examples include C. B. Black, *The Riviera* (London: A. and C. Black, 1898) and Beeby and Reynolds-Balls, *The Levantine Riviera* (London: Reynolds-Ball's Guides, 1908).
89  D. Moreno, *Dal documento al terreno. Storia e archeologia dei sistemi agro-silvo-pastorali. Attualità di una proposta* storica (Genoa: Genova University Press, 2019).

## Chapter Three

## 'A RUDE PEOPLE SUBJECTED TO NO RESTRAINT': IN TANIMBAR WITH ANNA KEITH FORBES, HENRY FORBES AND SO'U MELATUNAN

### Will Buckingham

In the 1990s, I flew to East Indonesia, to the Tanimbar archipelago in south-east Maluku, to try to make myself an anthropologist. For the previous two years, I had read everything I could get hold of about Tanimbar: travel accounts, academic papers, reports written by missionaries, obscure anthropological monographs. There wasn't much to read; this was part of the appeal: Tanimbar seemed always on the periphery, a corner of the world perpetually on the fringes of great events.

What I did read allowed me to piece together a picture of life in the place that later became my home. From anthropologist Susan McKinnon, who carried out fieldwork in Tanimbar in the late 1980s, I learned of the Tanimbarese adventurer So'u Melatunan, who travelled through the world of the colonial Dutch powers, bringing back valuables, riches and stories. From McKinnon, also, I learned how warfare was a 'persistent fact of life' in the Tanimbar islands, as if there were something about Tanimbar that was, and had always been, war-like.[1] It was a picture corroborated by the travel narratives of the nineteenth-century travellers Henry and Anna Forbes and by their tales of inter-village warfare, headhunting and violence. So when, in her elegant account of her stay in Tanimbar, Anna Forbes concluded the Tanimbarese were 'a rude people subjected to no restraint', I took the war-like nature of the Tanimbarese for granted.[2] Even after I returned home, after I started to weave stories of my own about Tanimbar, I worked on the assumption that this is just how things were, and it was how they always had been. But more recently, I have started to wonder. What if this tale of the war-like Tanimbarese is more complex than it first seems? What if, like everything else, violence has a history? What if I, and everybody else, had got Tanimbar wrong?

What follows is a story of getting things wrong. It is a story about Henry and Anna Forbes. It is a story about So'u Melatunan, whose own tale was darker than I ever imagined. And it is a story about how I – a rude person, subjected to little restraint – played my own small part in this history of violence.

## Arrivals

On 13 July 1882, after several days of rough seas and fog, Scottish ornithologist Anna Keith Forbes and her naturalist husband Henry Ogg Forbes arrived in Tanimbar on board the steamer *Amboina*. It had been a miserable journey. In her 1887 book, *Insulinde: Experiences of a Naturalist's Wife in the Eastern Archipelago*, Anna writes how the ship rolled in the heavy seas. They secured the cabin windows closed to keep out the spray and the rain.[3] But as they drew level with the island of Larat, the southmost island in the Tanimbar archipelago, things were looking brighter. The sun started to come out, and Anna started to feel more cheerful. From the deck, they could see the mangrove thickets and the coconut palms, and behind the low, scrubby forests, so different from the lushness of central Maluku.

They looked ashore, knowing this was to be their home for the next three months. The boat anchored near the village of Ritabel. The local people, who knew enough to be apprehensive about new arrivals, came to meet them in small dugout canoes. The Tanimbarese climbed on board, 'talking in exuberant Papuan fashion',[4] curious to find out about the new arrivals. It was Anna and Henry's first meeting with their new neighbours. Anna was initially ambivalent towards the Tanimbarese. She was impressed by the physique of the Tanimbarese men. They were, she wrote, 'powerful, athletic fellows, having rich chocolate-coloured skins and flowing manes of gold-hued hair, which gave them a most prepossessing air'.[5] But the women she found disappointing, with their 'untidy mops and dingy sarongs'.[6] Two elderly men came on board the *Amboina*. They made gestures of raising a cup to their lips and asked for *laru*, or alcohol. Anna and Henry obliged, serving them gin from the ship's supplies. Then passengers and crew from the Amboina clambered down into the waiting canoes and went ashore.

In Ritabel, Anna and Henry first went to meet the local post-holder, the resident official for the Dutch colonial regime, 'an official who, by residence among the savage inhabitants, upholds the authority of the Government, and meanwhile impresses on the natives the benefits of civilisation'.[7] The post-holder was himself from Maluku and had only been in Tanimbar for a few months. He was accompanied by his wife, their child, two police officers with their wives and two hunters. He was, Anna said, a 'dreamy sort of man'; but his wife was more practical and was a 'wonderful little woman, full of energy and tact', who got on with the local people far better than her husband.[8] The post-holder's house was still unfinished, but Anna and Henry rented a room, until they could find a site for a place of their own.[9] Inside the post-holder's house, they sat and chatted for a while. The post-holder filled them in on the difficulties they had endured over the previous few months. Then the crew and other passengers from the *Amboina* rose to leave, and Anna and Henry waved them off from the shore.

They sat down on a packing case and watched the steamer disappear over the horizon, 'with feelings somewhat of desolation, and not without misgivings, left as we were without the possibility of communicating with civilization for at least three months to come'.[10]

I was 23 when I arrived in the Tanimbar islands in 1994, more than a century after Henry and Anna Forbes. For the previous few years, I had been a student of fine arts.

But most of those years I spent in the library, haunting the anthropology stacks, reading up on the Mbuti and the Ik, the Nuer and the Azande, the Trobrianders and the Sa'dan-Toraja. I was entranced by anthropology, by the way it threw light on the parts of my own culture that seemed most unarguable, most necessary and showed them to be contingent. I immersed myself in books that sung the wonders of human malleability, of the diversity of cultures. And I decided I wanted to join this great tradition and to become an anthropologist myself.

After some scouring of the map, I settled on south-east Maluku. I would go to the Tanimbar islands and I would study the work of sculptors, those who carved in wood and stone. And if information on the Tanimbar islands was scarce, that was part of the point. In the gaps between what little information I could glean – the travellers' tales, the monographs, the scholarly papers – my mind spun fictions and fantasies. I visited the stores of the British Museum to see their holdings from Tanimbar. I wrote to museums in the Netherlands and took a research trip where I gazed at Tanimbarese wood carvings: *tavu* household altarpieces and *loru* prow-boards from war-canoes, adorned with spirals and fighting cocks. In the art school, I painted images from Tanimbarese myth, stylised representations of the culture hero Atuf as he speared the sun into ten thousand parts. My tutors, understandably, were baffled.

Over the final years of my degree, I scraped together the funds for the research. I tracked down a bunch of small grants that, when added to my small earnings from busking, made a pot sufficient to cover my expenses. I persuaded the Universitas Pattimura in Ambon to sponsor my research and the Indonesian Institute of Sciences to issue me a permit. Then in 1994, shortly after graduating, I flew out to Indonesia.

It was a windy day in September 1995. The tiny Merpati Airlines plane from neighbouring Kei circled over the rusted rooftops of Tanimbar, battling against crosswinds. The forest pitched and reeled beneath me. I thought about Henry and Anna Forbes. I thought about the artworks I had admired in shadowy museum stores. I thought of the foreigners who had come before me.

The plane came into land, hitting the tarmac hard. There were only eight or nine of us on the flight, but we clapped enthusiastically as we landed. The man in the seat across the aisle grinned at me: *masih hidup*, he said: 'still alive'.

At the airport, a minibus was waiting to take us into town. The minibus dropped me off at the Harapan Indah, the 'lovely hope' hotel in the centre of town. I went in and booked the cheapest room they had: a dark, airless place on the first floor.

## Warfare

When Henry and Anna arrived in Tanimbar, they had been married for two years. Henry had proposed in their native Aberdeen before leaving on his expedition. Shortly afterwards, in 1878, he had departed for the Dutch East Indies on a scientific voyage that was to last five years. Three years later, Anna followed him. She arrived in the Indonesian archipelago in 1881, and on 5 April that year, the two of them married in the Javanese city Buitenzorg, now known as Bogor.[11]

After their wedding, Henry and Anna travelled, cataloguing the rich fauna and flora of the region. Henry – despite having only one eye, and thus a poor aim (he lost the other eye while he was a medical student) – took charge of shooting specimens. Anna's job was to take the specimens and prepare and preserve them.

Once they had settled in to Tanimbar, Anna and Henry took their leave of the post-holder and went to explore. They were excited and apprehensive, and they were eager to find a place to build a house, so they could work undisturbed. As they attempted to leave the village of Ritabel, they were apprehended by the local villagers. In his book *A Naturalist's Wanderings in the Eastern Archipelago: A Narrative of Travel and Exploration from 1878 to 1883*, Henry told the story like this:

> All round the village we found a high strong palisade, with a portion removable, however, on the shore side in the daytime. In attempting to pass out by the landward gateway we were at once restrained by several of the villagers following us, who pointed to the ground in an excited manner, demonstrating to us its surface everywhere set with sharpened bamboo spikes, except along a narrow footpath. Their gestures instantly opened our eyes, with an unpleasant shock, to the truth that we were environed by enemies, and the village was standing on its defence.[12]

Unperturbed, the Scottish visitors edged along the footpath and left the village, heading out into the forests and plantations beyond. From the first, Henry was entranced by the richness of the flora and the fauna. He netted a swallow-tail butterfly (*Papilio aberrans*). He found an iridescent beetle (*Cyphogastra splendens*). In the trees, he spotted a scarlet lory (*Eos reticulata*), a bird that later he would pride himself on being 'perhaps the First European' to see alive in its natural environment and 'certainly the first to shoot'.[13]

It was close to sunset when they climbed the cliff path to the village of Ridol. As they did so, they were stopped by a group of men from Ritabel. The villagers, Anna wrote, 'with the most earnest insistence tried to hinder us from going farther'.[14] But Anna and Henry were too eager to see what lay at the top and would not be stopped. At the end of the path, they found the village abandoned, half-burned to the ground, 'and from the branch of a high tree before us a human arm, hacked out by the shoulder-blade dangled in the breeze, and at no great distance further were recently-gibbeted human heads and limbs'.[15]

Anna and Henry clambered back down the hill. The men from Ritabel were waiting for them and solicitously accompanied them back to the village. 'I often recall my impressions of that hour with pleasure,' Anna wrote imperturbably, as if coming across the site of a recent massacre was something of no consequence:

> You could see us on the sea-beach at sundown – would that I could fill in the picture so that you could distinctly imagine the group accompany us, and see the savage at home. Twenty lithe, handsome young fellows, their golden manes bound – some with scarlet cloth and some with yellow leaves – with bright feather or gay flower decorations stuck at the side and floating on their dark brown skins, capering round, waving their bows and arrows in the air, and

brandishing their spears, and now and again drawing near to examine our clothes and touch our hands and faces.[16]

One of the first people I met in Tanimbar was the Dutch Catholic pastor – the last of a lineage stretching back 80 years. I went to visit him in the *pastoran*, the church house just outside of Saumlaki. It was an enviable spot for a house: there were breezes coming in from the sea, and the little cottage was surrounded by low, scrubby gardens. Nearby, a group of seminarians was playing volleyball. They called out and waved as I passed them. I waved back.

The first official Catholic mission arrived in the Tanimbar Islands in 1910, just over a quarter century after Henry and Anna. The Dutch priests Father Cappers and Father Klerks came with petrol, gunpowder and a small entourage of servants and assistants. Three years later, the first baptisms took place. A monument in the village of Olilit Tua still marked the place. The monument read: 'a milestone in the history of the development of the Catholic religion in Tanimbar'.[17]

I knocked on *pastoran* door. A slight, serious-looking man in his sixties appeared, and we introduced ourselves. His name was Pastor Cornelius Bohm. 'Come in,' Pastor Bohm said, ushering me over the threshold. He pulled out a chair for me to sit down. 'Beer?'

'Yes, please,' I said.

As he went to fetch the beer, I examined the plastic sugar bowl on the table. On the bow was sign in Indonesian. 'Please keep closed,' the sign said. 'Ants like sugar too.'

Pastor Bohm handed me a beer and cracked one open for himself. We drank and chatted as the sun set, and the priest filled me in on what I needed to know about Tanimbar. He had been in the islands for years, and he was more knowledgeable about them than any outsider. When he found out I was interested in sculptures, he went over to a cabinet and took out some wood carvings. He handed them to me, one by one. They were made from *kayu hitam*, the local black wood, and were very finely carved. There were figures of women carrying baskets, of headhunters, of warriors with spears. 'These are all from the village of Tumbur,' Pastor Bohm said, 'There are many sculptors in the village. Once I tried to get the sculptors to make religious figures, you know? But they were derivative and without creativity. But these ... these are something special.'

'This one,' the pastor said, picking up a sculpture, 'is a head-hunter. The Tanimbar islands used to be a war-like place. But these days, the people play football instead.'

Before I left, the pastor gave me a large, yellow book that looked as if it had been run off on a photocopier. It was the Indonesian translator Petrus Drabbe's ethnography of the Tanimbar islands, first published in Dutch in 1940. 'You will find this interesting,' he said. 'Also, do you need a typewriter? We have one somewhere that you can borrow. It might be useful. I'll see if I can find it. Come back in a few days' time.'

I thanked him and left, the book under my arm.

A week later, I caught a boat out to the island of Sera, a little way to the west. I had heard that there was a sculptor in the village of Rumah Salut, and I was eager to meet him. The sculptor was called Matias Fatruan, and he carved strange, fantastical creatures that he wouldn't allow me to photograph. We spent a week or two together, talking about art and Tanimbarese history. Matias was disabled. Several years before, he had fallen from a coconut palm and shattered his legs. For several years, he had made a scant income from carving images. It was clear he was bored. He enjoyed the company and the attention. But he was also suspicious of me. He told me he didn't trust me, because I had come to steal from him. I protested that I was there only to find out about his work, to tell the world about the sculptors of Tanimbar. But Matias stopped me. 'I do not think that you have come to steal with the hands,' he said. 'I am afraid that you have come to steal with the eyes.'[18]

I travelled back to Saumlaki a few days later and moved back into the Harapan Indah. But Tanimbarese friends told me I shouldn't waste my money on hotel bills, so they fixed up for me to stay nearby in the village of Olilit Baru, where I rented a room from Ibu Neli, a local schoolteacher who lived alone with her son Lucky. Ibu Neli's place was perfect. She was a solicitous host. At breakfast time, she gave me hot, sweet tea to drink and platefuls of bread and margarine sprinkled with crystal sugar. She treated me like an adopted son, usually indulgent and sometimes stern. She set me up with a room of my own, a small corner of the middle room of the house with a curtain that I could pull closed in the evening. I had a desk and a chair set up by the window. I picked up the typewriter from Pastor Bohm and settled into the routine of work.

I started to make networks of friends. People invited me out for picnics. They included me. They suffered my faltering Indonesian with good grace. They put up with my idiot questions. And they ribbed me gently about how I was not getting any younger and should think about marrying a local woman before it was too late.

My main base was in Ibu Neli's house. But I took trips out by bus, by boat and on foot to remote villages. I recorded conversations on my small portable tape-recorder. 'We are impressed,' my Tanimbarese friends said kindly. 'You have come all this way to find out about our lives. You have come all this way for knowledge.'

One evening, I was sitting at my desk and working when I heard a commotion outside. I got up and went to see what was happening. Ibu Neli was ushering a small group of people into the house. They were distant relatives and had come on foot from the village of Wowonda, a distance of 12 miles. Ibu Neli gave them tea and asked them what had happened.

They were afraid, they said. They were fleeing out of fear for their lives, because the village of Wowonda was at war with the neighbouring village of Ilgnei. The skirmish had arisen out of a dispute in the pool hall in Saumlaki. An unmarried man from Wowonda, in his early twenties, was sent into town by his family to buy rice. He staked the money on a game of pool, and he lost. In an attempt to win back the lost money, he played again, this time staking his jeans. Once again he lost. He stripped off his trousers and handed the prize over to the victor. Then he walked home along the sea shore, barelegged and humiliated. He reappeared in Wowonda after dark, without rice, money, trousers or dignity. His relatives beat him. Then they asked him what had happened. He told them about the pool game and said his opponent was from the neighbouring village of Ilgnei. So the men folk of Wowonda gathered together and dressed for battle, armed with bows, spears and arrows. Then they marched on the neighbouring village. The people of Ilgnei either fled or else barricaded themselves into their homes, praying their enemies would not burn their houses down while they were inside. The warriors from Wowonda waved their spears, yelled belligerently and torched a few unoccupied buildings. Then they returned to Wowonda. But now the village was on a war-footing. And so some of the women and children from Wowonda, fearing reprisals, had slipped away southwards, to end up on our doorstep.

Ibu Neli gave the refugees tea and said they could stay as long as they liked. She said that her connections in the Catholic church would be able to mediate the dispute, and there was nothing to worry about. A few days later, the refugees drifted back to Wowonda, and I heard nothing more of the dispute. But when I travelled north through Ilgnei on the bus a couple of weeks later, I saw the remnants of the burned-out building.

**Headhunting**

In Tanimbar, for a long time, warfare has been tangled up with the hunting of heads. Writing in the early 1990s, Susan McKinnon argued that even if headhunting was no longer an integral part of warfare in Tanimbar, it remained 'an integral part of people's consciousness'.[19] In the dry season, the traditional season for the taking of enemy heads, there were regular headhunting scares. If headhunting was no longer practised, the fear of headhunting was still alive. Tanimbarese friends still told tales and circulated rumours of headhunters from elsewhere. And it was possible to detect a strange nostalgia for these days of heady violence. 'Today,' my Tanimbarese friends sometimes told me, 'we are modern. We no longer do these things.' And when they said things like this, it was possible to detect a note of sadness.

One day, Ibu Neli and her friend, Suster Astrid, invited me to the school kitchen to teach her to make courgette cake. Suster Astrid was one of my favourite people in Tanimbar. She was a nun who worked both in the school and the local clinic, and she seemed almost supernaturally cheerful. I never met anybody who said a word against her. She teased and cajoled Ibu Neli and seemed to overflow with an ebullient liveliness that knew no limits. I had been talking with Ibu Neli about courgette cake, and she suggested I teach them how to make it, so they could raise funds for the school. So I took an afternoon away from my desk, and we grated courgettes in the school kitchen, and Suster Astrid chatted about her work in the hospital.

'We get a lot of men who have fought with people in next-door villages,' she said. 'Some of them have bad injuries. People get drunk and angry, and they forget they are no longer headhunters.'

It took less than three weeks for Anna and Henry to build their new house. It was just by the tideline, raised up on stilts and spacious enough to carry out their work and to receive guests, who came crowding in large numbers trying to gain intelligence about these new arrivals. There was a certain mutual suspicion between the Scottish naturalists and their Tanimbarese hosts. But from their written accounts, it seems that Anna was more at home in Tanimbarsese society than was Henry. Anna seems to have got on well with the people of Ritabel. She spent time with the young mothers of the village. She played with their babies (the babies, she said, were 'good, interesting little creatures, profusely adorned with beads').[20] But Henry was more preoccupied with matters of science. For him, the Tanimbarese were not so much people to hang out with as they were fascinating specimens to be studied. 'The people that came about us to gaze,' he wrote, 'were all subjects deserving the closest study.'

> Their every gesture and every custom had to be watched with microscopic acuteness, if we were to improve our opportunities and not fail in deciphering the story – only thus recorded and to be ere long blurred and blotted by foreign contact – of their race, incessantly being unfolded before us in their every unconscious word and commonest action.[21]

Henry soon made clear to the people of Ritabel that he was keen to accumulate natural history specimens to add to his collection. And of all natural history specimens, it was human skulls that interested him the most.[22] Over the three months he was in Tanimbar, he gathered together 11 skulls which were later ferried back to the British Museum, where they were studied by Dr J. G. Garson from the Royal College of Surgeons. Because when you have a person's skull in your hand, you can at last begin to understand them. You can have their person at your disposal. You can finally know with whom you are doing business. It is almost as if you have a part of their soul.[23]

When Henry's enthusiasm for collecting skulls became clear to the people of Ritabel, the Forbes's new home became frequented by visitors eager to sell body parts. Anna, who was at the time suffering from fever, wrote that 'it having got abroad that H. wanted skulls', the Tanimbarese 'imagined that skulls and bones of any kind would be equally acceptable, and gathered from the refuse-heaps near the village all they could find, offering them with such a clamour that I was quite irritated in my weakness'.[24]

But not all sellers were equally eager. Sometimes, they would only part with these natural history specimens with reluctance. Henry wrote of how he bartered with a man to buy his father's skull. 'It seems,' he wrote,

> as if there existed in these countries a superstitious dread of any part of their person being in possession of another. One day, when I purchased from a man his father's skull, something of the same dread appeared; for as soon as the bargain was completed, the seller took from his *luvu* (or siri-holder) a piece of areca-nut, and, setting the skull before him, he placed the nut between its teeth, and before handing it over to me he repeated a long and devout invocation.[25]

## A Boy Named So'u

Almost everybody agrees that Tanimbar has been, from the very beginning of time, a place suffused by violence, by warfare and by headhunting. Beginning in the seventeenth century, travellers to the region have all told the same story: the villages on cliff-top positions, surrounded by tall defensive palisades; the inter-village feuds; the traditions of hunting heads.²⁶ And my friends in Tanimbar told me the same story. Tanimbar, they said, was a place with a proud warrior past. Once the Tanimbarese were indeed a rude people, subjected to no restraint. They were naturally given to hunting heads and to acts of savagery. Brave and courageous, they were in need of taming. And so – through baptism, through football, through the benevolence of the colonial regime, through the good offices of the Indonesian state – the people of Tanimbar slowly entered into the shared circle of humanity and civilisation.

But there is good reason to think that this story doesn't add up. And here, the story of So'u Melatunan – adventurer, trickster, storyteller, traveller – may be instructive. I first stumbled across So'u in McKinnon's *From a Shattered Sun*, a work of beautiful and intricate ethnography that, as a young anthropologist a quarter century ago, I carried with me through the Tanimbar Islands like a bible. From the stories that McKinnon tells, So'u emerges as a kind of culture hero, a trickster figure who journeys among savages and brings home treasures and tales. According to McKinnon, So'u – who was also known as Falaksoru Melatunan – was from the village of Rumya'an. It was in his home village that he first met the people the Tanimbarese called the Portugis, but who were in fact the Dutch. According to the story, a small fleet of Dutch ships arrived in the village, and So'u went on board. Quick-witted and adventurous, he remained on ship, and he went off adventuring with these savage outsiders. So'u took with him a stinking hunk of ambergris that had been found on the beach at Nus Wotar by the people of the Bungaa lineage. The ambergris was named 'Fish Shit', because of its stench.²⁷ The Bungaa folk did not know what to do with it, so they gave it to So'u, so he might exchange it with the Portugis.

When the Portugis departed, So'u left with them. And because the Portugis were savages, who didn't know how to speak his name, they inducted So'u into their rites and gave him a new name: henceforth, they said, you will be Cornelis Falcksoor. And this is the name he came to be known as in the strangers' books. So'u travelled to Ambon, to Banda, even as far as Batavia. He was skilled in the arts of exchange. With the Portugis, he traded Fish Shit for 160 elephant tusks. He journeyed to the island of Roti, far to the west, where the people are said to be more cunning than any snake;²⁸ and there he tricked the noble households out of their heirloom gold – their shining breast pendants and their armbands made of shells. He went to Banda, to the place where the Portugis fashioned intricate valuables from gold. He snuck in to the place where the strangers fashioned gold, and he made the gold stick to his feet. Then he walked right out, bold as anything, and nobody noticed his deception.²⁹

In this way, So'u became famous. And when he at last returned to Tanimbar, he brought with him great riches. He brought back the 160 elephant tusks, keeping one hundred himself, giving the other 60 to the people of the Bungaa folk. He brought a box carved from ivory. Carved on the lid of the box was a naked man who stood by a tree, around which was wrapped a great serpent. He brought a knight's armour and a dagger, the hilt made of copper.³⁰ And he brought many stories of his travels.

For years, I imagined So'u as a kind of trickster-storyteller, the Odysseus of Maluku, sailing the outer fringes of Dutch imperial might in the middle of the seventeenth century, getting himself in and out of scrapes. But when you look more closely, Sou's story is more complex and unsettling: from the Dutch colonial records, a darker picture emerges. In a letter dated to 1685, sent from the Banda islands in central Maluku, So'u is implicated in a massacre of 150 people in the village of Alouta in Babar, to the west of Tanimbar, and in the selling of the survivors into slavery – presumably to the Dutch.[31] He crops up several more times in the records, where he invariably got involved in murder, slave trading and havoc, a lone operator who is increasingly a thorn in the side of the colonial powers. The last time he appears is in a letter at the end of the seventeenth century. It is 1692, and by now, So'u is back in Tanimbar, where he has come to the attention of the Dutch authorities for having committed several murders, including that of the merchant Aarnout de Begue.[32] The authorities are unsure what to do with him. On the one hand, they propose to send a militia to arrest him; on the other hand, So'u is popular in Tanimbar, and his arrest will cause consternation among the Tanimbarese who – being 'strong, stout and courageous' – might well resist. So in the end, the order to arrest him remains unexecuted.

Later, in his *Beschrijvinge van de Oostindische Compagnie 1639–1701*, or 'Description of the East Indies Company 1639–1701', Pieter van Dam writes of the people of the Tanimbar Islands, how they are 'warlike, strongly-built, tough and treacherous', and he adds that out of all of them, 'the greatest and most prominent rabble-rouser and scoundrel' – the word in the original is '*roervinck*', literally meaning 'stir-finch' – is Falcksoor.[33]

After this, So'u disappears from the records for good.

## The History of Violence

What, then, of the history of violence, here in the margins of the world? Scholar Antoinette Schapper writes of how the defensive villages found by Henry and Anna Forbes in the Tanimbar Islands are part of a broader pattern of fortification that stretched from the eastern tip of Timor in the west to the Aru islands in the east. Across this whole region, from the seventeenth century, almost all villages in southern Maluku were fortified. And this is weird: sporadic fortification of villages took place elsewhere in the Indonesian archipelago, but in southern Maluku, 'stone walls fortifying villages were the rule rather than the exception'.[34]

Visitors to the area from the middle of the seventeenth century generally assumed this had always been the case. And yet the evidence gathered by Schapper suggests otherwise. Accounts from very early in the seventeenth century suggest that fortifications were uncommon, and that they emerged only towards the end of first half of the century, with the building of fortifications intensifying as the century continued. This is corroborated by carbon dating of fortified sites in Timor, in the far west of the region. Schapper writes that 'village fortification began in the early 17th century and was in full swing by the mid 17th century'.

If this is so, the question is why this sudden militarisation of the villages of southern Maluku? Schapper identifies one cataclysmic event: the massacre on Banda carried out by the Dutch in 1621. In this year, claiming treaty violations, the governor-general of the Vereenigde Oostindische Compagnie (VOC), or Dutch East Indies Company, Jan

Pieterszoon Coen, turned up with a Dutch fleet, sixteen hundred soldiers and one hundred Japanese mercenaries, and he seized direct control of the islands. It was necessary, he wrote, 'that Banda be once and for all subjugated, and populated with other people'.[35] In other words, his aim was to wipe out the population and turn the islands into a slave colony. Of the fourteen thousand Bandanese, many died fighting, many more died of sickness and starvation and thousands fled to the relative safety of other parts of Maluku. By the end of Coen's campaign, only 480 people remained. Schapper argues the massacre was a 'triggering event' that 'sent shock waves through Maluku as the Bandanese survivors fanned out across the Maluku islands'. And it was in the wake of this trauma that the rush to village fortification began.

But the story of So'u Melatunan adds another piece to this history of violence. A buccaneer on the fringes of colonial Dutch power, So'u takes advantage of the growing chaos brought about by the Dutch, as he murders, enslaves and trades in human lives, equally parasitic on local populations and on the Dutch infiltrators. There must have been other So'u Melatunans as well, riding the cresting waves of violence and disorder for personal gain. In the face of this – caught between the stir-finch So'u and the brutal Dutch colonial powers, between violence and violence – what else is there other than to build walls and ramparts and defences?

By the time Henry and Anna arrive two centuries later, violence is well embedded in Tanimbar, and the Scottish travellers marvel to find themselves among war-like headhunters. And as Henry goes round politely asking to buy up heads, the local people are obliging: not because they don't care for the remains of their ancestors but because the polite, good-humoured requests of this mild-mannered Scotsman are backed up by a history of over two hundred years of violence and exploitation. So the people of Tanimbar hand over the skulls of their fathers, their loved ones, in exchange for a few bits and pieces, a few scraps; they wait for the next turn in the cycle of violence; and they hope for the best. And when, towards the end of the century after, at the tail end of this history of violence, a young English anthropologist – a rude person, subjected to no restraint – sits in the dark of a sculptor's house, and the sculptor says, 'You have come to steal ... not with the hands, but with the eyes'; the anthropologist smiles and nods and begins to understand a little.

A little, but not enough.

## Notes

1 S. McKinnon, *From a Shattered Sun: Hierarchy, Gender and Alliance in the Tanimbar Islands* (Madison: University of Wisconsin Press, 1991), 7.
2 A. Forbes, *Insulinde: Experiences of a Naturalist's Wife in the Eastern Archipelago* (Edinburgh: William Blackwood and Sons, 1887), 178.
3 Ibid., 138.
4 Ibid., 126.
5 Ibid., 139.
6 Ibid., 178.
7 Ibid., 140.
8 Ibid., 147.

9  Ibid., 140.
10 Ibid., 142.
11 R. Ellen, 'The Contribution of H. O. Forbes to Indonesian Ethnography: A Biographical and Bibliographical Note', *Archipel* 16, 1 (1978): 135–59.
12 H. O. Forbes, *A Naturalist's Wanderings in the Eastern Archipelago: A Narrative of Travel and Exploration from 1878 to 1883* (New York: Harper and Brothers, 1885), 303.
13 Ibid., 304.
14 Forbes, *Insulinde*, 143.
15 Forbes, *Wanderings*, 304.
16 Forbes, *Insulinde*, 144.
17 W. Buckingham, *Stealing with the Eyes: Imaginings and Incantations in Indonesia* (London: Haus, 2018), 24.
18 Ibid., 54.
19 McKinnon, *From a Shattered Sun*, 8.
20 Forbes, *Insulinde*, 155.
21 Forbes, *Wanderings*, 307.
22 S. Pannell, 'Travelling to Other Worlds: Narratives of Headhunting, Appropriation and the Other in the "Eastern Archipelago"', *Oceania* 62 (1992): 162–78.
23 This is a well-worn theme in the literature. See, for example, R. Roque, *Headhunting and Colonialism: Anthropology and the Circulation of Human Skulls in the Portuguese Empire, 1870–1930* (London: Palgrave, 2010). Garson's findings are published in his paper, J. G. Garson, 'On the Cranial Characters of the Natives of Timor-Laut', *Journal of the Anthropological Institute of Great Britain and Ireland* 13 (1884): 386–402.
24 Forbes, *Insulinde*, 164.
25 Forbes, *Wanderings*, 309.
26 McKinnon, *Shattered Sun*, 4–8.
27 Ibid., 50.
28 This comes from my friend Grace Susetyo, herself of Rotinese heritage: the saying goes that if you see somebody from Roti contending with a snake, you should first save the snake.
29 McKinnon, *Shattered Sun*, 60.
30 J. B. J. v. Doren, 'De Tenimber-eilanden, ten zuid-westen van de Keij-eilanden', *Bijdragen tot de Taal-, Land- en Volkenkunde van Nederlandsch-Indië* 12 (1864): 67–101.
31 *Generale missiven van gouverneurs-generaal en raden aan heren XVII der Verenigde Oostindische Compagnie*, vol. 4 (1675–1683, GS 134), 173. See also the note in McKinnon, *Shattered Sun*, 60.
32 *Generale missiven van gouverneurs-generaal en raden aan heren XVII der Verenigde Oostindische Compagnie*, vol. 5 (1686–1697, GS 150), 518.
33 Thanks to Alexia Lagast for the translation here and for her help in unpicking this sorry tale.
34 A. Schapper, 'Build the Wall: Village Fortification, Its Timing and Triggers in Southern Maluku, Indonesia', *Indonesia and the Malay World* 47, 138 (2019): 220–51 (240).
35 Quoted in J. A. M. Straver, *Vaders en dochters. Molukse historie in de Nederlandse literatuur van de negentiende eeuw en haar weerklank in Indonesië* (Leiden University, doctoral thesis, 2018), 90.

# Chapter Four

# SENT TO COVENTRY: A JOURNEY HOME?

## David Civil

In the autumn of 1933, author, playwright and social commentator John Boynton Priestley began a journey through England. His travels took him to the 'ancient metropolis' of Bristol and the 'smouldering carpet' of the Black Country, from the 'Lilliputian' bleakness of Stoke-on-Trent to the 'Dickensian atmosphere' of Norwich.[1] Priestley's account was jointly published by Heinemann and Gollancz a year later in 1934. Titled *English Journey*, the book's subtitle promised the reader 'a rambling but truthful account of what one man saw and heard and felt and thought during a journey through England during the Autumn of the year 1933'.[2] Although he deployed a populist image to great effect, Priestley was not just 'one man'. While he was scorned by the modernist Bloomsbury set as the ultimate 'middlebrow', responsible for the cultural fragmentation and decline associated with commercialisation and democratisation, by 1933 Priestley was one of the nation's most popular journalists and novelists.[3] His novel *The Good Companions*, published in 1929, made him famous overnight and had already been reprinted 16 times just a year later.[4] *English Journey* was a follow-up to this success and was Priestley's first ostensibly nonfiction book. It immediately rose to the top of the *Bookseller*'s bestseller list and, by 1956, had sold 96,000 copies in hardback, making it his most successful book in that format between *Angel Pavement* in 1930 and *Bright Day* in 1946.[5] This success was predicated on the very populist traits that the likes of Virginia Woolf, Graham Greene and even George Orwell railed against.[6] Priestley's cultural authority ensured *English Journey*'s often radical national portrait was immensely influential.

Priestley's more-than-400-page portrait, therefore, deserves pride of place in the large historical gallery showcasing accounts by public intellectuals and social commentators who have used the process of travel to convey to readers something fundamental about the nation in which they lived. Alongside *English Journey* could stand Daniel Defoe's *A Tour thro' the Whole Island of Great Britain*, published in three volumes between 1724 and 1727; H. V. Morton's *In Search of England* from 1927; or John Higgs's more recent *Watling Street: Travels through Britain and Its Ever Present Past*.[7] Yet, in its style and ideological purpose, *English Journey* is a book born from the radical 1930s. Priestley's narrative is indicative of the shift, identified by Helen Carr, away from the instructive tales of heroic adventure associated with travel accounts during the last decades of the nineteenth century and towards the less didactic, more subjective, more literary texts of the interwar period.[8] By the middle of the 1930s, travel writers had abandoned the 'pseudo-scientific, journalistic method' that had dominated the genre prior to the First World War and embraced a more 'imaginative, introspective, essayistic and argumentative' kind of travel book that focused as much on the traveller's responses or consciousness as the journey itself.[9] The most prominent example of this, of course, is George Orwell's 1937 novel *The Road to Wigan Pier*.[10] While Orwell's bleak semi-sociological account of living conditions in the industrial north prior to the outbreak of the Second World War has clearly been more influential, it owes a significant, unacknowledged debt to *English Journey*.[11] As Kristin Bluemel has argued, reading Priestley's *English Journey* against Orwell's *Wigan Pier* 'shows us how thoroughly Priestley had mastered by 1934 the techniques, forms and purposes of documentary literature for which Orwell is now famous'.[12]

An explanation for Priestley and *English Journey*'s relative obscurity, when compared with the likes of Orwell, should be sought in the former's historiographical metamorphosis from political radical, exposing the burning injustices of poverty in interwar England, to nostalgic conservative, defending a narrow vision of English identity from the hostile forces of modernity.[13] As John Baxendale has argued, writing in 2001, by the end of the twentieth century, the progressive Priestley had been well and truly subsumed by an 'almost reactionary figure' who 'put forward a deeply conservative construction of Englishness, which echoed that of Tories like Stanley Baldwin and Arthur Bryant'.[14] At times, however, Priestley's account in *English Journey* provides ample evidence to support this construction. In the book's conclusion, Priestley breaks down the diverse array of geographical locations he visited into 'Three Englands': the first is an old, rural England associated with the natural beauty of the Cotswolds; the second, an industrial England, exemplified by Priestley's fond memories of growing up in Edwardian Bradford; and, finally, a 'Third England', a nation of

> arterial and by-pass roads, of filling stations and factories that look like exhibition buildings, of giant cinemas and dance-halls and cafes, bungalows with tiny garages, cocktail bars, Woolworths, motor-coaches, wireless, hiking, factory girls looking like actresses, grey-hound racing and dirt tracks, swimming pools, and everything given away for cigarette coupons.[15]

'Its real birthplace,' he claimed, was America.[16] For Priestley, the 'old brick boxes' of his Edwardian youth in Bradford had 'more solid lumps of character inside them' than the clean, well-ordered, 'chromium-plated' factories of interwar Britain. While the individuals who represented this 'New Britain' were always 'very nice', Priestley did not always enjoy meeting them. 'It is not pleasant,' he recollected, 'suddenly seeing yourself as impatient and weak, greedy and egoistical.' It is no coincidence that as he summarises these feelings he begins to feel dizzy, returning to his 'fog-bound' car which was 'crawling and halting in a world of sepia vapour, in which lost cars, making no time at all, hooted their despair'.[17]

While Priestley clearly felt uncomfortable with aspects of this 'Third England', he embraced others. Of most significance was its increasingly democratic nature, symbolised by the rise of Woolworths:

being cheap it is accessible; it neatly achieves the famous equality of opportunity. In this England, for the first time in history, Jack and Jill are nearly as good as their master and mistress; they may have always been as good in their own way, but now they are nearly as good in the *same way*. Jack, like his master, is rapidly transported to some place of rather mechanical amusement. Jill beautifies herself exactly as her mistress does. It is an England, at last, without privilege.[18]

In this sense, what Priestley valued in this 'Third England' was its essentially democratic character, elements of which reminded him of his idealised Bradford youth. Throughout his life, Priestley sought to defend what John Baxendale has described as a 'culture of the people: a vital and energetic people, rooted in the community'.[19] For Priestley, it was this culture which was under threat from the forces of 'mass society'. He was not blind, however, to the squalor, injustice and poverty which characterised many industrial communities in the wake of the Great Depression. One of *English Journey*'s most memorable passages came when Priestley visited the town of Jarrow, three years before the influential Jarrow Crusade of 1936.[20] With its 'thick air, heavy with enforced idleness, poverty and misery', Jarrow reminded him of the devastation of war:

> The whole town looked as if it had entered a perpetual penniless bleak Sabbath. The men wore the drawn masks of prisoners of war. A stranger from a distant civilisation, observing the condition of the place and its people, would have arrived at once at the conclusion that Jarrow had deeply offended some celestial emperor of the island and was now being punished. He would never believe us if we told him that in theory this town was as good as any other and that its inhabitants were not criminals but citizens with votes.[21]

What lent Priestley's account of Jarrow such authority, however, was that he was not a 'stranger from a distant civilisation'; rather he was the 'every man', as ordinary as you or I. No one, Priestley implied, could remain unmoved when confronted with 'The Town That Was Murdered'.[22] In contrast to the likes of Chris Waters, who portray *English Journey* as representative of a rural, nostalgic conservativism, one of the book's central targets was 'Old England'.[23] Meeting an ex-army officer from a long line of farmers in the Cotswolds, Priestley reaffirms his identity as a 'child of the streets, of the hotch-potch urban and industrial life'. While his acquaintance thought the reestablishment of a peasantry would help to cure the nation's ills, Priestley attacked his vision of a 'romantic, literary man's peasant' as failing to reflect the 'actual, ignorant, stupid, mean peasant of reality'.[24] If the Cotswolds was nice to look at, it should be kept firmly in its place. Unfortunately, 'the upper-class, country-house image of Englishness', a 'fake old Hollywood Britain', was beginning to assert itself and dominate the image of national life among tourists and visitors as well as, more dangerously, the population itself.[25] The problem with 'Old England', for Priestley, was that its idyllic rural beauty came with the heavy price of an arcane social system which sought to stifle progress. It was this system which *English Journey*, in part, sought to expose. At the end of his visit to the Cotswolds, Priestley does exactly this, condemning the patronising mythology of the 'craftsmen' and defending the ability of the machine, if coupled with a more egalitarian social system, to do away with the 'horrible dead weight of miserable toil'.[26]

In a similar vein to *Wigan Pier*, and with similar force, *English Journey* stands as a powerful denouncement of the governing ideologies of interwar Britain. By drawing on his populist image, Priestley invites the reader to draw the same conclusions from the carefully woven vignettes which made up the account of his journey. On a trip to the Cadbury chocolate factory in Bourneville on the south-west side of Birmingham, for example, Priestley uses the occasion to criticise paternalist private employment practices as well as those intellectuals and politicians who considered state ownership to be a panacea for the ills of poor conditions or national productivity.[27] Priestley's was a particular brand of social democracy, one profoundly uncomfortable with the language of class or the development of large, centralised economic units, yet remarkably comfortable denouncing the affluent society and articulating a vision of community and nation. This was a radical Englishness which 'defined the real nation as the people, and the true history of England as their struggle against privilege'.[28] Whereas *Wigan Pier* conveyed a feeling of 'social distance' between reader and subject by obscuring the names of places Orwell visited between North and South, the origin and destination of Priestley's *English Journey* was one and the same, that is, the nation. The industrial north is not, for Priestley, as it was for Orwell, a 'strange country'.[29] From June 1940, Priestley would project this broad, national, social democratic image during his influential series of BBC radio broadcasts. Through the Battle of Britain and the first phase of the Blitz, Priestley was 'probably the most famous voice of the BBC and second only in popularity to Churchill'.[30] The vision of the nation Priestley developed over the course of the 1930s, the descriptions of poverty, squalor and injustice, as well as the nascent affluence contained in *English Journey* appeared to anticipate the tenor of the postwar world. For historian Paul Addison, this world could be defined by the image of 'Colonel Blimp being pursued through a land of Penguin Specials by an abrasive meritocrat, a progressive Churchman and J. B. Priestley'.[31]

As that rather elaborate introduction demonstrates, *English Journey* remains an underexplored historical source, and J. B. Priestley an endlessly complex figure who serves as a symbol for the diverse ideological strands of interwar radicalism. Historians could analyse *English Journey* in any number of ways: as a profoundly detailed and radical source, describing the social life of Britain in the aftermath of the Slump; as a literary text, reflecting a shift in the style and purpose of the popular travelogue; or, how I approached the text as part of my research into the concept of meritocracy, as reflective of Priestley's distinct ideological concerns and emblematic of developments within a broader social democratic or socialist tradition in the interwar period. This collection, however, seeks to move beyond what Joseph North has identified as the 'scholarly turn' in literary studies since the 1980s.[32] While situating a text and its author in their intellectual context remains the primary task of the historian, *Travels in Isolation* aims to break free of a narrow historicism and explore how travel accounts like *English Journey* resonate far beyond their contemporary moment.[33] In this sense, texts often have long and underexplored afterlives: they escape the narrow confines of when they were written, as well as the intent of the author who produced them, and continue to haunt the present. This is particularly true for travel literature produced during the 1930s, the product of what is often regarded as a uniquely radical decade of totalitarian ideologies, capitalist crisis and rapid technological advancement.[34] A good example of this afterlife is the way journeys of the 1930s are frequently evoked and repeated, whether in Stuart Maconie's 2017 reconstruction of the Jarrow Crusade, David Sharrock retracing Orwell's steps to Wigan Pier 75 years later, or even Beryl Bainbridge's own 'English Journey', 'the Road from Milton Keynes', during the height of Thatcherism in 1984.[35] These journeys are treated as national barometers, said to yield eternal political lessons and to help us navigate moments of profound social change.

It remains tempting, however, to dismiss an account like *English Journey* and an author like Priestley as merely reflective of their contemporary context. To limit our approach to the text, picking apart its constructions until nothing remains. As David Robinson makes clear in his introduction, this collection seeks to explore how our own subjectivities as readers and authors impact on our interpretations of texts. In short, it emphasises not only how texts intrude on the present but also how we intrude on texts. Travel accounts are an ideal genre with which to attempt this approach. These accounts often bring our subjectivity to the surface by describing a journey which many of us would have undertaken at some point in our lives or by visiting a place which we have invested with significant memories or special resonances. Unlike Orwell, Priestley's rich geographical detail, especially the inclusion of the place names of those villages and towns he visited in 1933, lends his account a direct link to the present. On his way northward, for example, he visits my home city of Coventry. As I was reading this account in *English Journey*, I was making my own difficult and unexpected journey back to the city. In doing so, my aim was twofold: firstly, to take stock of what has changed and what has remained the same since Priestley's account of Coventry was published over 85 years ago. To see, as Priestley did, what lessons a city like Coventry holds about English identity and national politics. Secondly, and more personally, to interrogate my own experience growing up in Coventry and to explore how this influences my interpretation of the city today. Approaching *English Journey* as I headed 'home', I found it easy to 'huff-and-puff' my way through Priestley's remarkably positive view of the city. Despite my historical distance from the text, my emotional proximity ensured that I could not help but treat Priestley as an uninformed observer: 'He doesn't understand what it's really like.' Throughout this journey, I was struck by one overriding question: who has the authority to tell authentic narratives about a place and its community? In Coventry's case, my instinctive answer was: 'Me … I'm from there!'

The Midlands lies at the geographical and cultural core of *English Journey*, reflecting, in microcosm, all of Priestley's 'Three Englands'. There's the 'Deep England' of 'hunting country' in Market Harborough, a chance for Priestley to lambast those 'contemptible fellows' who pretend fox hunting is valuable to the countryside or a 'solemn duty' when 'in reality they are indulging and enjoying themselves'.[36] More memorable, perhaps, is the heavy industrial landscape of the Black Country. 'I was glad', Priestley claimed,

> that I did not know the names of the towns there in the smoke … no doubt at all that the region had a sombre beauty of its own. […] But it was a beauty you could appreciate chiefly

because you were not condemned to live there. If I could do what I liked with the whole country, I would like to keep a good tract of this region as it is now, to be stared and wondered at, but I would find it difficult to ask any but a few curators to live in it.[37]

Reflecting on this landscape from the ruins of Dudley Castle, Priestley's position as an observer is more explicit here than at any other point in *English Journey*. While the places he saw had names, 'Wolverhampton, Wednesbury, Wednesfield, Willenhall and Walsall', he struggled to identify where one ended and another began: 'You could call them all wilderness, and have done with.'[38] Priestley's account of the Midlands ends in Nottingham and a visit to the famous Goose Fair. Here, the trappings of the emerging 'Third England' make themselves felt among the fair's 'great many coloured lights'.[39] For all its 'glitter and blare and ingenuities', Priestley argues, it is 'no true carnival'.

> It is at heart, cheap, nasty, sordid. It offers no grand release from ordinary realities. It does not expand man. It cannot light the mind in retrospect. It does not suggest a people letting loose their high spirits, but a people trying to keep away low spirits.[40]

Priestley therefore uses the Midlands to make a series of political interventions, from his rejection of complete state ownership of industry after a visit to Bourneville, to his condemnation of cheap commercialisation after passing through Nottingham. Yet, it is also here, as his account of the Black Country suggests, that Priestley appears most self-consciously as an observer. While at times *English Journey* presents the Midlands as a distinct region with its own identity, at other points it feels squeezed between the two geographical poles of English identity: the North and the South.[41] As Tim Hall has argued, the Midlands contains elements as 'English' as the 'deep England of the Herefordshire, Worcestershire and Warwickshire countryside' and 'elements as un-English as Black Country factories and Birmingham workshops'. Accommodating the Midlands within 'the North-South geography of English culture involved little more than consigning the former elements to the cultural South' and the latter to the 'cultural North' where those unpleasant offshoots of the Industrial Revolution were enclosed in wider English consciousness.[42]

Coventry is a city which exists in this liminal space between the cultural poles of North and South, previously associated with the former due to its concentration of industry but increasingly connected to the latter, thanks to its quick transport links to the capital, the affluent surroundings of the Warwickshire countryside and its apparent lack of a defining regional accent. Priestley's account of the city in *English Journey* is remarkably positive. On arriving in the city, he paints a portrait for the reader:

> Coventry itself, ancient steeples and motor-car factories and all, was stated so emphatically against the green hollow and the silken sky that to see it gave one a sharp jolt of pleasure. There was the famous old city of the three steeples, and the equally famous new city of bicycles and motor cars and wireless sets, and all so clear that it might have been transported into Italy.[43]

Reading this, I was making my own journey back to Coventry after more than four years living and studying elsewhere in the United Kingdom. Despite my physical distance during these years, the city always remained 'home' throughout this period. As Priestley began *English Journey* in 1933, my grandad Brian was born in the same hospital his son Paul and I, 60 years later, would begin our own 'journeys'. Yet, during my time away, the meaning of 'home' had also changed and my relationship with the city of my birth transformed in fundamental ways. Coventry was somewhere I had left both physically and emotionally. For me, the process of social mobility I had experienced was bound up in my mind with leaving the city. Now, like many graduates, I was returning home with no income and less than rosy job prospects, a bundle of frustration and disappointment. While I was incredibly lucky to have been born to a loving, lower-middle-class family in one of Coventry's suburbs and to receive a good education from a local comprehensive school, my experience at university had opened my eyes to networks of privilege and patronage from which people like me were excluded. Romantically, I always related to Richard Hoggart's description of the 'uprooted and anxious Scholarship Boy' in his influential 1957 book *The Uses of Literacy*.[44] His account of the alienation engendered by social mobility, the profound discomfort individuals can experience in both the home environment they've left behind, as well as their new surroundings resonated deeply with me and probably explains the reason I pursued these questions in my PhD research. This narrative of 'escape', fundamental to myths of meritocracy and social mobility, explained why I struggled to recognise the city Priestley described in *English Journey*.

All journeys begin with a set of expectations. Priestley's expectations of Coventry were evidently low. Initially he did not even intend to visit the city, but took a 'little detour' to visit a place 'I did not know at all'. He had been prepared, however, 'for a dull day and gloomy vistas', prepared to 'overhaul' his 'stock of sombre adjectives'. First impressions are important when travelling, and even random factors like the weather can radically alter our perceptions. The 'exquisite luminous azure' which welcomed Priestley in 1933 clearly had an impact. 'The brick walls full in the sun,' he claimed, 'might have been newly painted by Vermeer.' The backdrop to my arrival in the city was less glamorous. Aboard a slow-moving train service from Nuneaton after numerous changes and delays, the backdrop was suddenly dominated by the imposing football fortress of the Ricoh Arena on the outskirts of the city. The perfect metaphor, I thought, with which to start my authentic account of Coventry and an excellent counterpoint to Priestley's Baroque-inspired entrance. The recent plight of Coventry City Football Club (or the 'Sky Blues' as they are affectionately known) appeared to encapsulate everything I thought about my hometown. It was a club trapped by the weight of the past (chiefly the years of Division One, later Premier League status and, of course, the 1987 FA Cup), disconnected from the community and in a state of terminal decline. As a regular season ticket holder growing up and attending games with my Dad, football was one of the main ways I connected and, when I moved away, disconnected from the city of Coventry. The club was relegated to League Two (the fourth division) in 2017 and, to top it off, in 2019 was forced to play their home games in Birmingham due to a rent dispute over the stadium.[45] The Ricoh Arena sat silent as I trundled past. 'They're playing well again,' stated the gentleman sitting opposite me, 'won't be long before they're back home.' He was right. Despite my gloomy prognostics, the football club was no longer a metaphor for decline but rebirth. The club was promoted from League Two in 2018 with a set of creative young players, many of whom were born and grew up in the city, playing attacking, stylish football. In 2020, the club would be promoted to the Championship.

I would have to search elsewhere for my gloomy metaphor. The train moved slowly passed the Arena Shopping Park, once home to Europe's largest Tesco superstore, and snaked towards the centre of the city. It is not exactly clear how Priestley entered Coventry in 1933, but clearly the city's famous spires made quite an impression. Over 85 years later, they were difficult to make out amidst the drizzling rain, the blue and yellow haze of the large IKEA and the creeping encroachment of several towering student accommodation blocks on the city's skyline. As I disembarked the train, I thought I caught a glimpse of another traveller passing through Coventry 65 years ago. Unlike Priestley, the poet Phillip Larkin was born in the city. He had difficult memories of growing up in Coventry, largely due to his relationship with his Nazi-sympathising father Sydney who served as city treasurer and kept a statuette of Hitler on his mantelpiece.[46] If Phillip tried to forget the city of his birth, the city did its best to repeat the favour.[47] Larkin was shunned after writing the unflattering portrayal of a childhood unspent in 'I Remember, I Remember'. The poem was the product of an accidental stop at Coventry train station in 1954:

> Coming up England by a different line
> For once, early in the cold new year,
> We stopped, and, watching men with number-plates
> Sprint down the platform to familiar gates,
> 'Why, Coventry!' I exclaimed. 'I was born here.'
>
> I leant far out, and squinnied for a sign
> That this was still the town that had been 'mine'
> So long, but found I wasn't even clear
> Which side was which. From where those cycle-crates
> Were standing, had we annually departed
>
> For all those family hols? ... A whistle went:
> Things moved. I sat back, staring at my boots.
> 'Was that', my friend smiled, 'where you "have your roots"?'
> No, only where my childhood was unspent,
> I wanted to retort, just where I started:[48]

As William Logan noted in a recent review of the poem in the *New Criterion*, 'the longing for home is so universal, rare are the fictions where the prodigal son refuses to return'. Looking back at that 'faceless childhood in Coventry Larkin saw nothing to suggest what lay ahead'. In 1954, 'it might have seemed that distinction much less genius, was beyond his grasp'.[49] The city stood as a symbol of this. Gradually the service in which I had spotted Larkin's spectre – a CrossCountry service to Crewe – pulled away and I passed through the barriers. I was finally 'home'.

If Larkin's disorientation was triggered by a combination of the damage wrought by the Blitz and his own decision to repress memories of a troubled childhood, upon exiting the station, my bewilderment stemmed from confronting the £700 million Friargate development. This redevelopment of the area around Coventry's train station comprises offices, hotels, bars and restaurants, as well as shiny new council premises. This further evidence of regeneration did not suit my narrative of the city as a bleak post-industrial wasteland. Even from this vantage point, I could see the appeal of Priestley's national topography. It requires updating, however, to reflect the transformations of the near century since the publication of *English Journey*. Coventry contains the old, the post-war and the postmodern. Recently there has been a lot of concern, however, that the balance between these three phases of Coventry's development is being tilted too far in favour of the latter with developments like Friargate obliterating the city's connection to its past.[50] A short walk from the station resides Spon Street, a medieval thoroughfare which used to run from Gosford in Oxfordshire to Birmingham. While it is not clear if Priestley visited the street, he was struck by the city's long history: 'I knew it was an old place – for wasn't there Lady Godiva? – but I was surprised to find how much of the past, in soaring stone and carved wood, still remained in the city.'[51] Today as the rain bounces off the pavement, however, the street is dominated by the flashing neon lights of the kebab shop and the shiny marble interiors of several hairdressers and beauticians. 'Ah,' I exclaim, 'I have finally found my symbol of Coventry's decline, of its failure or unwillingness to preserve and illuminate its past.' Yet, upon closer inspection, Spon Street is not the ancient thoroughfare I thought it was. A couple of plaques, which, confident with my status as a born-and-bred Coventrian I frequently ignored on the way to the pub, informs visitors that, although the street is lined with medieval buildings, several of them started life elsewhere in the city. After the devastation of the Blitz, the decision was made to try and preserve Coventry's ancient past by dismantling those medieval buildings that survived and to reassemble them in Spon Street. In fact it is thought Hitler targeted Coventry, not because of its industrial capacity but precisely because of the city's medieval legacy. As the poet Jackie Litherland has argued, 'the obliteration of the medieval city centre was so complete that nothing of it seems to remain in the national memory of the British people'. In this way, she claims, 'Hitler seems to have achieved his aim.'[52]

The Blitz obviously lies at the centre of the city's modern memory.[53] A short 10-minute walk from Spon Street lies a visceral portal to that night of Thursday, 14 November 1940, when Coventry was subjected to the longest, most devastating air raid Britain had yet experienced.[54] Bombs from this attack left the city's fourteenth-century cathedral in ruins. The decision to construct a new one, however, occurred only a day later. Built alongside the ruins, the 'new' cathedral was designed by the architect Sir Basil Spence, who commissioned artistic work from the likes of Graham Sutherland, John Piper and Elisabeth Frink, among others.[55] I had not intended to visit the cathedral. Priestley had not referenced it in *English Journey*, and growing up in the city, I had grown to take it for granted. As I clopped through the cobbled streets of Bayley Lane which surround the cathedral, however, a smile began to play on my lips. Maybe Priestley was right, this does have an Italian feel! As I turned the corner, this was reinforced by the arrival of a large tour bus. Umbrellas opened, guidebooks fluttered, cameras flashed. Defining oneself against the ephemeral tourist is a common trait of travel literature.[56] As Tim Hannigan points out in his contribution to this collection, we 'travellee-readers' – those from the place described by the travel writer – certainly presume the supremacy of local knowledge, particularly when confronted by confused flocks of tourists seeking authentic experiences in the nearest Wetherspoons. This attitude certainly conditioned my response to *English Journey*.

As I was leaving the cathedral past Jacob Epstein's towering bronze statue depicting St Michael's victory over the devil, two elderly tourists asked where Volgograd Place was. I thought these two strangers had either confused the destination of their holiday with the former USSR or had somehow uncovered my sympathies for Marxist analysis. 'Sorry, where?' I replied. 'It's a monument for the bond of friendship between Stalingrad and Coventry,' they answered, reading from their guidebooks. In 1942, with both Stalingrad and Coventry suffering the ravages of war, a group of ordinary women and the female Lord Mayor raised more than £4,000 to buy mobile x-ray units for the Red Army. In response, and before Stalingrad was devastated, 36,000 women sent a signed album dedicated to the people of Coventry. By 1944 the two cities became the first ever to be twinned in the world, an initiative established and encouraged by ordinary Coventrians.[57] I had no idea that this mural commemorated this link, or that this link even existed. The idea of building my authentic account of Coventry on the supremacy of local knowledge looked increasingly problematic. One of the most important reasons for my scepticism of *English Journey*'s account of the city was the lack of local voices. Priestley describes encountering two workers in the city:

> The Daimler young man, who took me back to my hotel, was not a Coventry man and did not like the place. Here he was in entire agreement with the head porter of my hotel, also not a Coventry man – perhaps there are no Coventry men – who answered my questions about a possible evening's amusement with the most sardonic negatives.[58]

Yet, as my encounter with the two windswept, rain-sodden tourists demonstrated, 'being local' or a 'Coventry man' (or woman) does not automatically give you a special form of knowledge or the authority to impose meanings of a place on others. You have to work hard to uncover a city's past, engage with its present and be invested in its future. 'I'm sorry,' I responded instinctively to the two travellers, 'I'm not from around here.'

Of course *English Journey* was published before the devastation of the Blitz and the city's post-war regeneration. The rebuilding of the cathedral, and the city's mazy ring road which sits above me at Volgograd Place stood as symbols of the social democratic postwar moment to which Priestley played such a fundamental part. Donald Gibson, the city architect responsible for much of Coventry's redevelopment, sought to disperse noisy, smoky factories to the outskirts of the city and to create 24 self-sustaining 'neighbourhoods' with shops, sports amenities and a village hall. Priestley, revisiting the city nearly a decade after *English Journey*, was struck by Coventry's success at creating a 'proud civic spirit'. He described to Home Service listeners his experience of investigating a municipal information bureau in the city:

> When I first looked in, I found a queue of old-age pensioners waiting to receive the fifty free bus tickets they are given every month, to encourage them to get out and about. One old lady,

wiping her shoes vigorously at the door, said to me: 'Mustn't dirty this nice place, y'know.' A good sign!⁵⁹

In this sense, Coventry stood not only for the hopes of a new type of rational social organisation but also for a new type of citizen, one transformed by the egalitarian and communitarian consequences of war. This history weighed heavily on the city as I was growing up in the late 1990s and early 2000s. I was frequently told how much Coventry had changed, how much it had declined from the heights of the postwar boom years. While I felt compelled to leave the city, my Irish grandparents were strongly attracted by the economic opportunities Coventry offered in the 1950s and 1960s. At the centre of this, of course, were secure, well-paid jobs in the automotive sector (Massey Ferguson tractors in my grandad's case). Deindustrialisation in the 1980s would hit Coventry hard and, despite not being born until 1993, coloured my perception of the city as one which had had its time. It was increasingly portrayed as a reactionary political space, liable to be captured by those seeking to propagate an exclusionary vision of English identity. Yet, if my journey so far had taught me anything, it is that the interpretation of my home city which I had carried around with me for decades was a fragile construction, liable to collapse as a result of even the most rudimentary of intellectual prodding. Firstly, it is clear that the dreams of social democratic planners, intellectuals and politicians never lived up to reality. Nick Tiratsoo, for example, has argued that, by the early 1950s, Coventry was a city with a thriving black market, with residents and migrants who were ever more individualistic and materialistic and who were much more interested in entertainment than any broader civic plans.⁶⁰ While it is clear Tiratsoo downplays the increasingly community-minded and internationalist outlook of the city in the immediate postwar decades, embodied in Volgograd Place, he is right to highlight the gap between social democratic aspirations and lived experience. Secondly, it is clear from my short journey that Coventry is no longer, if it ever was, the post-industrial wasteland I had told myself. It remains a diverse city and, like most large urban conurbations in the United Kingdom, relatively progressive, voting to remain in the Brexit referendum of 2016 and returning Labour MPs in my constituency of Coventry North West consecutively since 1974. It is also easy to find evidence of increased economic activity – from the success of Coventry University to the recent industrial investment embodied in the National Automotive Innovation Centre.⁶¹ A symbol of this regeneration can be found in the fact that Coventry has been selected as the UK's City of Culture for 2021.

Stumbling home to the suburbs, I realised that Priestley's broad judgement of Coventry was correct. It was one of those cities 'that have often changed their trades and have had many vicissitudes, but, unlike nearly all the rest, it has managed to come out on top'.⁶² If it's hard to make a case for Coventry being 'on top' today, the city is certainly an improvement on the bleak, post-industrial landscape of my imagination. As I crossed a bridge over the ring road and out of the centre, I reflected on my overriding question: who gets to tell authentic stories? I thought I enjoyed the authority, by virtue of growing up in the city, to tell a particular story of Coventry's post-industrial decline without interrogating my own subjectivities and ideological hang-ups. It was clear from my experiences chasing

Priestley that I had constructed a particular narrative of Coventry which suited my own personal mobility story. In this sense, the notion of home was a cultural resource I could manipulate. In short, I deployed this narrative in certain circumstances to help navigate the complex feelings of alienation engendered by my experience of both physical and social mobility. Coventry was never social democratic utopia or post-industrial void. Cities are dense, complex and messy spaces where competing identities and narratives jostle together. While the travellee should continue to uncover the particular intellectual preoccupations of the traveller, they should also seek to connect and reconnect with their home and its community. As I stood on the bridge and faced the sparkling lights of the city, Priestley's final image of Coventry came into view: 'the new Morris works, a tower of steel and glass, flashing above the city of gears and crank-shafts'. While this skyline may have been joined by new buildings of 'steel and glass' in recent years – whether student accommodation blocks or upmarket hotels – 'the old constellations' remain, in Priestley's words, 'remotely and mildly beaming'.[63]

## Notes

1. J. B. Priestley, *English Journey* (London: Heinemann, 1934), 26, 111, 208, 378.
2. Ibid.
3. R. Fagge, *The Vision of J.B. Priestley* (London: Bloomsbury, 2012), 5–6. For the notion of 'middlebrow', see M. Savage, *Identities and Social Change in Britain since 1940: The Politics of Method* (Oxford: Oxford University Press, 2010), 55–57.
4. J. B. Priestley, *The Good Companions* (London: Harper and Brothers, 1929); J. Baxendale, *Priestley's England: J. B. Priestley and English Culture* (Manchester: Manchester University Press, 2007), 22.
5. Baxendale, *Priestley's England*, 52.
6. For Priestley and Woolf, see J. Baxendale, 'Priestley and the Highbrows', in *Middlebrow Literary Cultures: The Battle of the Brows, 1920–1960*, ed. E. Brown and M. Grover (Basingstoke: Palgrave Macmillan, 2012), 69–81 (74); Priestley threatened Graham Greene with a libel suit for Greene's portrait of a popular novelist in his 1931 book *Stamboul Train*; see V. Brome, *J. B. Priestley* (London: Hamish Hamilton, 1988), 127; G. Orwell, 'Review: J. B. Priestley, *Angel Pavement* (1930)', in *Seeing Things as They Are: Selected Journalism and Other Writings*, ed. P. Davison (London: Harvill Secker, 2014).
7. D. Defoe, *A Tour thro' the Whole Island of Great Britain* (London: Penguin, 2005); H. V. Morton, *In Search of England* (London: Marshalsea Press, 1927); J. Higgs, *Watling Street: Travels through Britain and Its Ever Present Past* (London: Weidenfeld and Nicolson, 2017).
8. H. Carr, 'Modernism and Travel (1880–1940)', in *The Cambridge Companion to Travel Writing*, ed. P. Hulme and T. Youngs (Cambridge: Cambridge University Press, 2002), 70–86 (75).
9. B. Schweizer, *Radicals on the Road: The Politics of English Travel Writing in the 1930s* (London: University of Virginia Press, 2001), 3–4; Carr, 'Modernism and Travel', 74.
10. G. Orwell, *The Road to Wigan Pier* (London: Penguin Classics, 2001).
11. J. Baxendale, '"I Had Seen a Lot of Englands": J. B. Priestley, Englishness and the People', *History Workshop Journal* 51 (2001): 87–111 (87–88).
12. K. Bluemel, 'Ordinary Places, Intermodern Genres: Documentary, Travel and Literature', in *British Literature in Transition, 1920–1940: Futility and Anarchy*, ed. C. Ferrall and D. McNeill (Cambridge: Cambridge University Press, 2018), 182–98 (197).
13. Baxendale, *Priestley's England*, 76–101. For an example of this historiographical shift, see C. Waters, 'J. B. Priestley (1894–1984): Englishness and the Politics of Nostalgia', in *After the*

*Victorians: Private Conscience and Public Duty in Modern Britain*, ed. S. Pedersen and P. Mandler (London: Routledge, 1994), 211–30 (212–13).
14 Baxendale, 'I Had Seen a Lot of Englands', 87.
15 Priestley, *English Journey*, 401.
16 Ibid. For Priestley's complex relationship with America, see R. Fagge, 'J. B. Priestley, the "Modern", and America', *Cultural and Social History* 4, 4 (2007): 481–94.
17 Priestley, *English Journey*, 406.
18 Ibid., 402.
19 Baxendale, 'I Had Seen a Lot of Englands', 100–101. See also N. Miles, '"To Tell the Truth": Locating Authenticity in J.B. Priestley's *English Journey*', *Literature & History* 25, 1 (2016): 41–55 (48).
20 For the Jarrow Crusade, see L. Beers, *Red Ellen: The Life of Ellen Wilkinson, Socialist, Feminist, Internationalist* (London: Harvard University Press, 2016), 336–46.
21 Priestley, *English Journey*, 313–14.
22 E. Wilkinson, *The Town That Was Murdered: The Life-Story of Jarrow* (London: V. Gollancz, 1939).
23 Waters, 'J.B. Priestley (1894–1984)', 212–13.
24 Priestley, *English Journey*, 49.
25 Cited in Baxendale, 'I Had Seen a Lot of Englands', 95.
26 Priestley, *English Journey*, 63–64.
27 Ibid., 89–100.
28 Baxendale, 'I Had Seen a Lot of Englands', 107. For a good overview of the political thought of social democrats in the 1930s, see B. Jackson, *Equality and the British Left* (Manchester: Manchester University Press, 2007), 117–40.
29 Bluemel, 'Ordinary Places', 189–90.
30 S. Nicholas, '"Sly Demagogues" and Wartime Radio: J. B. Priestley and the BBC', *Twentieth Century British History* 6, 3 (1995): 247–66 (247).
31 P. Addison, *The Road to 1945: British Politics and the Second World War* (London: Quarter Books, 1977), 189.
32 J. North, *Literary Criticism: A Concise Political History* (Cambridge: Harvard University Press, 2017), 2.
33 A similar approach is encouraged by Benjamin Kohlmann and Matthew Taunton; see B. Kohlmann and M. Taunton, 'Introduction: The Long 1930s', in *A History of 1930s British Literature*, ed. B. Kohlmann and M. Taunton (Cambridge: Cambridge University Press, 2019), 1–14 (6–7).
34 For a good account of the 'long 1930s', see R. Overy, *The Morbid Age: Britain between the Wars* (London: Penguin, 2009).
35 S. Maconie, *Long Road from Jarrow: A Journey through Britain Then and Now* (London: Ebury Press, 2017); D. Sharrock, 'The Road to Wigan Pier, 75 Years On', *The Guardian*, 20 February 2011, www.theguardian.com/books/2011/feb/20/orwell-wigan-pier-75-years; B. Bainbridge, *English Journey: Or, The Road to Milton Keynes* (New York: Duckworth, 1984).
36 Priestley, *English Journey*, 117.
37 Ibid., 112.
38 Ibid., 113.
39 Ibid., 149.
40 Ibid.
41 For the 'North–South divide', see H. M. Jewell, *The North–South Divide: The Origins of Northern Consciousness in England* (Manchester: Manchester University Press, 1994); A. R. H. Baker and M. Billinge, *Geographies of England: The North–South Divide, Imagined and Material* (Cambridge: Cambridge University Press, 2004); T. Hazeldine, *The Northern Question: A History of a Divided Country* (London: Verso, 2020).

42 T. Hall, '(Re)placing the City: Cultural Relocation and the City as Centre', in *Imagining Cities: Scripts, Signs, Memory*, ed. S. Westwood and J. M. Williams (London: Taylor and Francis, 1997), 201–18 (208–9).
43 Priestley, *English Journey*, 68.
44 R. Hoggart, *The Uses of Literacy* (Harmondsworth: Penguin, 1958), 291–304.
45 S. Gilbert, *A Club without a Home* (Brighton: Pitch, 2016).
46 A. Piette, 'Childhood Wiped Out: Larkin, His Father, and the Bombing of Coventry', *English* 62, 238 (2013): 230–47 (235).
47 S. McClarence, 'That's Enough Larkin About', *The Guardian*, 2 September 2001, https://www.theguardian.com/travel/2001/sep/02/walkingholidays.poetry.observerescapesection.
48 P. Larkin, 'I Remember, I Remember (1954)', in *Phillip Larkin: The Complete Poems*, ed. A. Burnett (London: Faber and Faber, 2012).
49 W. Logan, 'Sent to Coventry: Larkin's "I Remember, I Remember"', *New Criterion* 36, 8 (2018): 8–16 (8, 13).
50 G. Darley, 'Going to Coventry', *London Review of Books*, 26 August 2020, https://www.lrb.co.uk/blog/2020/august/going-to-coventry.
51 Priestley, *English Journey*, 69–70.
52 J. Litherland, 'Why Hitler Sent Bombs to Coventry', *The Guardian*, 9 October 2009, https://www.theguardian.com/world/2009/oct/09/coventry-blitz-hitler-munich.
53 For example, Coventry City fans will frequently be heard chanting to opposition supporters: 'In our Coventry homes, we speak with an accent exceedingly rare, you want a cathedral we've got one to spare.'
54 F. Taylor, *Coventry: Thursday, 14 November 1940* (London: Bloomsbury, 2015). After the bombing, Joseph Goebbels talked of other cities being 'Coventried'. Logan, 'Sent to Coventry', 15.
55 On the art and architecture of the cathedral, see L. Campbell, *Coventry Cathedral: Art and Architecture in Post-War Britain* (London: Clarendon Press, 1996).
56 P. Hulme and T. Young, 'Introduction', in *The Cambridge Companion to Travel Writing*, ed. P. Hulme and T. Youngs (Cambridge: Cambridge University Press, 2002), 1–14 (7).
57 T. Baker, 'A Tale of Twin Cities: How Coventry and Stalingrad Invented the Concept', *The Guardian*, 4 March 2016, https://www.theguardian.com/cities/2016/mar/04/twin-cities-coventry-stalingrad-war.
58 Priestley, *English Journey*, 74.
59 Cited in D. Kynaston, *Austerity Britain, 1945–1951* (London: Bloomsbury, 2008), 603.
60 N. Tiratsoo, 'Coventry', in *Urban Reconstruction in Britain and Japan, 1945–1955*, ed. N. Tiratsoo, J. Hasegawa, T. Mason and T. Matsumura (Luton: University of Luton Press, 2002), 24–25.
61 For a good discussion of the city's prospects, see D. Morris, 'Towards a New Knowledge Economy', in *Revival of a City: Coventry in a Globalising World*, ed. J. Begley, T. Donnelly, D. Jarvis and P. Sissons (London: Palgrave Macmillan, 2019), 229–54.
62 Priestley, *English Journey*, 68.
63 Ibid., 75–76.

Chapter Five

# BEDOUIN IS A PLACE: FREYA STARK'S TRAVELS WITH NOMADS

## EmmaLucy Cole

If life gets tight, loosen it by travel.[1]

In 2020, with the opportunities for any form of travel to local areas and micro-adventures reduced by the onslaught of Covid-19, it feels as if vicarious travel has taken on a greater urgency. With many people isolated for months of the year and unable to connect and socialise, experiencing travel as a solo activity has perhaps felt abnormal for many readers. However, there are those of us who have always valued that peculiarly effervescent glow that comes from exploring the world on our own. As Freya Stark wrote of her first morning in Baghdad, Iraq, in October 1929: 'To awaken quite alone in a strange town is one of the pleasantest sensations in the world. You are surrounded by adventure.'[2] To feel immersed in the unfamiliar with a yearning to know and learn is what took me in 2011 to Nuweiba', South Sinai, Egypt, to discover more about the Tarrabin Bedouin tribe and a traditional dance called *Dahiyya*. After many years of 'downward exploration' in small communities across the world – and occasionally cities – I had recognised not only the thrill of travelling alone but also how it enabled me to connect and communicate with local people in a slow, quiet way.[3] Travelling alone, especially as a woman, is not a *brave* decision as many continue to insist but, in my opinion, can be a necessary one. Admittedly, there is a deep personal satisfaction to completing solo journeys, but that is far outweighed by the mesh of encounters created by entering an unknown environment armed with only our individual tool kit of language, empathy and experience, and with no recourse other than to choose to be vulnerable and put our faith in those around us.

Freya Stark was an individual who, with little money and few connections, forged an impressive career as an ethnographer, traveller and writer, driven by a deep-rooted belief that travel creates understanding across cultures. She believed that this subtle understanding is essential for compassion towards and consideration of others and should comfort and guide all travellers. Many of her later employments revolved around improving relations between cultures or groups. In 1979, the year that I was born, Stark, at age 86, was climbing mountains in Nepal with a BBC film crew. She travelled and learned ferociously, publishing more than two dozen books and living to a hundred years old: 'She was, quite simply, a classic,' states Jane Robinson.[4] Her innate ability to reconnect that which had become alienated, and her admirable determination as a female explorer, continues to inspire successive travel writers, such as the formidable Lois Pryce who was inspired to ride a motorcycle solo across Iran (in part tracing Stark's journey in search of the 'Assassins') and titled one of her book chapters 'Following Freya'. In the frontispiece, Pryce quotes Stark: 'I have no reason to go, except that I have never been, and knowledge is better than ignorance. What better reason could there be for travelling?'[5]

Arguably the most frequent question asked during talks by travellers and explorers is 'What is the most important thing you took with you?' For Stark, and for me, the answer is unequivocally language skills. No matter how basic, how inaccurate, how rusty, the ability to communicate is a thread woven throughout Stark's writing, a tool that facilitated a welcome into homes and communities and ultimately earned her the respect and support of institutions, such as the Royal Geographical Society. Stark initially decided to learn Arabic while convalescing from illness, mainly because it was interesting and would be useful in many different countries. I taught myself to read and write Arabic while living in Canada, scraping together enough money for a coffee so I could sit in one of the many cafes in Toronto, practising my awkward script years before my move to Egypt. There were so many times when I was grateful for the basic skills to enable connections, and occasionally to evade them.

Stark and I have a vague geographical connection: she split her childhood between Asolo, a small mountain village in Italy, and Chagford near Dartmoor in Devon, not far from where I grew up and now live across the border in Somerset. Her father built the exquisite Ford Park on the edge of the moor in the late nineteenth century, and it was a favourite home for Stark. She draws Dartmoor and Devon into her writing, finding connections between cultures and intertwining her own story within the travel narrative. While visiting *fellahin* (farmers) in Rustum, Iraq, Stark suggested that she shared a reverence of fire with the local people, relating back to the practice of controlled burning on the Devon moorland: 'I was properly brought up to worship fire. I remember as a small child being taken out to our Dartmoor "cleaves" after supper to watch the "swaling", and to dance with my sister around the burning furze bushes.'[6] As I sit looking out at the south-west countryside, writing this chapter in pandemic isolation, it seems to me that these themes of *home* and *place* resonate throughout both of our experiences of travel with the Bedouin, despite being almost a century apart.

Although I had initially planned only for a six-week research trip in Sinai, this quickly changed as I became increasingly welcomed and immersed in village life. It was an addictive process of learning that meant it was not until two years later that I finally dragged myself back to the United Kingdom. This chapter looks back on my own journey with Bedouin in Sinai, alongside Freya Stark's travels with *Beduin*, predominantly in Iraq in the 1930s.[7] I have used Tarrabani spellings when transliterating Arabic into English, and as it is not permissible in the Tarrabani community to use a woman's name in public, I use 'my friend' when referencing my female Bedouin friend because, although she is aware that I write about our lives, it is not my place to give her a pseudonym. Any men mentioned by name are also aware of my writing; however, I have not used family names so as to respect my friend's privacy.

Stark was a woman who I like to imagine would happily sit for hours beside me on insect-ridden rugs, drinking *shai* flavoured with *mermeria* from a tiny yet sturdy mass-produced tea glass, periodically topped up from a battered blue enamel pot kept hot in the embers, the lid broken but carefully reattached with a paperclip.[8] Although, in practice, we spent time with different tribes in different countries, there are many moments that echo between us. The differences themselves only prompt me to wonder further about the placedness of Bedouin culture and whether their nomadism – even where eroded into forced settlement – might be the very point that locates them in the land, wherever that happens to be geographically. As if to be Bedouin is a place in itself.

Strong as the desert, soft as the sea, moving with the wind, forever free.[9]

Search any social media profile of young Bedouin today and you will most likely come across this quote. It is roughly painted on the walls of Red Sea tourist camps in South Sinai, the paint trailing down plywood walls, roughly erected in sand and roofed with dry palm fronds. The words are a statement of presence, of ownership and of pride in cultural heritage, yet they are as transitory as the buildings they adorn. The camps are built quickly and in cheap materials with only a few wealthy Bedouin taking the risk of building in concrete and brick. The likelihood of camps being bulldozed by the Egyptian government is, according to some, always a possibility, and it is harder to rebuild with brick than with wood. Nevertheless, progress continues and I witnessed the installation of the first generator in a Bedouin-owned camp in 2011, later followed by one hot-water (open-air) shower, which caused great excitement for all of us just before the winter chill arrived. The words on the walls speak of stability yet flexibility, a connection to the land but freedom to move within it. They are also a form of self-exoticisation for the benefit of the tourists, prompting wide-eyed questioning and the opportunity for the young Bedouin men to sell trips into the desert to experience 'real' nomadic life: trips that are vaguely traditional but which are more about creating the orientalist dream for visitors, providing them with the Arabian Nights version of Bedouin culture that they had hoped to find. Throughout Stark's travels with the Bedouin, even she is unable to escape repeatedly referencing this Arabian Nights fantasy: 'Rutba is the palace planted in the wilderness when Aladdin's uncle rubbed the lamp; how else can it have got there? It is 200 miles from anywhere.'[10] According to Jane Robinson, it was a copy of the Arabian Nights that inspired her travel to the Middle East, and although Stark later claimed that she went out there because of oil, it is clear from her writing that, as for so many of us, the tales were a significant part of her early literary, and imagined, cultural education about the East.[11] There is ongoing discourse around the authenticity of travel writing and whether we should assume that the words of travel writers are factual observations, or fictionalised memories, but whichever stance we take, there are undeniable tiers of influence on the individual and how they approach travel, people and the power dynamics of travel. Stark claims: 'I am going the cheap way, being poor and also democratic by nature,' yet she perpetuates the exoticised othering of local people – including the Bedouin – through her use of Arabian Nights references and by her comments on different social and ethnic groups in the region.¹² She somewhat blindly follows the carefully cultivated 'imperial myth' of the English innate connection with the 'noble Arab' (Bedouin) which, according to Kathryn Tidrick, was in essence a way to justify interfering in their affairs, and yet Stark also refers to them as 'primitive' in comparison to their urban relatives.[13]

If travel literature benefits from the reader identifying with the writer on an emotional level, then it is safe to say that I feel an urge to identify with Stark and her travels, particularly given how often I recognise the situations and sensations she describes. However, her claim to a 'democratic nature' remains problematic given the prejudices and preconceptions ingrained in her writing. In questioning Stark's objectivity, I am of course questioning my own.

> Whereas the tourist generally hurries back home at the end of a few weeks or months, the traveler, belonging no more to one place than to the next, moves slowly, over periods of years, from one part of the earth to another. Indeed, he would have found it difficult to tell, among the many places he had lived, precisely where it was he had felt most at home.[14]

This quote from Paul Bowles's *The Sheltering Sky* resonated with me during my travels as I attempted to understand and avoid the negative associations of being a 'tourist'. I found that when I committed to a place and communicated that publicly, there was often a collusion of placing, and friends might begin to refer to me as being 'from' that area. After a year in Sinai, my friends began to make comments such as '*Inti Bedaweya*' (you are a Bedouin [female]). This was sometimes said in front of tourists, and while it was generally spoken in jest or perhaps simply as a way to make me feel welcome, I was also aware that in the eyes of the tourists this *located* me. Where the decision to travel (voluntarily) implies a certain level of privilege and number of resources, do we subconsciously credit those who travel without such privilege with more authority or authenticity? Stark rather unfavourably compares tourists to snails, implying that they take their culture, home and habits with them and that they only ever look *out* on the world and are not truly *in* it: clearly she viewed herself more as a traveller.[15] That urge to immerse oneself in a new culture can drive a traveller – as opposed to a tourist – to take surprising risks in order to stay or learn more. By being determined to follow her goals, Stark challenged acceptable behaviour for European and American ladies in Iraq and risked the serious disapprobation of the British Civil Service. Yet, no matter how well-seasoned a traveller is, there are still moments when the invisible threads of home reach out to us, as Stark recalls: 'I have not felt so near home since the day when […] we discovered marmalade in Jericho.'[16] After 18 months in Tarrabin with only a small village shop for supplies, I took a bus north to spend a few days on my own in wintry Alexandria. The bus driver sat me at the very front of the vehicle because I was the only woman, but an hour from the city, an Egyptian woman boarded, so we chatted away in Arabic for the rest of the journey. She was keen to show me her city and proudly took me to an enormous French supermarket where – with only a few pennies to spend and overwhelmed by vats of olives, shelves of coffee, snacks, breads, notebooks and clothes – I eventually bought one piece of gold tinsel. Stark seemed almost to resent the presence of the marmalade, and yet there is a suggestion that it was also comforting to have a familiar cultural presence appear where least expected. Like so many things, the tinsel gradually disintegrated in the devastatingly dry heat of the desert, but a small piece of it survived on my suitcase for some years after I left Sinai. It was originally a reassuring reminder of English culture, but with my own movement back towards home, it shifted into becoming a poignant relic of my life in Egypt.

The tribes visited by Stark in Iraq claim to be descended from the ancient Sumerians but, in Stark's writing, are referred to as desert people – even when living in the marshes. Culturally she considered them to be 'Arab' nomads and therefore Bedouin. Explorer Leon McCarron's capacity for drawing characters with words is exceptional; he has travelled extensively throughout the Middle East, including spending time in Iraq with the Marsh tribes that Stark met, and he has published *The Land Beyond* telling the story of walking 1,000 miles through the Middle East, including through Sinai. His guide during the Sinai section of the trip was my friend's brother, Msellem, who, while sat in Ain Khodra oasis, says: '"I will tell you a story here," said Musallem, "before we go. This is how the history of the Bedouin is kept, by telling stories under trees while we eat dates."'[17] There are historical resources documenting the background of Bedouin tribes, but to follow Msellem's lead, this is their story as told to me by friends in the village.[18]

All Bedouin came from Yemen, but over time, being nomadic, the tribes spread out across the Arabian Peninsula, partly due to fishing and sea trading and partly through overland trade. The Tarrabin tribe were originally called the Boqom tribe and were directly descended from members of the Quraysh tribe, to which the prophet Muhammed belonged. The Quraysh inhabited the area around Mecca in Saudi Arabia, and the Boqom families were based in the Turba valley, just outside Mecca. Three hundred years ago, they left the area and moved north-west with one of the five leading families eventually settling in Sinai.[19] I was told that my friend's grandfather had led this migration, which caused me some confusion until I began to understand that the word 'grandfather' may be used interchangeably with 'ancestor' and that high numbers are almost equivalent to *Once upon a Time*, hence are not always meant to be taken literally. The tribe who settled in South Sinai adopted the name *Tarrabin*, meaning 'people from Turba', and developed a pattern of nomadism that covered three specific areas, challenging the concept that nomadism is somehow random.

> 'This is Spring,' said the women, 'this is the Arab's paradise', and came laughing and chatting.[20]

In spring, the Tarrabin families would travel up to the mountainous plains where flowers burst forth in sheets of colour across the red earth, and grazing was good for the goats, sheep and camels. Weather allowing, the older women still do this every year from March to May, either by truck or by walking many kilometres from the coast with their goats and sheep.[21] It has become a period of peace and retreat for the women, an opportunity to feed the animals fresh plants so that they can make organic dried cheese for use throughout the year, and to enjoy the women's traditions – distinct from the orientalised hyper-Bedouin culture sold by the men to tourists.[22] An older Bedouin woman told me that even once settled, every year they all used to go into the mountains for several days to 'honour the ancestors'. They would camp in traditional black goat's hair tents, make sacrifices of goats and sheep, cook, eat, sing and dance the *Dahiyya*. This celebration has not been allowed for many years according to my friend, and the *Dahiyya* itself is rarely seen even at weddings now as some individuals consider it to be inappropriate. I was at a wedding party in Tarrabin in 2013 when the father of the bride angrily drove his truck into a group of guests to prevent the dance from continuing. Tourists and travellers who rush from place to place may miss out on the opportunity to see or take part in local dances, or will only be sold a parody at events put on for tourists, but for those who remain in a community for a length of time, the rewards of seeing these moments are unparalleled. Stark mentions experiences of dance multiple times in *Baghdad Sketches*, both within Bedouin society and linking back to her Dartmoor home, for the repression of dance, and pagan customs can be found in so many locations. In Devon and Somerset, for instance, community practices such as winter wassailing (appeasing the apple trees/cider gods) were replaced in the nineteenth century by Christian carolling and have only relatively recently been resurrected, mostly by cider farms and much to the joy of local revellers.

During the summer heat, the tribe would move to Nuweiba' on the coast of the Red Sea, where there were dates, fish and fresh water (*Nuweiba'* means 'place of two wells' and is now the permanent settlement, of which Tarrabin is a village). When the temperature dropped in the winter, they would move inland where they were protected from the worst weather and could tend their permanent orchards ready for next spring and the move back up onto the plains.[23] Daniel Miller, a rangeland ecologist, writes about Tibetan nomads: 'The purposeful movement of nomads' herds is often viewed as wandering [...] Nomads themselves are often perceived as backward and ignorant.'[24] He gives research evidence to challenge this and goes on to point out that, like the Bedouin, these nomads have over many centuries learned how to live in incredibly harsh environments, demonstrating an intelligence and resourcefulness in their capacity not only to survive but also to ensure that there is no negative impact on the land. Stark understood that these were nomadic but not landless people, noting that the 'tribe's grazing grounds lie to this side of the Tigris'.[25] These tribes still live in the area, but, due to critical environmental damage, are always prepared to relocate as dams upriver reduce water flow, cause drought and then industrial pollution in the scarce water poisons their animals. Even in the 1930s, Stark was commenting that 'a notice will soon be required – indeed is required already – to beg people not to strew paper bags about the desert'.[26] Previously, due to the rotation of sites, it might be six months before the tribe returned to any given area, by which time the organic human and food waste would have biodegraded or been eaten by desert animals. Now there is plastic and paper spread across the sand, washing up on the coastline, coating the village roads and blown into piles like sand dunes against cliffs; the community is not equipped to deal with waste that no longer returns to nature.

Bedouin tribes have always been nomadic to varying degrees, yet there is a presence and placedness which is intrinsic to their culture and which those in power have at times sought to repress. Despite regular communication with my friend, she had not mentioned that the Egyptian government had launched *Operation Sinai* – an attempt to take control of the peninsula under the guise of driving out extremist individuals. In 2019 they gave the families in Tarrabin a matter of months to prove that they owned the land on which their houses were built. In Egypt only Egyptian citizens with Egyptian parents are able to own land, but, of course, for nomadic groups without formal ID or even birth certificates, this can be impossible to prove (many people in the village do not know exactly how old they are for this same reason).[27] As a result of not being able to 'legally' provide evidence, many houses were demolished. Fortunately, my friend's house was outside the strip of land seized by the government and is still standing, for now. According to the elders in Tarrabin, the cycle of nomadism stopped around 40 years ago when the government first began to prevent them from moving freely across what the Bedouin consider to be their own land. Aesh, who owns a popular camp outside Tarrabin, ruefully told me one day that his land in North Sinai was spilt in half by the border (which I believe was when the Gaza–Egypt border was confirmed in 1979). He can stand on one side and look at his land but never visit the gardens and orchards that remain.

During this same period, there was an influx of tourists from Israel and Europe which encouraged the tribe to remain close to the coast where there was potential income, and as the families earned more money, they were able to build more permanent housing with water tanks, generators and furniture. My friend remembers when she was a very young child and they still lived in a tent on the beach. She recalls wooden sides being added to the tent, then a small breezeblock house was built, and a palm-frond shelter replaced the tent. The first house I rented in the village was next door to this original site that, in the evenings, was still the preferred place for the women of the family to meet, drink tea and chat after dinner. 'There was a pleasant sense of security, the safety of the tribe lapping us round,' wrote Stark.[28] The elderly aunt who still lived in this site used on occasion to wander into my 'living room' – a bare, and invariably sandy, concrete room with no frames in the windows – at any time she wanted. Oblivious to me lying prostrate in 40 degrees under the single wonky ceiling fan, she would grunt a greeting and head into the garden to pick guava or *nabug* (small nutty berries that are best eaten dried, similar to dates). The women often choose to cook and eat outside even if their kitchen is fully kitted out with gas cookers and marble surfaces, and in good weather, most people will eschew the television in the living room in favour of sitting outside all evening with a fire for making tea, especially if there are visitors, and possibly even driving into the mountains for dinner, or just to sit and brew tea, simply because they can. It is not just about staying cool in the summer but is more about maintaining a quality of life, a connection with the natural environment and the freedom to move as they choose. Stark in the 1930s commented on how the Bedouin were reacting to the impact of 'modern' life: 'The old way holds because the old life is still lived. The fact that instead of horses two motor cars are tangled in the tent ropes makes no very great difference.'[29] Yet, the concern in Stark's time is no different to now, when the impact of globalism and the lure of city life carries the risk of young people moving away. Stark met with Sheikh Ajil, whose son had gone to study at Beirut University and who the father tried to encourage to spend each summer in the tents with his family:

> 'But,' said Ajil with a smile that was half a sigh, 'when he comes back to us after three years, no doubt he will tell me that I am a savage, and will want to go and live in the towns.'[30]

'The old order goes,' Stark tells us, yet that progress is not always negative.[31] In 2011 there was only one member of the Tarrabin tribe living abroad: one of my friend's older brothers was living in Switzerland, and having spent about a decade away, then returned home to run his own business. A few members of the tribe have lived and worked abroad, and yet the drive seems still to be to return home and bring the experience back to the family.

In 2019 McCarron travelled with the Marsh Arabs in the same area which Stark had visited and, while sitting in a *mashouf* (wooden canoe) with an aged and singing Abu Hayda, poetically noted, 'The only concession to modernity is the engine, and perhaps, his stash of chocolate bars.'[32] So often, those who write about the Bedouin fall back into a paternalistic colonialism which would prefer that they remain in their historically familiar traditional ways, but McCarron observes quietly and listens. We see where modern developments have impacted on the tribe both negatively and in ways which have made life easier and safer for the people. In 2012 I sat and watched a young European woman walk past a Bedouin man who was working on a laptop in a tourist camp one evening. She paused, visibly shocked, and without asking began to take photos. To reuse Tim Hannigan's words, still we see 'the modern equivalent of Wilfred Thesiger proclaiming that "his" Bedouin had been "spoilt" by the arrival of the internal combustion engine'.[33] Many visitors to Sinai assumed that the Bedouin would be subject to cultural and technological immobility; they were more comfortable with this image and searched for evidence of it, yet at the same time they also expected to be able to rediscover their own freedom through experiencing the Bedouins' nomadic geographical mobility, usually via the culturally curated desert trips. When McCarron walked from Jerusalem to Mount Sinai in 2015, a local Bedouin man, Nasr, joined the group to guide them to the summit of *Jebel Musa* (Moses's Mountain or Mount Sinai). '"The Bedouin are very clever," he said. "But modern things are not natural for people here. Sometimes it takes a long time. I think it's good, probably. We have things here that don't need updating."'[34] Each of us chooses whether to engage with technology and recent developments to some degree, and it is no different for people in Sinai. That agency to decide seems to trouble visitors however, who so often prefer to pay extortionate amounts to be taken by jeep or camel into the desert for a night of 'traditional' Bedouin entertainment. The locals play along, creating the fantasy for the visitors, even to the point of pretending not to speak much English just to add to the illusion: most of my Bedouin friends are fluent in at least three languages. As Stark sagely wrote: 'if we listen to words merely, and give to them our own habitual values, we are bound to go astray'.[35] I was expected to collude and trusted not to break the spell, which I found equally amusing and distressing. Eventually I recognised that, to some extent, my friends were protecting themselves, for who among us would truly be comfortable with their entire life made visible and on sale day-after-day?

> What we see in the desert are a few permanent threads which, overlaid and hidden by many patterns, run unrecognized through our more complicated lives and hold them together.[36]

To what extent do past representations impact on what we observe while travelling in the present? Nicholas Howe points out that, despite it not being the aim of his travels,

Charles Montagu Doughty was 'always looking in *Arabia Deserta* for the traces left by those who were there before him. Following was for him a shadowy and metaphorical act.'[37] Regardless of how much we might wish to challenge the notion, nevertheless we all still carry a litany of preconceptions, second-hand imagery, historical and ideological expectations of our destination. Stark makes repeated references to the Arabian Nights tales (and other literature) in her writing, yet when she first went into the desert in Iraq, she stated with admirable insight: 'This is my first journey across the desert, I have no useful knowledge.'[38] For many travellers and writers, that litany of preconceptions is unnecessary baggage, and at a time when decolonising travel writing is finally at the forefront of discourse, an ability to experience and observe without applying damaging stereotypes is perhaps one of the hallmarks of 'great' travel literature. Ted Simon asserts this approach in *Jupiter's Travels*: 'The challenge was to lay myself open to everybody and everything that came my way. The prize was to change and grow big enough to feel one with the whole world.'[39] In 1834 when Alexander Kinglake (who was born in my hometown of Taunton, Somerset) travelled in the East as part of a brief rebellion against conforming to societal expectations in England, he visited his mother's childhood friend Lady Hester Stanhope, who was proudly declining into poverty and mysticism on a hill in Lebanon. While there, he encountered several Bedouin tribes and encampments but found them living in squalor, 'poor and wretched creatures'.[40] Mildly disappointed not to find the 'noble Arabs' of British imagining, he concluded that these could not be true, pure Bedouin.[41] Ultimately Kinglake fails to find the honourable image of the Bedouin intact, but is not exceptionally distressed by this, and neither is he drawn into the romance of the desert as an esoteric experience, instead viewing it primarily as an opportunity to revel in his own sense of accomplishment. Throughout the nineteenth century, explorers and Arabists continued to develop the narrative of an Arab and English sympathy. Sir Richard Burton published *Personal Narrative of a Pilgrimage to Al-Madinah and Meccah* in 1855, and Tidrick accuses him of being 'a snob about his relations with Bedouin'.[42] She claims that Burton demonstrated admiration for the Bedouin and that 'in Burton's hands the detested bandit became a romantic rebel against society'.[43] Twenty years after Burton's *Pilgrimage* was published, his wife Lady Isabel Burton regaled readers with a tale of hostage-taking in the desert. Lady A—— and her party were robbed at gunpoint by bandits (a party of 'Bedawin') near the Dead Sea, and yet Lady Burton claimed that the 'proceedings were more the action of the bad characters round the town, who call themselves Bedawin, than that of real Bedawin'.[44] What then does it mean to be a 'real' member of a tribal group? When Tarrabani friends call me *Bedaweya*, are they devaluing their own culture, even in jest, by admitting someone unrelated to them, or are they possibly making an obscure reference to the state of *being* Bedouin? Men from Tarrabin and Sawarka tribes say that the families around Cairo are no longer *real* Bedouin, either because they have adopted city life or because they have become farmers (fellahin). Stark echoes this contrast between the ways of life: 'for they [fellahin] are still religious, having neither the self-reliant independence of the Beduin, nor the weak open-mindedness of the town', although she later goes on to suggest that it is the availability of water that causes the shift from Bedouin nomad to farmer.[45] Water's transformative capacity is recognised in a comment that at once unites and contrasts English countryside and the desert, as a 'clear little brook that you would scarcely notice in Devonshire is here as rare and precious as a rainless day in the Lake District'.[46] Stark's expectations of characteristics and culture, no doubt as a result of reading previous works on Bedouin by Burton and others, resulted in a claim that, in comparison to the Iraqi fellahin, the Bedouin's 'finer features and nobler walk still distinguish them'.[47] It is perhaps worth noting at this point that, according to Tidrick, Burton actually did not know much about the Bedouin people:

> Much of his information (about Bedouin ed.) seems to have come from questioning his companions, especially one Sheikh Masud, a Bedouin camel-man hired for the journey from Medina to Mecca. Perhaps it seems presumptuous to suggest that Burton, who can truly be considered one of the great pioneer anthropologists, hardly knew the people on whom he considered himself an authority, but the fact is that at this period of his life he did not know the Bedouin well.[48]

Howe insists that authors 'depend on the moment of encounter between author and place, of course, but they also move within a flow of other places and other times [...] they offer neither the innocent claim of being somewhere first nor the world-weary one of being there last'.[49] Regardless of how we approach travel, these layers of temporally placed pre-knowledge can trigger astounding moments of recognition. There is ongoing discourse about the impact on travellees (local people in travel texts), and, of course, many writers still act as if their subjects will never know what is written about them. Indeed, as Hannigan asks, will they even care? 'If "Thesiger's" Bedouin had had the space to speak maybe this is how they too would have responded: "Wilfred who? Lawrence of what???"'[50] Msellem also spent time working with Dr Clinton Bailey, contributing to his research on Bedouin culture in Sinai. Msellem used to own a copy of the books which were published and read them frequently, but they were stolen some years ago to his great regret. He speaks of his pride at having been consulted and that, through the collaboration, his family history and culture has been recorded and acknowledged – as he would like it to be. Now that there is global internet access and a growth of affordable communications technology, it is an outdated arrogance to assume the people we visit will never read our words about them. Yet, it still surprises people to hear that I keep in touch with Bedouin friends via WhatsApp. Indeed, during a trip to Ain Khodra oasis – the same oasis where McCarron listened to Msellem's tales of Bedouin history – we were able to access mobile reception and post on social media. However, there was a furore from people online (in Europe) who did not want their image of untouched desert life altered or modernised. Unfortunately for them, in my experience, the internet connection in Sinai is far better than it is in Somerset. It should not be assumed that people within Bedouin communities are unaware of, or somehow incapable of understanding or managing, modern technology or conveniences. As mentioned previously, there is a complex process of choosing when to interact with technology, vehicles, food, culture or even clothing. For instance, while visiting the 'Azza tribe in Iraq, Stark observed a convergence of modern conversation and traditional dress, and when I have asked Bedouin men about choosing traditional dress over jeans one day but not the next, the question is met with some confusion: Why should we not wear both?[51] Under traditional all-covering black *abayas*, many younger Bedouin women will wear a range of clothing equal to the variety of dress we might see on any high street in the world – from traditional dresses to tight leggings with high heels. Essentially it comes down to personal choice, style, priorities and, of course, economic means. *I was sat with my friend one afternoon watching an Arabic music video with a young woman in scanty clothing driving a jeep in the desert.* I asked my friend what she thought: 'I don't like the clothes,' she told me, 'but I would like to drive.'

There are so few widespread modern representations of Bedouin and fewer still that also reflect the full range of modernity: so that, even one century later, many people seem only to have one point of reference for Bedouin culture: Lawrence of Arabia. Mythologised in word and image, T. E. Lawrence's own views on Arab people were themselves saturated by the nineteenth-century influence of Gifford Palgrave and Wilfred Scawen Blunt, two men who travelled in the East while 'proclaiming their Englishness with an exaggerated unconcern for the possibly unpleasant consequences'.[52] Tidrick contends that our inability to clarify the facts around Lawrence stems in part from certain people refusing to believe the more 'vulgar version' and preferring to think that he was simply able to manipulate and manoeuvre the Bedouin.[53] Lawrence himself was blunt in his description of the Arab people in *Seven Pillars of Wisdom*, referring to them as 'limited' and 'narrow-minded', inconsistent and yet also unable to compromise.[54] Knowing which version of the legend is most true will probably always remain a mystery for, as Hulme and Youngs point out, 'the real power of travel writing lay(s) in its independence of perspective'.[55] It is not only for readers of travel writing but also for the Bedouin themselves that these legends remain. I was sat in a small tourist camp at the edge of the Red Sea reading Tidrick's book *Heart Beguiling Araby* which carries a photo of Auda Abu Tayi on the front cover. Auda was the leader of the Howeitat tribe in the Arabian Peninsula and a key warrior in the Arab revolt of 1916, who rode and fought alongside Lawrence. A young Bedouin man from the Howeitat tribe in Saudi Arabia had come to Sinai to visit his cousins and was drinking tea next to me. We had spoken politely and then he leaned over to look at the book. 'Ah,' he said. 'That's my grandfather.' He was vaguely interested to see that his photo was on a book, but I was frankly astonished: here was a living descendent of what to me had been legend, telling me about how there are individuals in his tribe who still remember Lawrence and refer to him with pride and affection, at odds with the somewhat harsh opinions Lawrence himself gave of their people and culture. So, to answer Hannigan's musings about whether the Bedouin would remember or care, the answer in this case would appear to be an unequivocal 'yes'.

Stark's attitude towards the culture around her, while often somewhat orientalist in nature, can also be wonderfully sensitive and appropriate. It is perhaps for this reason that she was known for her ability to draw people in and to build rapport with those she met and spoke with. She was invited to visit Sheikh Habib of the el 'Azza tribe, which caused great consternation among the British community in Baghdad and prompted the appearance of an entire document advising her of how she ought to comport herself while residing in the area. Her very acerbic response to the document is a pleasure to read, and there is a definite sense that she enjoys playing the part of a woman who is potentially leading the 'wives' astray by encouraging them to join her on her expedition. 'I began to feel like a Disturber of the Peace,' she writes, with emphatic capitalisation.[56] That said, she convinced one female friend to accompany her out into the desert in an antique car, which she helped to push when it was stuck in the mud of a damp and misty journey. After the group attempted to rescue two Kurdish members of parliament also stuck in the deep mud, she was witness to the general prejudice towards Bedouin, as the politicians begged the group not to 'leave us to the Beduin'.[57] It must be said that she appears to have had very little sympathy for their fears and continued on towards the encampment with no trepidation at all. Stark writes about the Sheikh's marigolds and vegetables, his dress, his conversation. Once ensconced in the Sheikh's hall, she describes a scene that I experienced so many times in Sinai, 80 years apart and in a different country: '[we] sat among the tribesmen in a half-circle around a fireplace [...] watching their faces in the flamelight and listening to the rebaba, the one-stringed ancestor of the fiddle, as it played one or other of their four modes of music, for love and war and tenderness and sorrow, as they say'.[58] On summer nights, when it was too hot to sleep, we would sit up all night around a small fire with a teapot constantly on the embers, playing music together or sitting quietly and listening to one rebaba or 'oud being played. Sometimes all present would take a turn at spontaneously composing or reciting short lyrical rhymes along with the music or rhythm (these are a type of poetry called *ghinawwas*).[59] These traditions, while locally altered over time to reflect a changed environment or political landscape, appear throughout journals and literature to remain at the heart of all Bedouin culture. Sitting around the fire with one, or many voices raised in poetic remembering and placing of an aural history, what falls outside the flickering light is changeable and changing.

Shortly before dinner is served, Stark was led out of the hall and formally presented with a shelf on which were four bottles of alcohol. The Sheikh had shown them great courtesy in inviting them to share part of what he understood to be their culture, within his own alcohol-free home. Stark returned the courtesy by refusing gently since, we assume, she preferred to be immersed in his culture and not reminded of her own. She claimed to be 'much touched by his thoughtfulness', and it is one of many examples of how perceptively she navigates other peoples' worlds, thus creating a trust and respect on both sides.[60] Twenty years after Stark's visit, Wilfred Thesiger was also invited to visit the tribe (transcribed as Al Essa in *The Marsh Arabs*), and the description is uncannily similar, albeit with more rifles and that obstinate referencing of the 'dignity' of the desert Arab: Burton endures.[61] On New Year's Eve 2011 I was invited to join a celebration at the camp of the Sheikh's brother. There were around 150 people under a goat's hair tent, almost exclusively men, sitting around several fires in traditional dress and wrapped in enormous *farwas* (an equivalent of winter coats that are floor length and large enough to entirely smother a body). They would originally have been sheepskin with the fleece on the inside but are now made from heavy cotton and fake fur, mostly imported from Saudi Arabia). I was sat next to the owner of the camp, who was enjoying himself immensely as he fished underneath his *farwas* to retrieve an illicit bottle of Jack Daniels, offering it to me before filling his plastic cup. I declined, and he approved.

> We stand upon the shore and collect such oddments as we find floating in chaos – her customs, religions, her clothes and trinkets and some, alas! of her virtues. We [...] encase them in an armour of words – and by so doing, not unhopeful of the future, yet wage our little losing battle against the fragilities of Time.[62]

If we accept the theory that mobility is one of the markers of modernisation, it is not difficult to see where this becomes a contradiction in references to nomadic groups, whether they are mobile, or settled and therefore *immobile*. As travellers and tourists, we often use the freedom to move globally as an indication of self-engendered modernity, and from the cultures we visit, we gather in such elements as are interesting, then curate them carefully to support our own narrative of the culture and of the journey. Where these narratives interact with nomadic groups, however, the temptation is to refute modernity by ignoring cultural change and progression and to focus on preserving traditions which, in their familiarity, make us feel comfortable. Presenting Bedouin culture as premodern reinforces our own progressiveness, yet as Stark points out in the quote above, the passage of time ensures that these 'fragile' representations of culture will always change and evolve. Members of the Tarrabin community are actively attempting to educate the younger generations in certain traditions – for instance, knowledge of how to use desert herbs for medicinal purposes, but they also share this knowledge globally via social media. Bedouin modernity is a balance of mobility and geographical placedness, of economic and political factors and of using technology where it is helpful or fun but also maintaining freedom of movement and the choice of simplicity. Stark saw this in the tribes that she visited 90 years ago: 'All here was a mixture of new things and very old.'[63]

Repeatedly throughout my two years in Sinai, I witnessed the desert evenings from a privileged position of being able to document the differences when tourists or visitors were present. I saw the change in language use, behaviour and how the Bedouin 'story' was told. I thought back to what I had learned in my early days in Sinai and was able to add layers and depth and humour to the narrative I could see developing around me. Are these repeated romanticised descriptions of nights around the fire a homogenising of Bedouin culture, or a desperate affirmation of what Western travellers hope to find when travelling in desert cultures? Or are they true and authentic representations of Bedouin culture that many in the communities hope to preserve and, therefore, pass on to younger generations? Stark believed that the young Arabs she met were not so interested in documenting their history but instead, and echoing the words of Msellem, value the oral retelling of their history for the *feeling* of it. This awareness of essential and historical human experience was, for her, connected to their innate optimism about the future. Surely, if ever there were an appropriate theme for writing about travel in a time of isolation, it would be this.

Despite some significant differences, I still like to believe that Freya Stark would have been a truly wonderful travel companion, and although I began writing this by imagining that she and I might sit together next to a fire and share tea, as it turns out, we share one unshakeable opinion: 'Beduin coffee flavoured with cardamom – the best drink in the world.'[64]

# Notes

1. Bedouin proverb from Clinton Bailey, *A Culture of Desert Survival*, quoted in B. Hoffler, 'Quotes and Proverbs', *Go Tell It on the Mountain*, accessed 20 September 2020, http://gotellitonthemountain.net/quotes-proverbs.
2. F. Stark, *Baghdad Sketches* (London: John Murray, 1939), 17.
3. Downward exploration is my own term to reflect the process of exploring small areas or individual communities in depth, as opposed to covering long distances. Kris Lackey uses the term 'vertical travel'.
4. J. Robinson, *Wayward Women: A Guide to Women Travellers* (Oxford: Oxford University Press, 1991), 30.
5. L. Pryce, *Revolutionary Ride: On the Road in Search of the Real Iran* (London: Nicholas Brealey, 2017), frontispiece.
6. Stark, *Baghdad Sketches*, 117.
7. Stark chooses to use 'Beduin', whereas I have always followed the Tarrabin custom of writing 'Bedouin' when using English. Neither is incorrect since the Arabic could be transliterated in several different ways.
8. شاي 'Shai' refers to black tea, sweetened with sugar, and in Sinai this is served in two-inch-high thick tapered glasses. The water is heated in a tall enamel teapot on the embers of the fire, and then tea leaves are measured in the palm of the hand and tipped into the pot along with double the amount of sugar. Occasionally Lipton's Yellow Label teabags are used, although this is mostly for tourists, and the majority of households use *Al Aroussa* loose black tea. The herb المريمية 'mermeria' may be added to tea which is a type of sage. This spelling is a dialect form of مرمارية 'merimia', which is mostly used in the winter months or to ward off colds. Other spices and herbs are used by the Tarrabin tribe as well, depending on the social occasion, health requirements of anyone partaking and time of year. When spring comes around, they use the herb هبق 'hebug' (Tarrabani dialect), which is a perfumed and sweeter relative of mint, then the classic strong mint plant نعناع 'na'na', which is used more in the summer. Both of these may also be used for stomach and digestion problems. In the winter, cloves (قرنفل) with mint in the winter. When serious food poisoning takes hold, it is not unknown for a small grain of opium to be placed in the sufferer's tea glass, said to stop cramping and diarrhoea. Tea is always drunk after dinner, when someone visits, and as a break while travelling in the desert. Like in so many places in the world, it is a ritual, and if there are large numbers of a family gathered together, it falls to the younger girls to make the tea, or if it is all men, then the youngest brother cooks and makes tea. Sometimes, when the youngest children pile in after dinner, glasses will be filled with a little tea, and a healthy portion of condensed milk, to give them a sugar rush so they will go off to play and leave the adults to talk.
9. Oft-heard quote from Bedouin in Tarrabin, Sinai and heard repeated by visiting Bedouin from Sawarka (N. Sinai) and Mzeina (neighbours to Tarrabin) tribes.
10. Stark, *Baghdad Sketches*, 6.
11. Robinson, *Wayward Women*, 29.
12. Stark, *Baghdad Sketches*, 5.
13. K. Tidrick, *Heart Beguiling Araby: The English Romance with Arabia* (London: I. B. Tauris, 1989), 1.
14. P. Bowles, *The Sheltering Sky* (Hopewell: Ecco Press, 1977), 14.
15. Stark, *Baghdad Sketches*, 17.
16. Ibid., 6.

17 L. McCarron, *The Land Beyond* (London: I.B. Tauris, 2017), 197. McCarron spells the name Musallem; however, this is a case of transliteration not being entirely possible and resulting in variants in English. *Ain Khodra* means 'the green spring' (water).
18 These statements are from my journal notes taken between 2011 and 2013 and from a number of male and female individuals of mixed ages. The story did not waver, regardless of who was speaking.
19 'Three hundred' years may not be chronologically precise but instead be a reference to 'a long time ago'.
20 Stark, *Baghdad Sketches*, 137.
21 If there is not enough rain, then inevitably the plants and flowers do not grow, and it is said that 'there is no spring this year'. In recent years, changes in global weather systems have meant that increasingly there is no spring.
22 In the village, goats and sheep are usually fed leftover food from the house, cardboard and occasionally imported hay; however, they often escape and eat from the enormous piles of refuse around the village, so their milk is rarely used as it is not considered clean.
23 Sinai does not really experience an 'autumn' season, which meant that towards the end of summer, we would all be eagerly awaiting the day when it would finally and suddenly be cool enough to wear jeans.
24 D. Miller, 'The Importance of China's Nomads', *Rangelands* 24, 1 (2002): 22–24 (24). Rangeland is categorised as land containing bushes or grasses suitable for grazing animals.
25 Stark, *Baghdad Sketches*, 130.
26 Ibid., 3.
27 A. Smith, 'Under the War on Terror Egypt Is Ethnically Cleansing the Sinai Bedouin', *Middle East Monitor*, 7 August 2019, https://www.middleeastmonitor.com/20190807-under-the-war-on-terror-egypt-is-ethnically-cleansing-the-sinai-bedouin/.
28 Stark, *Baghdad Sketches*, 141.
29 Ibid., 131.
30 Ibid., 134.
31 Ibid., 135.
32 L. McCarron, 'Subterfuge', *BBC*, 25 May 2019, https://www.bbc.co.uk/sounds/play/p07bb836.
33 T. Hannigan, 'The Shepherd's Life: A Challenge to Travel Writers', *Tim Hannigan*, 22 August 2016, https://timhannigan.com/2016/08/22/the-shepherds-life-a-challenge-to-travel-writers/.
34 McCarron, *The Land Beyond*, 222.
35 Stark, *Baghdad Sketches*, 85.
36 Ibid., 139.
37 N. Howe, 'Deserts, Lost History, Travel Stories', *Southwest Review* 85, 4 (2000): 526–39 (527).
38 Stark, *Baghdad Sketches*, 5.
39 T. Simon, *Jupiter's Travels* (London: Penguin Books, 1980), 404.
40 Tidrick, *Heart Beguiling Araby*, 47.
41 Sir Richard Burton (1821–1890) was a writer, explorer and Arabist. He wrote a translation of the Arabian Nights, entered Mecca disguised in Arab dress and wrote lengthy assessments of the 'Arab character'.
42 Tidrick, *Heart Beguiling Araby*, 69.
43 Ibid., 70.
44 I. Burton in J. Robinson, *Unsuitable for Ladies: An Anthology of Women Travellers* (Oxford: Oxford University Press, 2001), 146.
45 Stark, *Baghdad Sketches*, 115.
46 Ibid., 153.
47 Ibid., 119.

48 Tidrick, *Heart Beguiling Araby*, 69–70.
49 Howe, 'Deserts, Lost History, Travel Stories', 527.
50 Hannigan, 'The Shepherd's Life'.
51 Stark, *Baghdad Sketches*, 75.
52 Tidrick, *Heart Beguiling Araby*, 67.
53 Ibid., 173.
54 T. E. Lawrence, *Seven Pillars of Wisdom: A Triumph* (London: Jonathan Cape, 1946), 36–37.
55 P. Hulme and T. Youngs, *The Cambridge Companion to Travel Writing* (Cambridge: Cambridge University Press, 2002), 4.
56 Stark, *Baghdad Sketches*, 71.
57 Ibid., 74.
58 Ibid., 76.
59 L. Abu-lughod, *Veiled Sentiments: Honor and Poetry in a Bedouin Society* (London: University of California Press, 1988), 27.
60 Stark, *Baghdad Sketches*, 77.
61 W. Thesinger, *The Marsh Arabs* (London: Penguin Books, 1967), 21–22.
62 Stark, *Baghdad Sketches*, xiii–iv.
63 Ibid., 75.
64 Ibid., 133.

# Chapter Six

# WITH WILKIE IN THE WEST: READING WILKIE COLLINS'S *RAMBLES BEYOND RAILWAYS* FROM A CORNISH PERSPECTIVE

## Tim Hannigan

Look – up ahead where the road bends: two figures, moving forwards, about to vanish from view.

At this distance, their forms are indistinct, but look harder and certain details will come clear: two young men, both carrying knapsacks. One of them is short – five feet, six inches to be precise (you can say this with some certainty). He is wearing a stovepipe hat (this is an informed supposition), dark jacket and trousers, loose about the thighs. If you could somehow leap ahead, meet him head on, you'd see a fleshy face, softly boyish despite a pronounced widow's peak; a broad and bulbous brow; and eyes set deep behind little wire-rimmed spectacles (there's excellent evidence here). The other figure is harder to discern. Taller, you might say; certainly a few years older; and probably dressed in similar garb. But just one small detail is absolutely clear: the square ruler, strapped to his knapsack.

Two figures, up ahead, about to vanish from view. Follow them!

The line of the road is perfectly familiar, though it lacks today's tarmac: the bend where the brook begins its sharp descent to the cove at Portheras, then the slight rise to the upper part of Bojewyan. But the jumbled grey cottages to the right have a strange, shape-shifting quality. There are buildings here, alright, as there should be. But when you try to fix them in their familiar positions, the rough-cut quoins tumble out, reconfigure elsewhere. But as the two figures move past the houses, stride towards the next bend at Keigwin, solidly familiar ground opens in the distance: the intersection of sea with coast; the rough rising hulk of Watch Croft, then the shallow saddle sweeping up to the twin granite crags of the Carn, all darkly tawny under a lowering sky.

The two figures are already around the Keigwin bend. Hurry! Follow them down the slope to the bridge on the parish boundary, past the turn to Chypraze. Watch them into the little hamlet clustered by the church, watch their response to this place. Watch it – and then watch your own reaction:

Imagine three or four large, square, comfortless-looking, shut-up houses, all apparently uninhabited; add some half-dozen miserable little cottages standing near the houses, with the nasal notes of a Methodist hymn pouring disastrously through the open door of one of them; let the largest of the large buildings be called an inn, but let it make up no beds, because nobody ever stops to sleep there: place in the kitchen of this inn a sickly little girl, and a middle-aged, melancholy woman, the first staring despondently on a wasting fire, the second offering to the stranger a piece of bread, three eggs, and some sour porter corked down in an earthenware jar, as all that her larder and cellar can afford; fancy next an old, grim, dark church, with two or three lads leaning against the churchyard wall, looking out together in gloomy silence on a solitary high road; conceive a thin, slow rain falling, a cold twilight just changing into darkness, a surrounding landscape wild, barren, and shelterless – imagine all this, and you will have the picture before you which presented itself to me and my companion, when we found ourselves in the village of Morvah.[1]

In the summer of 1850, Wilkie Collins set out from his home in London to make a walking tour of Cornwall. At the start of the year, shortly after his 26th birthday, he had published his first novel, *Antonia, or the Fall of Rome*. It had done well,[2] and though he was still notionally a student of law at Lincoln's Inn, Collins clearly intended writing to be his career. A portrait by John Everett Millais painted that same year shows the emerging literary star striking a pensive pose. The short, rather chubby fingers are pressed into a steeple. The eyes behind their spectacles are cast downwards. But the face is very much that of a cossetted child, thinning hair notwithstanding. He's trying to look serious, but he doesn't quite pull it off.

Collins seems to have set out for Cornwall intending to produce a book, for he was accompanied by Henry Brandling, a young artist from the Royal Academy. Brandling would produce the plates; Collins would take care of the text. The pair took the train as far as they could – to the end of the line in Plymouth. Then they crossed the River Tamar by boat and set out walking, carrying their notebooks, sketching equipment (including a square ruler to help when drawing houses) and spare clothes in knapsacks – the original backpackers. They made their way along the southern coast, through Looe, Liskeard, Lostwithiel, Fowey, St Austell, Truro, Falmouth and Helston, then pushed on through Penwith, the terminal crook of Cornwall's long limb. At Land's End they turned right, following the northern littoral through St Ives and Newquay, before cutting cross-country to Launceston, heading back over the Tamar and returning to Plymouth to catch a home-bound train.

Collins wrote up his notes back in London, at his mother's house on the edge of Regent's Park.[3] Elsewhere in the city, Brandling prepared a dozen lithographs. They show stylised landscapes of cliffs and crags beneath florid skies. In two of the images, a small figure appears. In the first he poses beneath the improbable granite stack of the Cheesewring; in the second he sits in conversation with another man – a local, or perhaps another sightseer – on the edge of a precipice at Logan Rock. His features are indistinct, but he is recognisable by his dress: stovepipe hat, jacket, baggy trousers.

*Rambles beyond Railways, or Notes in Cornwall Taken A-foot* was published in early 1851. Like the novel 12 months earlier, it was a success.[4] Wilkie Collins was off to a flying start. Soon he would forge a fruitful collaborative friendship with Charles Dickens, and within a decade, he would publish the first of his enduring mega-hits, *The Woman in White* (1860).

But back to the travel book. *Rambles beyond Railways* appeared at a significant moment in the history of British travel writing. The first-person, notionally factual account of a journey was already a very old form. But its traditional role was as the vehicle for what Carl Thompson has called a 'knowledge genre'.[5] From at least the sixteenth century onward, travel writing – or 'voyages and travels', as it was usually known at the time – had been overwhelmingly concerned with a 'fairly summative reporting of incidents and observations'.[6] Any aesthetic quality that the text might possess was generally incidental, a happy accident – the facts were the thing. This approach was not restricted to stories of exploration and adventure in far-off lands. Even narratives of journeys which did not stray beyond British shores tended to the strictly informational, their aim to enhance public knowledge of some obscure shire, seldom visited by travellers from the burgeoning imperial capital. You can see this in the work of an earlier travel writer in Cornwall, the Reverend Richard Warner, who visited in 1808. Warner was an acolyte of Richard Gilpin, who popularised the concept of the 'picturesque' in Britain. But the account of his Cornish journey is emphatically a matter of facts and figures. Even the picturesque itself appears reduced to a quantifiable resource – and there was precious little of it in Cornwall, as far as Warner was concerned, a deficit mitigated by the abundance of valuable minerals hidden beneath 'the deformity of [the] exterior'.[7]

But by the middle of the nineteenth century, a change was underway. Serious science, geography, economics and ethnography were beginning to peel off into their silos in professionalised academia, leaving the old first-person travel narrative reduced to 'anecdotalism and amateurism'.[8] But as its serious scholarly purposes were stripped away, it found a new impetus: it became 'more aesthetically ambitious';[9] it began to move towards entertainment as its primary function. Literary travel writing as we know it today was coming into being.

In the 1850s, this shift was barely underway. But with *Rambles beyond Railways*, Wilkie Collins was ahead of the game, for – a single grudgingly informational chapter on the pilchard fishery aside – he seems to have been firmly fixed on entertaining his readers. Even a visit to a tin and copper mine – which the Reverend Warner, four decades earlier, would have made a matter of measurements and economic data[10] – is played here for drama and laughs.

The book's humour often emerges from the way Collins portrays himself. Here is the familiar figure of the self-deprecating and decidedly unheroic British travel writer, already perfectly formed a full century ahead of Eric Newby. The one statistic that Collins does reveal in the description of the visit to the mine is his own height – five feet, six inches. The set of borrowed work clothes he dons for the descent belongs to a much taller man. The shirt hangs down to his ankles 'like a bedgown', and the trousers flow 'in Turkish luxuriance' over his feet.[11] Below ground, 'fettered as I was by my Brobdignag [*sic*] jacket and trousers', Collins suffers a moment of paralysing panic on a narrow ledge and has to be rescued by his guide:

Our friend the miner saw my difficulty, and extricated me from it at once, with a promptitude and skill which deserve record. Descending halfway by the beams, he clutched with one hand that hinder part of my too voluminous nether garments, which presented the broadest superficies of canvas to his grasp (I hope the delicate reader appreciates the ingenious cleanliness of my periphrasis, when I mention in detail so coarse a subject as trousers!) Having grappled me thus, he lifted me up in an instant, as easily as a small parcel, then carried me off horizontally along the loose boards.[12]

Beyond the self-deprecation, *Rambles beyond Railways* is also remarkably playful in its form – innovative, even, for a book written so early in the era of 'aesthetic' travel writing. Collins talks directly to his readers. He trips back and forth between past and present tenses, and between first, second and third persons, all in the space of a few paragraphs.[13] And he skips over whole chunks of the journey that he deems of insufficient interest[14] – eschewing both the 'total knowledge' approach of imperial travel writing in its monarch-of-all-I-survey mode, and the plodding linearity of many less-inventive authors.

*Rambles beyond Railways* is, in short, a very good and very clever travel book. But it is also a book about a very particular place, and this is where things get complicated, contentious – and, for me, personal.

For the historian Bernard Deacon, Cornwall – this long, tapering peninsula, jutting out into the Western Approaches – is 'a kind of halfway house between English county and Celtic nation'.[15] This peculiar ambiguity surely has its origins in actual historical distinction. When Cornwall's border was fixed at the River Tamar in the tenth century, it was largely occupied by Britons (as opposed to Anglo-Saxons), speaking an entirely distinct Brythonic language (as opposed to Old English). The second syllable of the name – Corn-*wall* – shares an etymology with Wales: *Wēalas*, an Old English word, usually translated as 'strangers' or 'foreigners'. (The Cornish word for Cornwall is *Kernow*; the Cornish name for England is *Pow Sows*, 'Saxon Land'.)

But some sense of Cornwall's separateness survived – *survives* – beyond the apparent end-point of a centuries-long process of Anglicisation. Collins himself – who was travelling at least two generations after the final extinction of Cornish as an everyday spoken language – reported that in Cornwall 'a stranger is doubly a stranger, in relation to provincial sympathies [...] a man speaks of himself as *Cornish* in much the same spirit as a Welshman speaks of himself as Welsh'.[16] This observation suggests a strong sense of difference emerging from *within* Cornwall in the nineteenth century. However, as Bernard Deacon acknowledges, any broader external idea of Cornish 'otherness' owes 'much to attitudes and processes in the centre, to travel writers, visitors, painters, novelists and poets who have "discovered"' the place over the years.[17] We need to look, then at the way Wilkie Collins 'constructed' Cornwall in his travel book.

In his introduction, explaining why he and Henry Brandling chose Cornwall for their summer adventure, Collins states it quite plainly:

> The main reason that urged us to choose Cornwall [...] was simply this – Cornwall presented to us the most untrodden ground that we could select for our particular purpose [...] I doubt

whether Cornwall will not gain by comparison with foreign countries, as an unexplored region offered to the curiosity of the tourist. Have we not, in fact, got under our thumbs, or in our circulating libraries, volumes of excellent books which amuse us with the personal experiences of adventurous travellers in every part of the habitable globe – except, perhaps, Cornwall and Kamtschatka? [...] Even the railway stops short at Plymouth, and shrinks from penetrating to the savage regions beyond![18]

Savage regions! Cornwall compared to the Russian Far East! What exactly is going on here? There is, as it turns out, a certain amount of scholarly disagreement on this point.

For Paul Young, Collins is to be taken as read: an author constructing a 'gothic location' of 'embodied, anachronistic time and space, set apart from the mechanisation of modernity'.[19] Cornwall appears in *Rambles beyond Railways* just as its author intended: 'as a fathomless, wild, at times grotesque place, inscribed with legend and mystery, affective as opposed to abstracted, its landscapes and peoples defying rational comprehension'.[20] This would certainly fit with a long-established pattern – one that arguably begins with that Old English word, *Wēalas*. It is certainly at play in the 1720s, when Daniel Defoe feels he sees evidence that the Cornish were once 'a kind of barbarians',[21] and 90 years later when Reverend Richard Warner typifies the place as 'one wide and wild scene of troubled ocean, barren country, and horrid rocks'.[22]

But Erika Behrisch Elce thinks that Young has missed the point. Collins's register is ironic throughout, she argues. When it comes to the image of Cornwall as a gothic, othered place, 'Collins's travelogue actively dismantles such stereotypes' and 'actually consistently pushes against this trope' – mainly, it seems, by making it clear throughout that Cornwall is a very nice place, and that the people he and Brandling meet there are friendly and intelligent. He is, in fact, aiming to 'domesticate' Cornwall and bring it in from the wild periphery, 'all the way home to the centre of English culture'.[23] (Behrisch Elce does not seem to acknowledge the obvious 'imperial dimension'[24] in such a strategy, when dealing with a historically distinct place such as Cornwall.)

For what it's worth, I think Young and Behrisch Elce are *both* right. You can always exoticise a place, other its people, while at the same time ironising the lurid portrayals of the writers who went that way before you. Isn't this what almost every self-deprecating comic travel writer of the twentieth century did – from the heights of the Hindu Kush to the heart of Borneo? When Collins compares Cornwall to Kamchatka and talks of 'savage regions', he *is* making a joke of it. But he still wants the place to be different, new, *other*. As the Cornish tourist industry developed in the later nineteenth century, a semi-comic conception of the place as 'West Barbary' came into play.[25] You wouldn't actually meet any barbarians if you took a holiday there (as Collins's narrative makes clear). You'd be perfectly safe; but you wouldn't be entirely *at home*; it was just different enough to be titillating. And that is precisely the Cornwall that Wilkie Collins constructs in *Rambles beyond Railways*.

But here's the key question: What does it feel like to be on the receiving end of all that? How does it feel to read such a travel book – not as an academic or a would-be tourist but as what scholars of travel writing call 'the travellee'?

Scholar Wendy Bracewell makes a fine observation:

> Any first-person travel account invites the reader to accompany the traveller and gaze through his or her eyes. But reading foreign travel accounts of one's own society means finding oneself simultaneously displayed as the object of the narrator's description and analysis.[26]

A 'travellee-reader' – that is, someone from the place described by the travel writer – finds themselves, Bracewell says, 'doubly written into these texts'. And this is a strange, even uncanny and often aggravating experience.

There is sometimes an inadvertent suggestion in travel writing scholarship – particularly that of the postcolonial bent – that the travellee is a mute and powerless figure, inevitably subaltern. This suggestion is there in the word itself, as coined by Mary Louise Pratt[27] for the local people encountered by the explorers of the colonial era: travell*ee* – the one passively travelled *upon* by the active travell*er*. But Wendy Bracewell's research (mainly on eighteenth-century travel writing about South-East Europe) brilliantly complicates this: travellees have often engaged with travellers' texts, and reading itself is an intellectually active process. But there's more: travellee-readers have sometimes penned their own 'travellee polemics'[28] in response to problematic travel narratives about their home places. Bracewell cites late eighteenth-century examples of this from across Europe, from the Balkans to Ireland.

When Kathleen Jamie, in her famous 2008 essay, 'A Lone Enraptured Male',[29] on Robert Macfarlane's *The Wild Places*, writes of the 'horrible mix of class, gender and ethnic tension' stirred up by reading the travel account of a middle-class Englishman approaching her own native Scotland, what she describes is the experience of the travellee-reader, of being 'doubly written'. And what she produces in response is a travellee polemic.

Everything I've written here so far is, to borrow Jamie's own words, 'preliminary to the admission of a huge and unpleasant prejudice'. I am from Cornwall (and not just from Cornwall: from the westernmost part, Penwith, a periphery of a periphery when viewed from any conventional centre). When someone asks me what I am, I tend to answer 'Cornish' – if not *exactly* 'as a Welshman speaks of himself as Welsh', then certainly in a *similar* spirit. I come to travellers' accounts of Cornwall as a travellee-reader. And when I encounter someone exoticising or romanticising the place, calling it 'savage', or simply addressing an intended readership manifestly situated outside of Cornwall, I often end up, like Kathleen Jamie, 'not just groaning but banging my head on the table'.[30]

But there's something to admit here: it isn't entirely unpleasant, this travellee-reading, this being doubly written. There's a certain sense of validation in knowing that at least you come from a place *worth* visiting, worth writing about. That's one reason I've reread Wilkie Collins's *Rambles beyond Railways* so many times over the last 20 years. There are other complications too. It's all too easy to accept the supremacy of local knowledge, to presume that the travellee-reader is always right. But it's not necessarily so. For a long time I missed the very obvious irony in the way Collins constructs Cornwall, as identified by Erika Behrisch Elce. And then there's the issue of time and distance. We tend to assume that the traveller and travellee always occupy the same space – what Mary Louise

Pratt calls the 'contact zone'.³¹ The traveller has to *go* somewhere, and the travellee has to be there, literally *in place*, before he or she arrives. That's the very dynamic from which so much academic discussion of travel writing arises, from which the wrangles over representation and agency and authority emerge. It's the dynamic in place for the eighteenth-century travellee-polemicists that Wendy Bracewell examines. And it's the dynamic in place for Kathleen Jamie when a lone enraptured male appears over the hill. But if the traveller and the travellee were *never* in the contact zone at the same time, then things aren't quite so simple. It leads, in fact, to an awkward question: when I read *Rambles beyond Railways*, 170 years after Wilkie Collins visited Cornwall, am I really the travellee at all?

There's only one way to try and work it out. Seated at a desk, fully 254 miles from my Cornish home place, and with the easy back and forth temporarily suspended in the age of Covid-19, I open the book, flick through to chapter 10, where Collins and Brandling make their way into Penwith – *my* bit of Cornwall – and start reading.

Look – two figures, up ahead. Follow them!

Wilkie Collins and Henry Brandling head west from Penzance, to Lamorna, to the Logan Rock at Treen, and on along the coast to Land's End. But with the light-footed, leap-frogging narrative of *Rambles beyond Railways*, it's hard to keep them in view. Which way do they go on their way out of town? Around the coast through Mousehole, or up the steep incline of Paul Hill? I don't know. I don't even know how long they took over this section of their journey, from Penzance to St Ives. I suspect an overnight stop – probably at Sennen or St Just. But there's no mention of it in the book. I can only catch them here and there, at specific spots along the coast.

At Lamorna, Brandling makes a sketch – one he'll work up later as a plate for the book. I peer over his shoulder here, smugly thinking I've caught him in the excessive exercise of artistic licence, for his picture shows no sign of the quarries on the hillside – the skirt of tumbled granite blocks that I can see quite clearly, running down towards the cove. But wait – were the quarries there in 1850? Check … *The first quarries opened in the Lamorna valley in 1849.* Just a year into their operation, the holes in the hillside wouldn't have been very big, might have been out of view of Brandling's vantage point. I frown as he closes his sketchpad, no longer so sure of myself. He shoulders his knapsack, calls to Collins and walks on – which way? Along the coast? On the field path through Tregiffian? Or up the valley and along the line of the modern road past the Merry Maidens? I don't know.

I catch them up at Logan Rock. I have some confidence here. Even at my distant desk, I can trace the weathered stone of the buildings in the Treen hamlet, half a mile inland, see the way the grass bends at the field edges in the breeze of an August day (it's August for both Collins and I). I can follow the path south across the fields, over the stiles set in the thick banks of earth and granite that we call 'hedges' hereabouts, push out onto the rough of the clifftop with the sweep of the bay to the right, the water on a cline from cobalt to turquoise as it runs in over the shell-sand shallows.

I scan the jumbled, lichen-bearded rocks of the headland. There's Brandling with his sketchpad out again. And there's Collins, sitting on a high crag, chatting to another man. I feel the local know-it-all's urge to intrude, point out to him the things he might have missed, the embankments of the Iron Age cliff-castle. 'And see that beach down there? That's a ....' But, of course, there are no nudists at Pedney in 1850. 'Look over there! You'll see ....' But no; there's no Minack Theatre on the cliffside across the bay either.

And that's when I recognise my own sloppy presumption. Hurrying through the Treen hamlet, I was all blithe confidence: *there's* the pub and *there's* the chapel ... But at a distance of 170 years, none of this can be assumed.

Looking at the granite buildings that stud the landscape of Penwith, it's easy to view them as ancient. I used carelessly to think that my own family home was 'hundreds of years old'. But that was before I took to exploring old maps of western Cornwall and saw the remarkable churning over that went on in these scattered settlements and farmsteads until the second half of the nineteenth century. Old cottages and barns were knocked down and new ones thrown up at a remarkable pace; every hamlet was a hive of construction and demolition, of constant change. Things only really settled down at the start of the twentieth century. Take a look at the 1840s map of a place like Treen, and chances are that you'll be able to identify none of the buildings that were recorded in the same place four decades later. As Wilkie Collins walks on towards Land's End, I have to acknowledge that he and I are travelling through entirely different places.

I let him lead the way, seeing what he sees for the first time, follow him into a fishing hamlet – where? He's making a composite here, with what can only be St Leven Church moved to a more convenient location. But the detail must come from Penberth or Porthgwarra, and it's all new to me; I've never *seen* it:

> Sturdy little cottages, built of rough granite, and thickly thatched, stand near you, with gulls' and cormorants' eggs set in their loop-holed windows for ornament; great white sections of fish hang thickly together on their walls to dry, looking more like many legs of many dirty duck trousers, than anything else.[32]

I watch Collins and Brandling up across the wide, windy expanse by Gwennap Head, where my grandmother's ashes are scattered ... but no, *no* – they haven't been scattered yet. The clifftops at least have the same heather and gorse, 'in brilliant clothing of purple and yellow'[33] (and what I wouldn't give to walk that way now). But once I follow them around Land's End and back eastwards along the harder coast, even the familiar flora is lacking: the land is stripped, soured with arsenic. And the configurations of the hamlets and villages are still less familiar. This is western Cornwall at the height of its industrialisation, with fuming mine-stacks all along the coast, and a working population shifting back and forth from parish to parish as speculative mining ventures open and close. The last few years have been bad for potato blight, and food shortages have prompted the first major waves of Cornish out-migration – to the Americas, to Australia, to South Africa – anywhere with hard-rock mining. But the local industry has yet to begin the long decline that will reach its sad terminus in my childhood.

I leave Collins and Brandling to descend the mine at Bottalack without me and wander off for a while, fascinated, trying to work out the lie of the land, to identify the exact spots where we will one day ride our BMXs, scramble down to fish for pollock off the rocks, slide across gravel heaps on bits of plywood. But it all looks so different ...

The two travellers come up to grass, wash with the soap and water laid out for them by their guide, change back into their own clothes, then push on, through Trewellard and Pendeen. We're getting very, very close now.

Follow them – follow them through Bojewyan, past the bend in the road at Keigwin, down over the bridge at the parish boundary and into Morvah.

This is the part of *Rambles beyond Railways* – the part that I placed up near the start of this chapter – that I go back to most often. Morvah, very specifically, is my home place. This small and stony parish – a narrow ledge of wind-flayed pasture perched 120 metres above the seething Atlantic, dotted with huddled grey hamlets and isolated cottages, home today to just 50 people – is where I am *from*, my original point of reference for what the world looks like. And Collins, in 196 well-honed words, gives a very hostile account of it. It is one of the few places in the book where he unquestionably *is* constructing Cornwall as a 'grotesque place'[34] without irony.

But it's also one of the finest passages in the book. It begins in the imperative: 'Imagine three or four large, square, comfortless-looking houses ….' The reader is pushed to believe that they are doing the work, that the author is simply guiding them as they create a collage of unrelenting negatives: miserable cottages; a grim church; people sickly, melancholy, despondent, gloomy; and a landscape 'wild, barren, and shelterless'. Only at the very end do they discover that they have been unwittingly putting together a detailed picture of what supposedly presented itself to Collins and Brandling, 'when we found ourselves in the village of Morvah'.[35]

For me, the passage always prompts a strange mix of outrage and amusement, and for years, I thought I was coming to it as a travellee-reader, that I was already there, waiting to be travelled upon by the outsider and ready to respond with a polemical counterblast. I've often, with perfect illogic, identified myself among those 'two or three lads leaning against the churchyard wall'.[36]

But Wilkie Collins came to Morvah long before this particular baby boy was driven by his parents one wild March day across the moors from the maternity home in Penzance to a granite farmhouse which – I know now from the old maps – didn't even exist in 1850. My claim to speak here as the travellee is very tenuous indeed. And here's the important thing: for years I was so caught up in my own emotional response to the text that I missed the most significant part of it: the presence of a *real* travellee, one who really was there in the contact zone at the same moment as Wilkie Collins. And what's more: there's just enough detail to suggest that something of who she was might be recoverable, 170 years later.

There is no inn in Morvah today; just a café in the old schoolhouse (though even that is shuttered this summer, too cramped to allow for the necessary social distancing). But the inn of Collins's visit is marked on the Ordnance Survey map of 1877: *Star (P.H.)*.[37] It is one of the few buildings in the parish, besides the church tower, with a relatively long pedigree. It is a private home now and still the largest house in the hamlet. The 1856 Post Office directory lists among Morvah's meagre tally of traders one James Trounson of the Star Inn.[38] Other Trounsons show up in the parish records of births, marriages, burials.[39] And the census data for Morvah, gathered the year after Collins passed through, includes one Sarah Trounson, 43 years of age, 'Inn Keeper's Wife'.[40] We have her, then, with some reasonable degree of certainty: Wilkie Collins's 'middle-aged, melancholy woman'.

What about the 'sickly little girl'? The census lists four Trounson children, but only one female, Elizabeth, who would have been 18 at the time of Collins's visit – hardly a little girl. But there are three boys, who would have been 3, 9 and 13 at the time. We might, of course, be looking at some other child altogether, the daughter of a neighbour or a relative. But isn't there also a chance that we're simply dealing with the fickle memory of a travel writer – never quite so accurate an instrument as we might like to imagine? Collins wrote up the scene weeks or months later, 250 miles away on the edge of Regent's Park. He wasn't entirely certain about the number of large houses alongside Morvah Church (was it three or four?), nor about how many lads were leaning up against the churchyard wall (was it two or three?). Perhaps he simply misremembered an infant gender. Perhaps the sickly child, staring into the fire that damp August evening, was actually little John Trounson, or 9-year-old James Junior – or even teenaged William (given certain details in the parish records, his being 'sickly' in 1850 might make sense).

Look, then: two strangers, wearing knapsacks, at the door of the Star Inn in Morvah at dusk, with a thin drizzle sweeping in across the fields, masking the crown of the Carn and the summit of Watch Croft.

Sarah lets them in, leads them through to the kitchen, for there are no drinkers in the bar tonight, and her husband is not here. Perhaps he is resting upstairs. Perhaps he is elsewhere, working on the land he holds jointly with Nicholas White in the neighbouring hamlet of Trevowhan, or gone into Penzance for supplies. It has been a busy time. Morvah Fair – the first Sunday of the month, 4 August in this year of 1850 – was just a few days ago, and though the vicar has been fulminating of late against 'idle and profane amusement', the revellers still turned up from all the farms and mines along the coast. They fairly cleaned out the cellar and larder of the Star Inn, and there's been no chance yet to restock.

Sarah offers the two strangers the little she has left – some bread, eggs, a jug of leftover porter, laid out at the kitchen table. They ask about rooms. But no, in the aftermath of the fair, the place is all disordered still; there are no rooms fit to let.

Does she wonder who these strangers are? Surely. They are a strange sight, with their knapsacks. People have stared at them the length of Cornwall, taken them for mapmakers, travelling salesmen. They appear to be educated gentlemen, though their clothes are a little weatherworn, their shoes scuffed. If she asks, they say they are from London, that they are making a tour of Cornwall. One of them is a very short man, with a boyish face. If Sarah had to guess she might say he was little older than her own Elizabeth. And where *is* Elizabeth this evening? Perhaps Sarah already knows of a certain flirtation with the boy Jelbert from Tregaminon, the adjoining hamlet to the west of Morvah Churchtown – though she doesn't know that the pair will marry, in five years' time.

The Trounson family, like so many others in this age of economic churn in western Cornwall, has led a mobile life within a small compass. Elizabeth, the first child, was born in St Just. William was born in Penzance. And by the time of James Junior's birth, the family were at Paul, above Mousehole on the south coast. Little John is the first to have been born here at the inn. As for Sarah herself, she comes from Gulval, on the other side of the moors, out of the hard winds that cut in winterlong from the sea at Morvah, and out of the mist and drizzle that creeps up over the cliffs even on mild August evenings.

There will be sadness in the Star Inn next year. In June, William, the oldest boy, will die. A few weeks later, another child will be born to the family, and they will name him after the departed William. But the baby will survive only until October. At his burial, his parents will be recorded in the parish register as Sarah and James, 43 and 48 years of age. But Elizabeth will be 19 by then, and the boy Jelbert is just along the road in Tregaminion, so who can really say for certain what arrangements might have been made?

Perhaps one day, before or after the bereavements, someone will drop into the inn with a book, newly published in London, open it at the start of the 12th chapter and point to a particular passage. It's nice to think so, nice to wonder at Sarah Trounson's reaction.

But all of that lies ahead. Tonight she just has these two unexpected customers to take care of. They finish their meagre meal, talk a little – about what? Perhaps about the visit they have made to a mine earlier in the day. But this will be of little novelty to Sarah. Most of the 367 people living in Morvah parish are miners, miners' wives or miners' children – whole families huddled up in tiny cottages built into the field corners.

The strangers drink the last of the old porter, hand over a few coins, rise to go. They ask about the road to St Ives, and Sarah shows them out through the empty bar. They do look ridiculous with their belongings all bundled on their backs. The taller man has a square ruler strapped to the outside of his pack. They walk out onto the road, turn right past the church and are gone, into the wet gloaming. Sarah closes the door, goes back to the warmth of the kitchen.

## Notes

1. W. Collins, *Rambles beyond Railways* (London: Richard Bentley, 1851), 227–28.
2. P. Ackroyd, *Wilkie Collins* (London: Vintage, 2013), 43.
3. Ibid., 44.
4. Ibid., 46.
5. C. Thompson, 'Nineteenth-Century Travel Writing', in *The Cambridge History of Travel Writing*, ed. N. Das and T. Youngs (Cambridge: Cambridge University Press, 2019), 108–24 (123).
6. Ibid.
7. R. Warner, *A Tour through Cornwall in the Autumn of 1808* (Bath: Richard Cruttwell, 1809), 346.
8. Thompson, 'Nineteenth-Century Travel Writing', 124.
9. Ibid., 123.
10. Warner, *A Tour through Cornwall*, 133.
11. Collins, *Rambles*, 206.
12. Ibid., 210–11.
13. Ibid., 24–28.
14. Ibid., 111–12.
15. B. Deacon, *Cornwall: A Concise History* (Cardiff: University of Wales Press, 2007), 2.
16. Collins, *Rambles*, 94.
17. B. Deacon, '"The Hollow Jarring of the Distant Steam Engines": Images of Cornwall between West Barbary and Delectable Duchy', in *Cornwall: The Cultural Construction of Place*, ed. E. Westland (Newmill: Patten Press, 1997), 7–25 (8).

18 Collins, *Rambles*, 7–8.
19 P. Young, 'Rambles beyond Railways: Gothicised Place and Globalised Space in Victorian Cornwall', *Gothic Studies* 13, 1 (2011): 55–74 (55).
20 Ibid., 60.
21 D. Defoe, *A Tour thro' the Whole Island of Great Britain* (London: J. M. Dent, 1724), 257.
22 Warner, *A Tour through Cornwall*, 337.
23 E. B. Elce, 'Cornwall and Kamtschatka: Domesticating Cornwall through Pedestrian Travel in Wilkie Collins's *Rambles beyond Railways* (1851)', *Wilkie Collins Journal* 14 (2017).
24 E. A. Bohls, 'Picturesque Travel: The Aesthetics and Politics of Landscape', in *The Routledge Companion to Travel Writing*, ed. C. Thompson (Abingdon: Routledge, 2016), 246–57 (250).
25 E. Westland, 'The Passionate Periphery: Cornwall and Romantic Fiction', in *Peripheral Visions: Images of Nationhood in Contemporary British Fiction*, ed. I. A. Bell (Cardiff: University of Wales Press, 1995), 153–72 (157).
26 W. Bracewell, 'The Travellees' Eye: Reading European Travel Writing, 1750–1850', in *New Directions in Travel Writing Studies*, ed. J. Kuehn and P. Smethurst (Basingstoke: Palgrave Macmillan, 2015), 215–27 (216).
27 M. L. Pratt, *Imperial Eyes: Travel Writing and Transculturation* (Abingdon: Routledge, 2008).
28 Bracewell, 'The Travellees' Eye', 218.
29 K. Jamie, 'A Lone Enraptured Male', *London Review of Books*, 6 March 2008, https://www.lrb.co.uk/the-paper/v30/n05/kathleen-jamie/a-lone-enraptured-male.
30 Ibid.
31 Pratt, *Imperial Eyes*, 8.
32 Collins, *Rambles*, 199.
33 Ibid., 198.
34 Young, 'Rambles beyond Railways', 60.
35 Collins, *Rambles*, 228.
36 Ibid.
37 Ordnance Survey, 'Cornwall LXVII.7 (Morvah; St Just in Penwith)', OS 25 Inch England and Wales, National Library of Scotland, https://maps.nls.uk/view/105995917.
38 'Kelly's Post Office Directory of Cornwall 1856, Morvah', West Penwith Resources, accessed 17 September 2020, https://west-penwith.org.uk/morvah56.htm.
39 'Morvah Documents', West Penwith Resources, accessed 17 September 2020, https://west-penwith.org.uk/morvah.htm.
40 '1851 – Transcript of Piece HO107/1919 (Part 1)', Cornwall Online Census Project, accessed 17 September 2020, http://freepages.rootsweb.com/~kayhin/genealogy/51919.html.

# Chapter Seven

# PICTURING ROME: WALKING THE ETERNAL CITY WITH THE LAST VICTORIAN

## Tory Hayward

We are about to walk through Rome. Not in a single day, or even in a single century, but through a flickering palimpsest of overlaid time, of records and recollection. We will walk down composite constructions of wisteria-draped ruins and secret courtyards and bone-lined crypts, and we will do this without having to go anywhere.

This is just as well, because as I write in the late summer of 2020, it is in fact very difficult (if possible at all) to go anywhere at all. To have been to a place is a precious thing – those memories warm us like the remembered heat of summer in a frozen winter.

I first arrived in Rome by night. Anywhere known as the Eternal City has quite a lot to live up to, but even in darkness, it was captivating. As the taxi rolled past the uplit, mighty Aurelian walls, I had the sense that I was *arriving*. Both into a place where the warm night felt thick with history, and into a role. To enter Rome feels like becoming part of a story, a complicated and ever-unfolding living performance that weaves itself continually along the weft of time.

In lieu of the physical place, we will walk through the Rome of my memories, and those of Augustus Hare, the 'last Victorian'.[1] He is an excellent companion, perhaps the best person one could pick for this walk. He has impeccable travel-guide-writer credentials and perhaps, more importantly, he is good company and knows all the gossip. A friend of his recalled that he always said, 'The moment you have become discreet, you ease to be interesting.'[2] He is in fact so committed to being the man in the know that, on leading a tour group to a favourite cafe only to find it had closed down, he actually swooned.[3]

Before we strike out, I will tell you a little more about Augustus and how he would advise us to prepare for our time in Rome. Let's start with the man. Augustus was born in Rome in 1834. A surplus child born to an eccentric family, he was sent to live with his widowed godmother, Maria Hare, in England, apparently on a whim. Maria was in mourning and made the request to adopt her godson to Augustus's birth mother, who responded accordingly, 'the baby shall be sent as soon as it is weaned; and, if any one else would like one, would you kindly recollect that we have others'.[4] If this seems callous to you, prepare yourself for the rest of the family. Aunt Esther is worse than anything dreamed up by Dickens or Dahl, but we'll save her for later. Suffice to say, it seems incredible that Augustus became the gregarious raconteur he did. He was also extraordinarily generous, both to strangers and to his friends. Shane Leslie wondered whether 'perhaps having been made to suffer as a child, he was careful of the feelings of others'. One friend recalled that 'no more faithful or affectionate friend ever lived. He would forgive again and again almost any injury, while he was morally absolutely fearless.'[5]

He was also, to his contemporaries, alarmingly candid. His autobiography (which ran to six volumes) contains copious amounts of gossip and anecdotes. He didn't hold back on shaming the ecclesiastical family who had abused him either – something which sent ripples of shock through contemporary society. Interestingly, not just because of *what* was done to him but because he revealed by *whom* it was done. An 1897 review titled 'Augustus Hare as a Gossip', stated 'Mr Hare has chosen to be very candid, to upset our complacent notions of many persons with venerable and saintly reputations.'[6] He was open about his feelings and had no qualms about sharing them frankly with the world, along with the minutiae of his interactions with the great and good. He may have been described as the 'last Victorian', but sometimes his biographies read more like those of the first millennial.

So how did a bullied and abandoned boy come to be one of the most prominent travel writers of his time? The book which will guide us, *Walks in Rome*, was first published in 1871 and was into its 18th edition by 1909. Augustus had connections first and foremost – he may not have had vast wealth at his disposal, but he had enough useful contacts to set him on his way. He produced several guides for the publisher John Murray, but to me, it seems that the publication of *Walks in Rome* gave him his first real break. If nothing else, writing and updating the guide gave him a chance to return to Rome, to escape both the scrutiny of his hateful family and the monotony of caring for his mother (a supposed hypochondriac). Augustus was an artist and a storyteller – his writing meant he became a celebrity, and he was celebrated. He knew everyone and everything. He was a man about town with a seat at the most interesting and fashionable tables. And I believe that the first place this happened in – the first place that allowed Augustus to *become* himself – was Rome. You can see the threads of this in his autobiography. Over the course of years, he moves from hoping that 'Walks in Rome' will grow into a book, to relief that its publication and success brought 'better days' at a time when he and his family were in financial difficulty, to an anecdote requiring dazzling heights of confidence most of us can only dream of pulling off.[7] Augustus recounts that he was apparently accused of plagiarising himself by a passionate fan who hadn't realised he was actually listening to the author of *Walks in Rome* lecture a tour group. Augustus responded by saying, 'Oh, I am *so* much obliged to you. I did not know there was anybody in the world who would defend my interests so kindly. I am Augustus Hare.'[8]

Rome was one of the first places I travelled solo overseas – on a business trip for my first job. From recollection, I did a presentation before being turned loose for the afternoon. I am the first person in my family to be awarded a degree, so the realisation that jobs where someone else would actually *pay* for you to go abroad exist was intoxicating. I recall stepping out into the sunshine and thinking, 'I am someone who can just walk around Rome!' There is something nice about being able to pretend that you have a reason for being in a place. It allows you to pretend that you are different, that you aren't encroaching on the atmosphere of the city in a way that the maligned tourist might.

In his guide, Augustus also urges travellers to do 'something which will give them an individual interest, a personal property in Rome itself'.[9] Years after that first trip, I still like to have a reason, however spurious for being in a place. I was in fact supposed to be in Rome this year, on a printmaking research trip funded by Arts Council England on folk beliefs, witchcraft and the occult. I like to think that Augustus would have approved of this undertaking, not just because he himself was an artist, working in watercolours and illustrating many of his own guidebooks, but because his autobiography is packed with ghost stories and contemporaries recount that he was a good teller of them (and also did the voices).

As well as finding a reason for going to a place, Augustus tells us not to try to 'do' Rome, to try and tick off lists of endless sights. If we do this he warns, 'The promised pleasure seems rapidly to change into an endless vista of labour to be fulfilled and of fatigue to be gone through; henceforward the hours spent at Rome are rather hours of endurance than of pleasure.'

Now we've done the preparatory work, let us open our guide book. *Walks in Rome* contains a section towards the front of the first volume amusingly titled 'DULL – USEFUL INFORMATION'. Leafing through my 12th edition, I indeed find useful details about hotels, dentists, chemists, hairdressers, shipping agents and booksellers. It feels very modern in format, until you get to the tiny section of restaurants which contains reviews like 'Inferior, but much frequented by Italians and by artists'.[10] There is also a listing for an 'English Dairy' which seems peculiar (why not just eat Italian cheese?) until you consider it in the context of the restaurant reviews and start to realise that there is something odd going on. Augustus (and Victorians more generally) had what with authority I am going to call 'weird views' about Italian food. Mullen and Munson quote an 1843 traveller who referred to mozzarella as 'a vile compound'.[11] Augustus cites another who was 'sick at stomach of sour bread, sour wine, rancid butter, and bad cookery'.[12] He himself also published an article with (to a modern eye) a bizarre segment where he teaches an Italian lady to boil an egg, and makes a statement which jeopardises this whole chapter, because it is such a major area of disagreement. In 1873, Augustus Hare wrote, 'One does not come to Rome to eat.'[13] I go to Rome precisely *to* eat – some of my most vivid memories of the city involve food. The telegraphing cheese of a split suppli, the crunch of a deep-fried artichoke, the saucy smack of bucatini all'Amatriciana. There's no accounting for taste, of course – but really, Victorians?

However, in the interests of ensuring you get to see some of the city, let's choose to ignore the food issue for now and stick with the areas of agreement. Let us escape to the ever-changing penumbra of Rome. The physical realities of a place are only a part of what it is – the living part we create ourselves in our imagination. So here are some memories – part of the flickering Rome of the mind, ever changing, ever moving but ever alive.

We are going to begin this walk in the environs of the Borghese Gardens. This is in fact where Augustus instructs visitors to Rome to start, informing them that 'a stranger's first lesson in Roman topography should be learnt standing in the Piazza del Popolo'.[14]

The Piazza del Popolo is a monumental oval, the ceremonial gateway to Rome by which travellers (before railroads) would enter the city. My impression of it was of gleaming whiteness against the azure sky. The building frontages are those of various eras and styles, but together achieve what the *Encyclopaedia Britannica* describes as a 'remarkable harmony'. Augustus describes it thusly:

> On the left side of the piazza rise the terraces of the Pincio [...] The terraces are adorned with rostral-columns, statues, and marble bas-reliefs, interspersed with cypresses and pines [...] From the platform of the Pincio terrace the Eternal City is seen spread at our feet, and beyond it the wide-spreading Campagna, till a silver line marks the sea melting into the horizon beyond Ostia.[15]

My memories of this place are of being lost somewhere behind the Borghese Gardens at night. An inky wash of indigo twilight blooming across the sky, the spike-sharp silhouette of a palm tree outlining itself against the horizon. Aperitivo hour had just passed. It was my 30th birthday, and I had just left the bar of a very expensive hotel where the lobby was filled with fresh-cut orchids and roses, walked past the fountains of the Palazzo del Popolo and up Monte Pincio past cypresses and evening birds.

In his guide, Augustus quotes another writer who describes how the Pincio has been overrun by 'barbarians from Gaul, Great Britain, and beyond the sea', but that is still 'the world's great watering-place [...] here are beautiful sunsets; and here [...] are scenes well worth gazing at, both in themselves, and for their historical interest'.[16] In his autobiography, Augustus describes 'the sunny Pincio terrace, with the deepest of unimaginable blue skies seen through branches of ilex and bay, and garden beds, beneath the terraced wall'.[17] This was also a special place to Augustus – he came often with his adopted mother and reflected on the meaning of the place to him after she died: 'no one could understand – all that that walk is to me [...] Nothing has been more our garden'.[18]

Augustus only briefly mentions the Hotel de Russie (location of my expensive cocktails) in *Walks in Rome*. He describes it in my edition only as 'very comfortable and well managed'.[19] This is pretty complimentary in the context of his restaurant reviews, but doesn't quite do the establishment justice. The Hotel de Russie features a beautiful nineteenth-century secret terraced garden, with almost 3,000 square metres of palm trees, yews and climbing roses. Pablo Picasso and Jean Cocteau stayed here in 1917 and leaned out of their windows to pick oranges, with the latter describing it as 'paradise on earth'.[20]

I am an interloper here. I like nice things, but no, I don't spend most of my time mooching around five-star hotels. This is a one-night performance – although an enjoyable one. We have a lovely view of the gardens from the courtyard and are surrounded by the sort of people who I imagine Augustus may have gossiped about. There is one eccentric hotel resident dressed in a tracksuit (looking a little like an ageing sporting celebrity) holding forth in Italian to a table of bemused, beautiful young people who glitter in expensive jewellery and designer clothing. I enjoy the combination and suspect that Augustus would have too.

We ended our evening wandering around the Borghese Gardens – and this is where, in Augustus's accounts, we get more of a sense of the flamboyant socialites of his time. It is strangely pleasing to know they haunt the same environs, then and now. In *Walks in*

*Rome*, Augustus gives us a fairly formal description of the Borghese Gardens' 'beautiful grounds'.[21]

It is in his autobiography that we get a little more colour and a sense of the 'enjoyment' hinted at in *Walks in Rome*.

> The Borgheses have had a magnificent fancy ball. Young Bolognetti Cenci borrowed the armour of Julius II. from the Pope for the occasion, and young Corsini that of Cardinal de Bourbon. The Duchess Fiano went in the costume of the first Empire, terribly improper in these days, and another lady went as a nymph just emerged from a fountain, and naturally clothed as little as possible. The Princess Borghese was dreadfully shocked, but she only said, 'I fear, Madame, that you must be feeling horribly cold.'[22]

This place, where we are starting our walk, feels almost where we should in fact end. With Augustus the social butterfly, flitting between fabulous people in lush gardens with twinkling lights, intriguing gossip with a little mild scandal thrown in for interest. This is where we see the Augustus that was made by Rome – or perhaps the Rome that was made by Augustus. He said in his guide that 'when one is in Rome, life seems to be free from many of the petty troubles which beset it in other places'.[23]

This would be a nice place to leave things, but for us to understand how Rome became a place of freedom for Augustus, we need to know a little more about what he was escaping. So we will leave these gardens and head south-east, towards somewhere a little more suitable for discussing darker matters.

We are now standing in a chamber decorated with human bones. And when I say decorated, I mean that the skeletons of 4,000 people have been disassembled, then placed into intricate, baroque patterns garlanding the walls and ceilings. There are also whole, robed skeletons amidst this, frozen for eternity in the performance of religious allegories. My recollection is that the ossuary smelt of preserved things. Not a bad smell, just something outside the realms of the usual. This is the crypt of the Santa Maria della Consezione dei Cappuccini, which sits at the foot of the Via Veneto. The skeletons belong to the friars of that order who died between 1528 and 1870. To access the crypt, you must pass through a museum about the order of Capuchin friars – which is well put-together and informative, but really, everyone is here for the bones. The chambers were 'decorated', as far as I can tell, by one artistic monk, whose gruesome crypt transformation project was somehow given the go-ahead by the monk leadership. Despite considering myself as being fairly competent at delivering an ambitious pitch, I'm not sure how I'd even start with that one.

I don't consider myself squeamish, but there is something dreadful about the sight of so many disassembled individuals. It's not the fact that they are bones themselves, it's that they no longer feel as if they were people. Like the husks of plants in winter, they've been divested of their form and meaning, of their essence in a profoundly disturbing way.

Uncomfortable as it may be to view, it is also fascinating. Anywhere with a crypt of pelvises is going to leave an impression, and it did on travellers of Augustus's time. The Marquis de Sade loved it, as did Mark Twain who described its 'picturesque horrors'.[24] I can't determine if Augustus, who enjoyed spending time with Twain in Rome, agreed with his contemporary, because he himself actually gives us very little detail of his own response to the place in his guide.[25] He does furnish us with a colourful extract from Hans Christian Anderson's autobiographical novel *The Improvisatore*, which he describes as 'pleasant to read on the spot'.[26]

> On the festival of All-Saints I was down in the chapel of the dead [...] I, with two other boys of my own age, swung the incense-breathing censer before the great altar of skulls. They had placed lights in the chandeliers made of bones, new garlands were placed around the brows of the skeleton monks, and fresh bouquets in their hands [...] I gazed for a long time on the pale yellow skulls, and the fumes of the incense which wavered in strange shapes between me and them.[27]

I am surprised that Augustus doesn't give us more of his own take on the crypt – it wasn't that he avoided horror. He loved telling people scary stories – in the course of researching this chapter, I discovered that he was the originator of a tale called 'The Vampire of Croglin Grange' – a story which has petrified generations of my family on dark nights on camping trips, as it was always told by my grandfather on these occasions. I wish I could ask him whether he knew of Augustus, but it was an unexpected and pleasant surprise to discover that link across the years.

But for once Augustus is silent on a topic – so I won't keep you in the crypts for much longer, While we're here however, I will make the most of the atmosphere to talk about the darkness in his early life. Contemporaries seem to have been horrified by what was done to the young Augustus – and really, if a Victorian thinks you've gone too far in punishing your child, you probably need to take a long, hard look at yourself. James Papp states in his introduction to the abridged version of *Story of My Life* that Augstus survived 'one of the most extravagantly cruel childhoods in one of the maddest of Victorian families'.[28] There was repeated physical violence, but it was the psychological torment that for me seems the most horrific, because of the level of calculated thought that went into it. His adopted mother 'submitted to the rule that whatever amused or interested a child must be wrong'.[29] It was his Aunt Esther who was the driving force behind what Shane Leslie has called the 'Pious sadism' which characterised Augustus's early life.[30] She was behind the idea that caring about something was inherently wrong, that any enjoyment must be punished and stamped out. This ranged from having meals taken away if you were enjoying them, to torturing and killing his pet cat simply because he loved it. We may have certain views or stereotypes of Victorian discipline, but that wasn't normal. To hurt and destroy a living thing simply because a child loved it wasn't acceptable at that time, or any time I know of. To be punished for caring about or enjoying something is very dark. I'm sure that anyone reading this already detests Aunt Esther for murdering his cat (she hanged the poor animal), but the historians and archivists among you will wince to learn that she also burned all of the family manuscripts and papers – for no other reason than because she knew they were of sentimental value to Augustus. I think we can waive not speaking ill of the dead in this instance – and I suspect Augustus's other biographers have come to feel the same across the course of their research. I can't top Shane Leslie's pithy summation of the end of Aunt Esther: 'she seems to have killed herself by an innocent habit of lying in the rain on the Archdeacon's grave' – which feels in many ways like all she deserves.³¹

In the end, however, Augustus triumphed. Despite the attempts to crush all love and interest out of him, his life was lived in pursuit of those things. He was kind and generous and, most of all, seemed driven by enthusiasm and enjoyment. And in his final document, his last will and testament, he pays special regard to the care of a dear pet – his 'little dog Nero'.³² I can't think of a life lived in superior riposte to his oppressive beginnings.

In the spirit of choosing to pursue things that are interesting and enjoyable, let us leave this dark place and move on, emerging into the light. There is a gallery near to this place where I saw a wonderful exhibition of the prints of Hiroshige. We spent hours in his exquisite floating world, exploring the *One Hundred Famous Views of Edo* and *The Fifty-Three Stations of the Tōkaidō*. One of the most remarkable things about Hiroshige's work is his ability to capture the fluidity of weather in something as solid as a woodblock. He evokes perfectly the feeling of light rain, the soft weight of snow cradling a building, the cool wash of a winter sky. When we left the exhibition (in the old stableyard of the Quirinal Palace), spring rain filled the air. Palm trees soared into the grey sky, and it felt a little as if we ourselves were in a print.

Let us walk back down the road, past the Capuchin crypt, onto the Piazza Barberini. We are in a different time now, in a warm late-summer evening. We are going to see a film at the 1930s Barberini Cinema. We arrive at the cinema to find a crowd outside. I was mildly irritated to find a queue when the film was soon to start. But as we got closer, we realised that the crowd wasn't queuing, just milling outside with cameras. We push our way through and take our red velvet seats inside the cinema. After a hushed wait, to our surprise the lead actors arrive in person to introduce the movie. They are beautiful and glittering with an air of old Hollywood, and the lead actress introduces the film in Italian, which the crowd loves. They walk back down the red carpet to watch the movie away from the public and pass within a few feet of me, sitting as I am at the end of the aisle. As they are leaving, the lead actor meets my eye for a moment. He looks tired, and I wonder how many times they have done this. I applaud politely with the rest of the audience, appreciative but no *too* much. It must be exhausting interacting with overexcited people all of the time.

We stopped for a drink outside a bar afterwards. Suddenly, a people carrier with blacked-out windows pulls up on the street next to us, and the actors, flanked by security, are whisked inside. When the women at the table next to us saw who had arrived, one leaped up and actually overturned their table, sending their drinks flying! We got to feel a little smug at that – of course *we* weren't hysterical, having been 'insiders' at this premiere. We weren't really, and we were just as bad as the table upturners, but in a different way. I was aware of that at the time, but it was still quite fun to pretend. I did feel sorry for the actors though – they could never melt into the city and become part of the fabric of it in the way we could. They would always be a bright light, attracting people and excitement as if they were moths.

Let us leave the bright lights of the fashionable Palazzo Barberini area (so iconically featured in Roman Holiday) and take a stroll somewhere quieter. This is a longer walk, so maybe we'll hop on the metro for this one.

We are going to Testaccio, where in my memory it is now April. Wild green parrots nibble the pink blossom in the trees lining the streets, which falls like spring snow. I have come to a graveyard scented with roses and cypress, cared for by a colony of cats and distinguished ladies. There is a tall white marble pyramid here, which should feel incongruous but seems to fit this place out of time. It was built for Gaius Cestius, a magistrate in ancient Rome.[33]

Augustus spoke about the Monte Testaccio, 'The extraordinary formation of this hill, which is entirely composed of broken pieces of pottery, has long been an unexplained bewilderment.'[34] The hill is formed of broken amphorae dating back to Roman times. Testaccio is a trendy neighbourhood undergoing gentrification, but this specific spot where we stand is also a place where, throughout time, people have taken their rubbish and their dead – it feels like a place of endings. The way Augustus describes it for me enhances the impression of a liminal borderland between life and death, between Rome and not-Rome.

> A wild and beautiful vineyard occupying the greater part of this deserted hill, and extending as far as the Porta S. Paolo and the pyramid of Caius Cestius. There are beautiful views towards the Alban mountains, and to the Pseudo-Aventine with its fortress-like convents. The ground is littered with fragments of marbles and alabaster, which lie unheeded among the vegetables, relics of unknown edifices which once existed here [...] The spot is beautiful, and overgrown by a luxuriance of wild mignonette and other flowers in the late spring.[35]

The peaceful cemetery we are standing in has been known by several names – the non-Catholic Cemetery, the Protestant Cemetery and even the Cimitero degli Inglesi ('Englishmen's Cemetery'). Shelley and Keats are buried here in what Augustus describes as 'a lovely spot'.[36] He tells us:

> It extends for some distance along the slope of the hill under the old Aurelian Wall, and is beautifully shaded by cypresses, and carpeted with violets. Amid the forest of tombs we may notice that which contains the heart of Shelley (his body having been burnt upon the shore at Lerici, where it was thrown up by the sea).

If this was a superhero movie, this would be the place where we come to for the Augustus Hare origin story. His uncle is buried here, and it was for that funeral that Augustus's adopted mother came to Rome and took a fancy to the young boy who would become Augustus Hare. It is because of what happened in this place that young Augustus was taken from Italy to England and subjected to the cruel upbringing we have spoken about. What would he, what would his life have been like had he remained in Rome? I wonder if the eternal city would have played such a part in his imagination and formation had she simply been a home, rather than an escape. We will of course never know, but this borderland feels to me to be the right place to consider it.

Let us travel to somewhere more lively, which I will let Augustus introduce:

> We now enter the Trastevere, the city 'across the Tiber' – the portion of Rome which is most unaltered from mediæval times, and whose narrow streets are still overlooked by many ancient towers, gothic windows, and curious fragments of sculpture.[37]

I came to an incredible slow food restaurant here, Spirito DiVino, in a picturesque vine-draped alley. We were told that the restaurant building is all that remains of a tenth-century synagogue, the first in Rome, dating to the time when Trastevere was the heart of Rome's Jewish quarter. There are faint Hebrew characters still visible on the entrance pillars. I remember walking down into the darkness of the cellars and being told that each footstep took us down centuries, until we arrived into a room pre-dating the Coliseum. On one visit, I have eaten a rich stew here by candlelight, on another sheltered from the summer sun in the cool darkness while sipping the moscato produced by the owner's family.

Augustus wrote about a famous archaeological discovery made in Trastevere in 1849 which included a bronze 'mutilated horse, found, 1849, in the Trastevere'.[38] In the same year at Spirito DeVino, a bronze horse was found along with a Roman marble statue of an athlete – I like to imagine it was the same discovery.

Now we walk north along the Tiber towards the Orto Botanico di Roma. I visited this place years ago to attend an evening reception in the gardens which was rather magical. I had no idea what to expect as my invite was checked at the entrance. I was used to the world of Brussels policy receptions at which the centrepiece was often a giant loaf of bread filled with tiny sandwiches (something I still don't understand and have never seen elsewhere). Here, with nobody else in sight, I followed a red carpet down a colonnaded courtyard out into perfumed gardens lit by burning torches. Tables covered in white linens were nestled among soaring trees and exotic plants and attended by waiters wielding trays laden with champagne glasses. I spent the evening in the very good company of an Italian judge and associated dignitaries, including a very elegant Calabrian gentleman who was impressed with my knowledge of 'Nduja, the famous spicy sausage of that region. This was just as well, because I don't speak Italian, so had no other chat. He dramatically illustrated the location of his region by stamping his foot on the ground to demonstrate where it was located in 'the boot' of Italy. The kind judge acted as a translator for me for the evening, and I recall her explaining how a particularly unusual plant got its name due to having thorns in the shape of a jet plane. It was certainly all a lot much more glamorous than a junior policy wonk like me had any right to expect and is one of my favourite memories from that time.

Augustus spoke of the gardens in *Walks in Rome*. He provides us with an extract which captures my experience of passing into what felt like another world.

> A magnificent porter [...] unlocked the ponderous iron gates of the gardens, and let them through, leaving them to their own devices, and closing and locking the gates with a crash. They now stood in a wide avenue of ilex, whose gloomy boughs, interlacing overhead, effectually excluded the sunlight; nearly a quarter of a mile further on, the ilexes were replaced by box and bay trees, beneath which the sun and shade divided the path between them, trembling and flickering on the ground and invading each other's dominions with every breath of wind.

It is strange to know that I have walked under the same trees Augustus did. Buildings seem different – there's something about a living witness that feels wistful. The trees persist across the centuries that separate our accounts and experiences.

We now head north to the Roman Forum, the legendary founding spot of this place. David Watkin described it as 'the heart of the ancient city, the hub of the Roman empire, the goal of tens of thousands of Grand Tourists. It is still visited by millions of people a year, yet it can be a baffling experience.'[39] The bafflement of travellers at this site is not new. Travel writer Philip Glazebrook wrote in 1989 of the 'uncomfortable obligation' of a traveller to respond to a place such as a Rome in such a way 'that will not shame him when compared with what great men down the ages have recorded of their tremendous sensations in the ancient capital'. Glazebrook also shares the interesting account of a nineteenth-century woman, Mrs. Hall, who accompanied her husband on a tour of Rome. Unlike his wife, he had benefitted from a classical education which enhanced his experience – he saw the projected historical figures and buildings in his mind's eye, whereas she was simply dragged around ruins. She recorded that sometimes she felt 'disgusted with myself for being so indifferent'.[40]

Augustus, you will probably not be surprised to hear, loved the Forum. He had the education to 'read' it the appropriate way, but also seemed to enjoy the atmosphere.

> The first days at Rome this winter were absolute Elysium – the sitting for hours in the depth of the Forum, then picturesque, flowery, and 'unrestored', watching the sunlight first kiss the edge of the columns and then bathe them with gold.[41]

My recollection of the Roman Forum was of blithely pushing my way through pendulous, purple grapes of wisteria, over and around ruins, marvelling at the ancient fragments underfoot and all around. I didn't know what I was looking at, and heresy – I didn't mind. The experience reminded me of an Anglo-Saxon poem believed to be about my home city – also a Roman town – Bath. The poem describes the feeling of walking through a ruined city and I love it, because the feeling of looking at the fragments of a lost world is clearly something that echoes across time. The people we wonder about, who lived and died a millennia ago, wondered about the people who lived and died a millennia before them. There have been many translations, but my favourite is by Michael Alexander which speaks of 'the work of giants' being destroyed by 'weirds' and mournfully recalls the builders of the ancient city. 'Earthgrip holds them – gone, long gone, fast in gravesgrasp while fifty fathers and sons have passed.' I thoroughly recommend seeking out the full version for some beautiful and evocative poetry about past civilisations.[42]

Augustus was a guardian of the past – his identity was built around knowing how things were, as much as how they are in his Rome. While Augustus encourages us to take a more relaxed approach to getting to know Rome, he is not relaxed about any changes made to the city in his time. In my 12th edition of *Walks in Rome*, he talks about 'destruction', 'fatal injury', ruins being 'bereaved' and, worst of all, of the city being 'modernised'.[43] Shane Leslie describes that at this time 'Rome was now becoming devastated and devastating to the sentimental pilgrim'.[44] An 1875 review of *Days Near Rome* expresses frustrations at Augustus's 'endless sneers' at the government and the modernisation of the city. The author seems baffled as to why Augustus would mourn the loss of the greenery previously growing across ruins in what feels like a very modern statement of sarcasm, 'Is Mr. Hare sorry to see the mosaic pavements? Or What?'[45]

Augustus may have been upset by the changes to 'his' city, but Philip Glazebrook argues that, while Augustus situates the blame in the new government, the feeling that Rome had been ruined seems to be endemic among those who have known the city for a certain length of time. As with Augustus, Glazebrook argues it is simply that they had grown old and didn't respond to the place in the same way. I think that he hits the nail on the head when he says, 'The traveler's heart, ever after, is drawn painfully back to places so much loved, not indeed as they now appear to him, but as they once seemed to be – and as the heart itself once was.'[46]

I wonder if we will now ever have the privilege to return to Rome and feel it ruined because it is changed. Perhaps this situation will make us more grateful to be there at all, and we will celebrate what it is rather than what it is not. History is alive, just as places are alive. The story of Rome continues, with or without us.

When I last visited, the beautiful terraced Farnese Gardens had recently been reopened. Created in 1550, they originally featured frescoed aviaries with rare and exotic birds, ancient sculptures and a theatre of fountains.[47] They fell into disrepair and were badly degraded by archaeological interventions made in Augustus's time. They have now been lovingly restored and planted with yew, cypress, laurels, vines and damask roses. And so we finish our walk hopefully – with time, things can grow better.

We end our tour in the place where this city started. We have travelled in a way that is unusual for historians, and I still count myself one at heart. We historians usually hide. The convention is that we shouldn't let you, the reader, see the marks of our tools on our work. We set ourselves up as an invisible source of authority – objective, analytical. But, of course, historians (and anyone else) can only tell you how things appear to them from when they're standing. One of the things this collection of chapters does is to tell you who is telling the story.

Most travel accounts we have, certainly leading up to the time in which Augustus was writing, were written by people who looked a lot like Augustus. It doesn't mean we shouldn't read these accounts, and it doesn't mean they can't tell us useful things – but it does mean that we should be aware of this. That the experience of Rome we are reading about is just one 'picture'. That to properly understand a place or a time, we need to seek out a whole gallery and explore many schools of art.

At school, I was taught in history lessons to look for 'bias', in sources – the hidden meaning behind a text, and why that rendered it somehow unreliable. At university, I was rapidly taught to unlearn this. I think that's right, because 'bias' implies that nobody can be trusted. Our perspective isn't 'bias' – it's just what the inside of our heads looks like. Many things form this – our family, friends, education and life experiences. And if we're always looking for bias in other people, we run the risk of not interrogating our own approaches and responses. Bias also implies that we are aware of the contexts and external factors that make us think or say various things, and of course we aren't. We should think more about perspective – both in terms of who and what we study, and who is doing the studying.

Why have I chosen the quotes I have? What have I chosen to exclude and why? Augustus left us more than a dozen editions of *Walks in Rome*, each subtly different, and six volumes of autobiography. Through necessity, I'm being selective about what to explore – but how? Even I'm not sure I can unpick that. To be frank, I've told you about the things that interested me when I was researching. The bits where I felt there was a moment of connection. Those things are subjective, and this approach could, of course, make me a bad, good or just honest historian depending on how you look at it. But I've shown you my workings – you know about my own experiences and self-fashioning, and therefore maybe why I have come to the conclusions I have. I think it is a good thing to be honest about who we are – as Augustus himself said, 'There is no use – none – in trying to be, or to do, two things at once.'[48]

Since you know I'm not trying to be objective, then I can conclude by telling you unequivocally that Rome is the best city in the world, and I feel sure that Augustus would agree. If you have never had the chance to visit, I hope that you one day do and that your first time there is so perfect that your fate will be to – later in life – consider it ruined as we are told we are all fated to do.

There has only ever been one Rome, and yet each of us owns a different one. I hope these sketches have served to illustrate one possible walk through this place. This is probably blasphemy against the History Gods, but I think that reality or accuracy of memories is secondary to the importance of the feeling a place leaves us with. Memory is after all a reconstructive process.[49] A criticism levelled at Augustus by a contemporary was that, 'To him, history and legend are very much the same.'[50] In fact, I believe it is indeed true for all of us. We make our own legends, some large, some small and everyday. But once we have made them, they silently frame what we actually experience. A reader noted out that my memories of Rome are very similar in tone to Hare's account. On reflection, it's true – I present you (and myself!) with a stylised, romanticised version of the place. But, that is the version I remember. Perhaps this is because it's the version I always imagined visiting. I grew up among the myth and ruins of my home city, Bath – a place shaped physically and spiritually by both the Romans and Victorians. This exists in parallel to the strange and unreachable glamour I associated with foreign travel growing up. Perhaps Rome, the first place I had the luxury of visiting independently, is always going to be left bejewelled with the gems of excitement and possibility of that first trip. I very much hope that this is the case.

There is something poignant in the encouragement Augustus gives us to read the accounts of people who have lived in, who have really known the city. All of these are written by people whose lives we will never know and whose experiences we may never have – whether because we are separated by centuries or because our world has changed so significantly over the course of this year that those places are lost. Because, of course, people make places. And the ease of travelling, of being in a place, of being with a crowd have been altered. This will feel different for a long time. Augustus bemoaned the loss of Rome to the encroachment of modernity – and we may feel that we have lost it too, that it is permanently changed. But, of course, the idea of a place is much bigger than the place itself. I will leave the last word to the man himself:

> It is not a rapid inspection of the huge cheerless basilicas and churches, with their gaudy marbles and gilded ceilings and ill-suited monuments, which arouses your sympathy; but the long investigation of their precious fragments of ancient cloister, and sculptured fountain, – of

mouldering fresco, and mediæval tomb, – of mosaic-crowned gateway, and palm-shadowed garden; – and the gradually-acquired knowledge of the wondrous story which clings around each of these ancient things, and which tells how each has a motive and meaning entirely unsuspected and unseen by the passing eye.

## Notes

1. Ted Morgan, *Maugham* (New York: Simon & Schuster, 1980), 74.
2. Shane Leslie, *Men Were Different* (London: M. Joseph, 1937), 83.
3. Ibid., 85.
4. Augustus J. C. Hare, *Story of My Life*, vols 1–3 (London: George Allen, 1896), accessed 27 September 2020, http://www.gutenberg.org/files/35589/35589-h/35589-h.htm.
5. Leslie, *Men Were Different*, 83, 127.
6. 'Mr. Augustus Hare as a Gossip', *The Sketch* 16, 206 (1897): 438, accessed 9 September 2020, https://www.proquest.com/docview/1638071323.
7. Augustus J. C. Hare, *Story of My Life*, vols 4–6 (London: George Allen, 1896), accessed 1 October 2020, http://www.gutenberg.org/files/42770/42770-h/42770-h.htm.
8. Hare, *Story of My Life*, vol. 5.
9. Ibid.
10. Augustus J. C. Hare, *Walks in Rome*, vol. 1, 12th edn (London: George Allen, 1893), 27.
11. R. Mullen and R. Munsen, *'The Smell of the Continent': The British Discover Europe 1814–1914* (London: Pan Macmillan, 2009).
12. Augustus J. C. Hare, *Walks in Rome*, 5th edn, vols 1–2 (London: Daldy, Isbister, 1875), accessed 1 September 2020, http://www.gutenberg.org/files/39308.
13. Augustus J. C. Hare, 'Pictures of Italian Life', *Good Words* 14, 12 (1873), accessed 16 September 2020, https://www.proquest.com/docview/3316480.
14. Hare, *Walks in Rome*, 12th edn, 35.
15. Ibid., 43.
16. Ibid., 45.
17. Hare, *Story of My Life*, vols 1–3.
18. Hare, *Story of My Life*, vols 4–6.
19. Hare, *Walks in Rome*, 12th edn, 26.
20. Rocco Forte Hotels, 'The Centrepiece of the Eternal City', accessed 4 October 2020, https://www.roccofortehotels.com/nl/hotels-and-resorts/hotel-de-russie/.
21. Hare, *Walks in Rome*, 5th edn.
22. Hare, *Story of My Life*, vols 1–3.
23. Hare, *Walks in Rome*, 12th edn, 13.
24. William Murray, *City of the Soul: A Walk in Rome* (New York: Crown Journeys, 2003), 46.
25. Hare, *Story of My Life*, vols 4–6.
26. Hare, *Walks in Rome*, 5th edn.
27. Ibid.
28. Augustus Hare, *Peculiar People the Story of My Life*, ed. Anita Miller and James Papp (Chicago: Academy Chicago, 2007), xi.
29. Leslie, *Men Were Different*, 90.
30. Ibid., 91.
31. Ibid., 112.
32. Wikisource, 'Last Will and Testament of Augustus Hare', accessed 16 September 2020, https://en.wikisource.org/wiki/Last_Will_and_Testament_of_Augustus_Hare.
33. Amanda Claridge, *Rome: An Oxford Archaeological Guide* (Oxford: Oxford University Press, 1998), 59.
34. Hare, *Walks in Rome*, 5th edn.

35 Ibid.
36 Ibid.
37 Ibid.
38 Ibid.
39 David Watkin, *The Roman Forum* (Cambridge, MA: Harvard University Press, 2009), 1.
40 Philip Glazebrook, 'European Overtures: Rome Revisited: Same City, Changing Perceptions', *Washington Post*, 19 March 1989, accessed 7 October 2020, https://www-proquest-com.ezproxy.nottingham.ac.uk/docview/140033732.
41 Hare, *Story of My Life*, vols 1–3.
42 Michael Alexander, *The First English Poems* (London: Penguin, 2008), 3.
43 Hare, *Walks in Rome*, 12th edn, 17.
44 Leslie, *Men Were Different*, 115.
45 'Hare's Days Near Rome', *Saturday Review of Politics, Literature, Science and Art* 39 (17 April 1875): 510–11, accessed 9 September 2020, https://www.proquest.com/docview/9630640
46 Glazebrook, 'European Overtures'.
47 World Monuments Fund, 'Farnese Aviaries', accessed 7 October 2020, https://www.wmf.org/project/farnese-aviaries.
48 Hare, *Story of My Life*, vols 4–6.
49 Joyce W. Lacy and Craig E. L. Stark, 'The Neuroscience of Memory: Implications for the Courtroom', *Nature Review Neuroscience* 14, 9 (2013): 649–58.
50 'Hare's Days Near Rome', 510–11.

# Chapter Eight

## *SU E ZO PER I PONTI*; OR, HOW HISTORY DOES NOT HELP

### David Laven

For Feruccio Berolo, ballet dancer and ballet master, who loved Venice so much; my friend who was one of Venice's first victims of Covid-19.

It is a great pleasure to write the word; but I am not sure there is not a certain impudence in pretending to add anything to it. Venice has been painted and described many thousands of times, and of all the cities of the world is the easiest to visit without going there.[1]

I am a historian of Venice. Since the mid-1980s, I have spent a lot of time in the Venetian state archives. In recent years I have barely crossed their threshold. I have stopped researching the city's past. I have, instead, spent a decade and a half researching what other historians said about Venice's past. Rarely does a day pass when I do not spend some time pondering what scholars wrote about the Republic of Saint Mark. Most of what they wrote is repetitive and dull. Historians spend a lot of time taking in each other's washing. They often launder it badly; sometimes they deliberately stain or tear it; sometimes they are just careless when it comes to folding. In the trade this is called historiography.

The Venetian Republic came to an end suddenly in 1797. Contrary to what many long-dead historians wrote, and a lot of living ones – unthinkingly and incorrectly – echo, the Most Serene Republic did not expire because of a century or so of decadence and decline. A myth persists that Venice's ruling elites had become effete and effeminate by the eighteenth century; that the men who ran Venice were either inflexible relics of a faded glory, or fops, addicted to coffee and gossip, the whorehouse and the gaming table. But repetition does not equate to fact. When Venice fell, it was a vigorous imperial power: to the west its territories stretched almost to Milan, encompassing the rich and populous mainland territories of the Po Valley; to the east, they reached deep into the Julian Alps, and down the Dalmatian Coast. In the 1790s, the winged lion still lurked, carved protectively into the walls of Adriatic ports; the Venetian *gonfalone*, the symbol of St Mark fluttered over the smattering of Greek islands that the Ottomans had never managed to seize. Late republican Venice had its reformers and warriors: Andrea Tron, 'el paron' – 'the boss' – closed religious houses with more vigour than Pombal in Portugal or Joseph II in the Habsburg lands; Angelo Emo used Venice's still powerful fleet to crush the Barbary pirates to whom the young American Republic offered protection money in silver dollars. Venice did not fall because it was corrupt or weak, or because it was the city of libertines like Casanova or populated by gossipy or scheming characters from Goldoni's plays. The Republic was not guilty of a slow suicide by neutrality and the *ridotto*. It was a victim of violence.

In 1796, a young Corsican artillery officer found himself commanding the Directory's *Armée d'Italie*. It was a reflection of the changes wrought by the French Revolution that the future emperor, who had recently day-dreamed of liberating his native island from French rule, had risen so swiftly to such rank. Nabuleone di Buonaparte's promotion was rapid not just because he was a brilliant and unorthodox general but also because revolution created opportunity. He defeated the Piedmontese and Austrian armies in northern Italy with ease. In the meantime, he started signing his name Napoleon Bonaparte. He had decided his fortunes lay with being French, only shortly before he decided it served his own and France's purposes to destroy a thousand years of Venetian independence. As a warmongering general, then First Consul, and finally emperor, Napoleon wiped hundreds of states permanently from the map as he visited over 15 years of conflict on Europe. Apologists for Napoleon tend conveniently to forget that his liking for war, often pursued for no other reason than his own narcissistic desire for victory, caused the unnecessary deaths of hundreds of thousands of soldiers and civilians.[2] Apologists for strong-willed, great men – and it is funny how rarely these apologists share the characteristics of their idols – always seem to find convenient excuses to justify their heroes' readiness to gamble with the lives of others. The violation of Venetian neutrality and the destruction of Venetian independence – Bonaparte soon bartered Venetia to the Habsburgs in return for Austrian recognition of Lombardy as a revolutionary satellite – set the tone for Napoleon's future career. With a few regiments, a signature on a treaty and a complete absence of scruple, Hegel's 'world soul on horseback' consigned the world's longest-lived republic to a bloated archive and the history books.

The Most Serene Republic had had plenty of historians before its collapse. Many were Venetian patricians, often official historiographers dedicated to maintaining the myth of Venice.[3] Others, frequently francophone, were much more critical, tracing the *Serenissima*'s famed stability and longevity, the loyalty of its patricians, citizens, plebeians and colonial subjects not to the political virtues of the mixed Venetian constitution or the wisdom of the senators but to the sinister operations of secretive magistracies. For Venice's critics, it was the Council of Ten or, at best, the mere lust for lucre of a mercantile oligarchy that fashioned a populace in its own meretricious image and made the Republic endure. When the Republic expired, its past garnered still more interest. The rise and fall of the oligarchic empire became a topic for debate among both earnest scholars and popularising hacks, and a great many writers who fell somewhere in the middle. These are the men – and the very occasional women – on whom I focus my research: the historians of the Venetian Republic in roughly a century and a quarter after young Buonaparte killed it. Between 1797 and the Fascist seizure of power in 1922, Venetian history became an industry, one that still thrives today. Studying it tells us little about the Venetian Republic, but it does tell us a lot about the culture of those who chose to write about it in the century or so after its fall.

The study of Venetian historians is, for me, a very personal matter. Sometimes I am obliged to adopt the label Italianist. (I did, after all, teach in an Italian department for five years.) But when I write more generally about Italian history, I write about a geographical and cultural expression, which political forces transformed into a state, a political structure made not because of any great passion among 'Italians' for unification but mostly because it happened to suit the ministries and chancelleries of Berlin, Paris, London. There are, of course, many things about the Italian peninsula and its islands that fascinate me, that I love or enjoy: I like the diverse cuisines, the different artistic traditions, the varied landscapes; I speak Italian competently, read it with ease. But I have no passionate intellectual or emotional engagement with *Italy as a whole*. Were I to find German easier, I may well have continued as a Habsburg historian rather than one who 'specialised' on the peninsula, although I would probably have given up when it came to trying to master Magyar and Czech, Polish and Croat. I would be just as happy to switch to writing about the history of Spain or Portugal or, indeed, Brazil or Argentina. I like many things about being in Italy. There are some other parts that I love besides Venice – the Venetian *Terraferma*, Naples, Calabria, eastern Sicily – but I have a similar affection for Schleswig-Holstein, Normandy, Galicia. Indeed, it is largely coincidental that I am a historian of *Italian* pasts. When I decided to write my PhD not on French radicalism but on Habsburg Venice, it was not because I wanted to be a historian of Italy rather than of France. It was because I loved Venice, because I feel a special commitment and affection, fashioned first through family trips as a child, for the lands that were once part of the Venetian empire.

Venice's past, you see, is a family trade. My late father wrote about Venice and Venetian rule on the mainland. My younger sister's first book was about Venetian nuns after the Council of Trent. And, in a strange way, I somehow feel that Venetian historians belong to my family, and that my family belongs to them. Sometimes in moments of vanity (or crisis), I wonder whether anyone will ever see fit to write about what I have written about Venice's past. I rather doubt it. I shall be forgotten, my work will slip into the great morass of academic overproduction in which articles and books are written but barely read except by referees and reviewers. (I sometimes wonder when I read referees' reports and book reviews whether even referees and reviewers read the history on which they comment.) I study my fair share of historians who are now largely – and generally quite rightly – forgotten.

I wondered recently whether, in the last 150 years, anyone but me has read the two-volume *Histoire abrégée de la République de Venise* that was published in 1811 by a young but battle-hardened Napoleonic officer.[4] Three years later, the author, Eugène Labaume, wrote a brilliant and damning account of the horrors and stupidity of the 1812 invasion of Russia. He based that book on the notes he took during the retreat, kept with a quill cut from the feathers of a crow he had found, glossy black against the frozen ground, and ink he made from gunpowder and mixed with snow in the palm of his freezing hand. Labaume's book on the Russian campaign[5] and even his study on the fall of Napoleon[6] are still quite widely read: they have an immediacy, a sense of having been in and of the events that are described that makes them live. But Labaume's doge-by-doge account of Venice is not vibrant. It does have its merits: Labaume could turn a phrase, wrote well about military conflict and – while protesting loyalty to the Emperor's stepson, Eugène Beauharnais, Napoleon's viceroy in the satellite Kingdom of Italy – he managed to slip in the odd dig against the evils of imperialism. Yet *Histoire abrégée* is also one of many unremarkable histories of Venice. The story is usually the same: a settlement rises from the swamps of the lagoon as a place of refuge against assorted barbarians; it gradually grows wealthy on trade, exploiting its position between the Eastern and the Western Roman empires; its ships penetrate first the Adriatic then the eastern Mediterranean; Venetians exploit the crusades, sinking a rival Pisan fleet in the process, and repeatedly fight the Genoese; Venice develops a network of small colonial outposts; it conquers the *Terraferma* and fights wars against rival Italian states; having helped seize Constantinople in 1204, the Venetians also resist the Turks when the Greek capital falls 250 years later; the League of Cambrai, the loss of Cyprus, Lepanto, the War of Candia, the impact of the rounding of the Cape, the ignominy of a policy of neutrality and, finally, comes the fall. The story does not change that much in most of these accounts. Often it unfolds in a fashion so similar that you could swap huge chunks from different authors (even those who lambasted each other in print as ignorant charlatans) with barely any effect on the overall narrative or argument.

I have probably read too many of these books by men with mediocre minds, but pretty prose. But my research addresses great names too, important figures not just for Venetian historiography but also for the development of the writing of history as a whole. Venice's archives in the nineteenth century became the premier research laboratory for a new style of archivally based 'scientific' history. Not all the people I study were especially keen on getting their hands dusty. The Archivio di Stato, located for the past two hundred years in the buildings of the ex-Franciscan Friary (with the later addition of the buildings of the oddly named San Niccolò della Lattuga – Saint Nicholas of the Lettuce), unsurprisingly keeps registers of those who have used it. To this day, those who use the archive must sign in. This means it is easy to see who actually spent their days transcribing or making notes on anything from tax returns to the famous *relazioni* of Venetian ambassadors. Not everyone I study was especially assiduous; some of them never went near the archive. Oddly, quite a few never went near Venice. But there are plenty of famous historians among them. One who did not care much for archives and, despite long residence in Italy, never visited Venice was Simonde de Sismondi, the Genevan economist; his history of medieval Italy stitched the Republic's story into the fabric of Italy's perpetual communal feuding.[7] Pierre Daru – Napoleon's favourite civil servant – did use documents, if not as many as he liked to suggest, to write his vast history of Venice, but he never set foot in the city. The manuscripts he used were those taken as part of Napoleon's policy of ruthless pillage.[8] Daru, like his model Machiavelli after the fall of Soderini in 1512, suddenly found himself cast from the centre of power. Writing history was a way that both the Florentine and the French bureaucrat accommodated themselves to restored rulers, who looked askance at men who had been too close to now fallen governments. Like Machiavelli, Daru wrote history both to defend past regimes with which he felt sympathy and to court favour with new rulers who suspected his motives: Daru was vastly more successful in government than Machiavelli, and much more talented at sucking up to those in power. The French aristocrat lacked the Florentine's provocative brio, but he was still a great stylist: as a prisoner of the French Revolution, Daru had translated Horace in his cell; his prose was good enough to get him elected to the Académie Française, an honour never visited on his now more famous cousin and protégé Henri Beyle, better known by his *nom de plume* Stendhal.⁹ When reading Daru's *Histoire de la République*, as is the case when reading Machiavelli, you know that every line is written by a man who had been near power and knew how it functioned.¹⁰

Then there is Ranke who liked to give the impression he 'discovered' scientific archival research, and that the Venetian archives were one of his favourite places. Believe his self-aggrandising narrative – which does not actually bear much resemblance to 'things as they actually were' – and you would assume he spent a lot of time in the former halls of the Frari. He was far from assiduous in going to the Venetian archives; he preferred to buy documents from the families of patricians who had once run the Republic and to work in the comfort of his own apartment. Ranke's Venetian research was patchy, *un*scientific, far from the exhaustive engagement with detail he advocated. His self-mythologisation is easily revealed: you simply check who signed the register. Someone who believed archives don't lie might have grasped this.¹¹ The Swiss Burckhardt boasted of being unlike Ranke. The Basler made a virtue of being 'unwissenschaftlich', of having 'keine Methode'. He was not a habitué of archives. But he did vividly capture life in renaissance Italy. Burckhardt, the native of a city-state, despised Prussian militarism and German nationalism and had no sympathies with the imposition of unity on Italy. Rather he took his readers by the hand and led them through the alleyways of renaissance Venice, filled with exotic goods, before arriving at the great trading centre of the Rialto, the hub of the city's incredible wealth. Read Burckhardt and you can smell the spices, feel the silks, hear the water lapping against the sides of merchantmen.

And then there were the resident scholars. Not all were born or raised in Venice – often they were merely honorary *veneziani* – but they became of the city. Rawdon Brown, the Englishmen, arrived in Venice in 1838 and made the city his home. In a famous sonnet, written in November 1883, shortly after the death of the first editor of the *Calendar of State Papers*, Robert Browning described the historian's obsessive attachment to Venice and his inability to be parted from the city: '*Bella Venezia, non ti lascio più!*'¹² Browning exaggerated – Brown did periodically leave Venice during the half century he lived there – but his poem contained a truth about Brown's obvious and obsessive attachment to Venice past *and* present: Brown lived in and loved Venice. He developed an intense sense of place and an understanding of the historical layering of the city, as well as a profound affection for its population.

> Day after day, year after year, the Vice-Librarian Lorenzi having regularly breakfasted with him, Rawdon Brown's truly English head […] would be seen poring over some dull and dusty delicacy; and equally day after day and year after year, did this tall, slim and well-knit figure, after his work was done appear on the Grand Canal rowing himself, gondolier fashion, to the Lido.¹³

Samuele Romanin was another Venetian by adoption: a Triestine Jew, whose family moved to Venice when he was 12. He really did know the archives in a way that shames

Ranke's hollow boasts. Romanin's judicious scholarship make his the shoulders on whom so many historians stand today. Few seem actually to have read his monumental *Storia documentata di Venenzia*.[14] They do not realise that their footnotes that cite another historian are citing ideas, documents and information often derived from histories that ultimately rest on Romanin's painstaking but joyful poring over the dusty delicacies he discovered in *fascicoli* in the Frari. The great Pompeo Molmenti *was* a Venetian by birth and education, although, perhaps curiously, for much of his life he chose to live on the mainland. His lifetime's work was a hymn of praise to a vanishing Venice. He was perhaps the first historian truly to capture the spirit of 'Venezia minore', the everyday world not of doges and senators, captains and condottieri (although he wrote about these too) but of gondoliers and fishwives, matrons and master artisans, prostitutes and sailors.

But how much of *my* Venice is really shaped by reading historians?

I first went to Venice before I could read. I think I was 4. I recall being annoyed most of the time. My parents had packed my toy soldiers in the boot of the Austin 1800, left on the Tronchetto, the vast ugly carpark, an expanse of ill-kept and blistering tarmac; they would not fetch my toys to the scruffy flat we had rented. Otherwise, I remember ice-creams, the fire station – and the plastic Venetian firemen's boat I was bought, presumably to stop my grumbling about the plastic soldiers left in the Austin. Above all I recall *Ai gondolieri*, the trattoria owned by Giorgio and Antonietta Zennaro, friends of my father – real *venexiani* who spoke Venetian not the bastard pompous Florentine that passes as a national language. My father met Giorgio through his younger brother Sergio in the early 1950s. Sergio was a fine exponent of Venetian rowing (*voga*) who never could break into the closed shop of gondoliers. At the time they met, Sergio was working in a bar; it was the only work he ever knew. My father, working for his PhD and – when not in the archives – generally in a bar, had left his satchel filled with his research notes in a *caffè*; and Sergio had run after him to return it. Their strange friendship – born of drinking wine, of rowing trips on the lagoon (my father as inept as Sergio was expert), of walking Sergio's huge Alsatian dog that lived with him in the tiny one-bedroom apartment shared with several chickens and four adults – grew strong. I suspect both the rowing trips and the dog-walking were really mostly pretexts for drinking. The Zennaro family later adopted the Lavens. The Zennaro prospered through hard work, beneficiaries of the post-war economic miracle, which brought growing wealth to northern Italy and of the city's prosperity built on tourism. Not that in those days tourists drank at the *Gondolieri*. Now it is transformed into a costly and pretentious *enoteca*; tourists slip in on their way between the Accademia and the Peggy Guggenheim. In the 1970s and 1980s, its clients were Venetians: artisans, bakers, shopkeepers, masons, bricklayers, even the odd gondolier, eating lunch, drinking slightly acid, black Merlot served in two-litre bottles, playing cards (*scopa*), smoking; everyone smoked. Sergio died young. Like many Venetian men of his era, he was killed by cirrhosis. A bachelor with no prospects, he drank too much. He had mournful eyes and wore a drooping, melancholy moustache. He always had something for me: a particularly pretty postage stamp, a toy car, a sweet, a tiny wooden *fòrcola* (the distinctive and essential Venetian rowlock). Sergio was a vision of sad generosity. He delighted in catching small green crabs, which he would secrete in his hand and pass to me – aged perhaps 6 or 7 – when I least expected them.

I would shriek, then laugh; he would giggle, scooping me up in his arms and threatening to throw me into the canal.

When I was 18 – with Sergio long dead – I lived with Giorgio and Antonietta for several months, learning a strange blend of Venetian and Italian, with a bad accent: 'anglo-venexian', my friends later dubbed it. And Zennaro hospitality, now in Campagna Lupia – a name that spoke of the poverty of its sandy soil – a village on the Terraferma, kept me well fed and comfortable when I started my PhD four years later. Each morning I would take the rickety commuter train to Venice. The old lady who ran the halt and sold the little card tickets of the north-eastern railway company would sometimes give me fresh eggs or offer to stitch a loose button on my polo shirt when I got back in the evening. Once she told me with pride that many years before she had been to Venice.

I did not read Venice through the eyes of others until many years later. I did no more than dip into Byron or Browning, Chateaubriand or Alfred de Musset, Goldoni or d'Annunzio until my thirties. When I began to read them, for the most part, I found their writings about Venice were just wrong. Byron especially is the curse of Anglo-Saxons who visit Venice. He was not interested in the city except for the cheap living, cheap sex, cheap wine. It suited his lifestyle, but his engagement, as he archly hinted, was with a literary Venice of the imagination. As he wrote in Canto IV of *Childe Harold*:

And Otway, Radcliffe, Shakespeare, Schiller's art,
Had stamped her image in me.

Byron knew full well that Otway had never got near to Venice, that Shakespeare probably never left England, that Radcliffe and Schiller had not set foot in the *Serenissima*. I have lost count of the people who have told me that they know Venice because they see the city through Byron's eyes. To do so is silly because in the years he lived in Venice – missing England and pretending he didn't, boasting about his sexual conquests (for which he paid a small fortune) – Byron never looked at Venice properly. He didn't much like Venice or Venetians, although he quite liked how easy it was to buy sex in an impoverished city. He paid for vast amounts of sex, wrote lots of letters that were amusing in a bitchy, self-satisfied way and only really dealt with one subject (Byron) except when being nasty at the expense of his friends, and verse that was often sublime and frequently very funny. Contrary to popular myth – like most Byronic myths of his own invention – he never learned Armenian – he failed to master the alphabet – but he did get drunk, swam, rode on the Lido, dined with the Austrian governor (which did not stop him calumnying the Habsburg authorities). What Byron really liked was the Venice of his own imagination, which basically meant he liked not Venice but his own imagination, because Byron really loved Byron more than anything else in the world. So, when people try to see Venice through a Byronic lens, all they really see is the fantasy of a drunken and priapic narcissist who'd read a lot, including a lot of history. It does not help that the British also tend to imagine Venice through the eyes of Turner – who spent almost no time there – and Ruskin – who really hated Venetians, although, unlike Byron, he did not ever have sex with them. The act disgusted him so much, he could not even bring himself to consummate his marriage, although he encouraged his young wife's flirtation with the Austrian officer who had bombarded the city in 1849 and requested that she copy out every reference to Venice in Sismondi's *Histoire des républiques italiennes*. It must have taken her a very long while. Still, Byron's *Beppo* makes me laugh aloud, and *Faliero* moves me; Turner's *Canaletti painting*, in the Tate, first exhibited at the Royal Academy in 1833, is a great visual joke on how we think we know places through art; Ruskin's *Stones of Venice* remain a fine guide to Venetian architecture. But none of these tell us much about Venice or help us to see the city. Ruskin was quite explicit not only that he despised his Venetian contemporaries but that he also loathed the Palladian and the Baroque, and thought almost everything after 1418 – he was precise on this date – was completely decadent. To read Venice through Ruskin is to resemble the British tourists observed by Dostoyevsky in Cologne Cathedral, who were so obsessed with their guidebooks that they never saw the beauty of the architecture. No artist or writer can capture the beauty of sunlight reflected on a canal, reflecting onto crumbling brick, which makes Venice's walls live; no architectural guide prepares you for the mosaics in the Basilica or catching sight of Titian's *Assumption* in the apse of the Frari, the virgin both orant and erotic, a sturdy peasant girl on the edge of ecstasy. You have to see Venice's beauty. Byron never did, because he was too busy looking for his own reflection; Ruskin never did because he thought the Venetians made Venice ugly; Turner never did because he was too busy sketching so that he could paint the city when back in his London studio.

I was lucky. I knew Venice before I ever read about it. And I had never studied its history before I began to study its history. I learned to love Venice with – yet without – my father when I was a schoolboy: he sent me off, aged 13, with money for a *panino* and a beer, and a few parroted Italian phrases, to explore its *campi* and *rii*, to walk up and down its bridges while he went to spend long days in the archive. I made myself lists of churches and walked Venice for hours, discovering that it is almost impossible to get lost because there are landmarks everywhere. At 18, I learned to live in Venice on my own; I also learned to live on my own in Venice. I was assiduous in looking for art, but I did so without a guidebook. I sat in freezing churches or *scuole*, the bitter damp cold of a Venetian winter seeping into my bones, but warmed by paintings by the famous colourists – Giovanni Bellini or Paolo Veronese, Titian and Tintoretto – but also by Gaspare Diziani and Antonio Zanchi. I get the impression that the latter are despised these days, but I took a liking to them. I learned to drink *ombre* in bars – *bàcari* – at the end of narrow *calli*, learned the value of an 11 a.m. *spriss con bitter* to challenge the blur of an evening spent with friends; I drank pinot grigio *ramato* with hunks of *mortadella* at the Schiavi, long before pinot grigio became the noughties version of nineties Chardonnay. I learned that *spaghetti alla busara* or *bigoli in salsa* tasted better when served in a friend's *osteria*, not just because of friendship but because, before the existence of TripAdvisor, many Venetian restauranteurs made little effort if they thought a customer was simply passing tourist trade. I discovered that eating *polenta* kept out the misery-inducing, bone-icing *bora*, the biting, damp wind from the north-east that slithers and pokes and jabs through the warmest of coats and the thickest of jumpers. I discovered that *grappa*, however disgusting, did an even more effective job of fighting off the bitter, bone-icing, damp, misery-inducing cold of Venetian winter. I learned that Venice in fog or under the piercing blue skies of clear winter day was more beautiful than Venice in the sticky heat of summer, that Venetian – Henry James called it 'the familiar soft-sounding almost infantile prattle of the place [...] this invertebrate dialect'; Arthur Symons called it 'unconsonated' – had a greater beauty than any of the melodious rhetoric or poetic pomposity of Italian. I learned that Venice can wrap you in its embrace, serene and alcoholic, shivering in winter and dripping with sweat in the breezeless, muggy summer heat, and hug you so tight that, like Browning's Brown, you do not want ever to leave.

I have since learned that my experiences were not mine, but Venice's. I began to read people who loved Venice and Venetians in equal measure: William Dean Howells's *Venetian Life*, the essays of Henry James, Horatio Brown's *Life on the Lagoons*, perhaps the greatest book by an English speaker on Venice. 'It is the people and the place' [...] which constitutes for many the peculiar and enduring charm of Venice', wrote Brown. Brown said, 'To leave her is a sure regret; to return a certain joy.'[15] As Venice loses its people, driven out by cruise ships and Air BnB lets, by the closure of butchers and greengrocers to make way for still more places from which tourists can buy tat, for faux Irish pubs and kebab shops, I no longer long to return; the city is still beautiful, but its people have been driven out.

Let me turn to Arthur Symons's essay in *Cities of Italy*.[16] Symons was a translator and poet, not a historian, and a better observer for that. His meditation on Venice is dated, sometimes it is frighteningly prejudiced: the beautiful Jewish women possessed of 'the finest type of Jewish beauty, in which the racial characteristics stop short just at the perfect moment',[17] 'the softness of the climate' permitted 'poverty, even beggary, to remain dignified',[18] women cluster 'with the mechanical movement of a herd of cows with the same deep sense of repose, of animal contentment'.[19] But his meditation is also fresh. Is this because he had lost his guidebook changing trains at Basel? 'A guide-book is a necessary evil; but it is not when I have had a guide-book in my hand that I have received lasting impressions.'[20] Is it, as he observed, because he had bothered to live there, to walk the city, to explore its canals and the lagoon by gondola? Is it because he recognised the melancholy of the city? Perhaps it is above all because he understood that it was pointless to paint Venice: 'I do not understand why anyone paints Venice, and yet everyone who paints, paints Venice. But to do so is to forget that it is itself a picture, a finished, conscious work of art.'[21]

I began this essay by quoting James who warned that we cannot really write anything new about Venice; I end by quoting Symons who warns against trying to portray it. Venice is not and was not Dickens's 'strange dream upon the water' or Byron's 'greenest island' of the imagination[22] but a city founded by refugees from the mainland, made rich by its inhabitants' contacts with the world, constantly replenished by new settlers. Venice's beauty was not as a collection of buildings housing canvases by Carpaccio and Tiepolo, or *calli* and canals with emotive names, but as a living city. The city I knew as a child and young man still had something of Francesco Pasinetti's beautiful documentary film of 1940, *Venezia minore*; the city now struggles to survive under weight of visitors, its resident population tumbling by the day. Covid brought a brief beauty back to the Venice; its waters were clear, and swans and ducks could be seen paddling on them; German and Japanese, English and Russian, Mandarin and French no longer drowned out Venetians in the *campi*. Venetians could once more walk across the Rialto without fighting with barbarian hordes taking selfies. Venice was spared the sword of Attila or sack by Charlemagne; it learned better than most states how to brave the plague, but is slowly being stabbed to death with selfie sticks. My friends begged me to visit while it was almost empty. I could not. But their invitations reminded me that 'it is the people and the place' that matter. You can read all the history you like, but it will not make Venice live again. Only Venetians can do that.

## Notes

1. Henry James, 'Venice', in *Italian Hours* (Boston: Houghton Mifflin, 1909), 3.
2. For examples of absurdly positive judgements on Napoleon, see the work of the right-wing historian A. Roberts, *Napoleon the Great* (London: Penguin, 2015), and the numerous works of the current director of the Fondation Napoléon, Thierry Lentz. See, for example, *Le Grand Consulat (1799–1804)* (Paris: Fayard, 1999); *Napoléon* (Paris: Le Cavalier bleu, 2001); *Nouvelle histoire du Premier Empire*: tome 1: *Napoléon et la conquête de l'Europe (1804–1810)*; tome 2: *L'effondrement du système napoléonien (1810–1814)*; tome 3: *La France et l'Europe de Napoléon (1804–1814)*; tome 4: *Les Cent-Jours (1815)* (Paris: Fayard, 2002–10); *Napoléon* (Paris: Presses universitaires de France, 2003). For more judicious assessments, see M. Broers, *Napoleon. Soldier of Destiny* (London: Faber and Faber, 2014); *Napoleon. Spirit of the Age* (London: Faber and Faber, 2018); and C. Esdaile, *Napoleon's Wars: An International History, 1803–1815* (London: Penguin, 2008). For a more critical assessment, see P. Dwyer, *Napoleon: The Path to Power, 1769–1799* (London: Bloomsbury, 2008); *Citizen Emperor: Napoleon in Power* (London: Bloomsbury, 2013); *Napoleon: Passion, Death, and Resurrection, 1815–1840* (London: Bloomsbury, 2018). The classic study of the way in which Napoleon divides opinion is P. Geyl, *Napoleon: For and Against*, trans. O. Renier (New Haven: Yale University Press, 1949), first published as *Napoleon: voor en tegen in de Franse geschiedschrijving* (Utrecht: Oosthoeck's Uitgevers Mij, 1946).
3. For Venetian historiography, see E. Dursteler, 'Introduction: A Brief Survey of Histories of Venice', in *A Companion to Venetian History*, ed. E. Dursteler (Leiden: Brill, 2014), 1–24.
4. E. Labaume, *Histoire abrégée de la république de Venise* (2 vols; Paris: Le Normant, 1811).
5. E. Labaume, *Relation circonstanciée de la campagne de Russie* (Paris: Panckoucke, 1814).
6. E. Labaume, *Histoire de la chute de Napoléon* (2 vols; Paris: Anselin & Pochard, 1820).
7. Widely translated, the key French editions of Sismondi are J. C. L. S. d. Sismondi, *Histoire des républiques italiennes du moyen âge* (8 vols; Zurich: Henri Gessner, 1807–9; 16 vols, Paris – vols 1–8, Henri Nicolle, 1809; vols 9–16, Treuttel et Würtz, 1809–16); *Histoire des français* (18 vols; Paris: Treuttel et Würtz, 1821–44).
8. B. Bergerot (with a preface by J. Tulard), *Daru, intendant général de la Grande Armée* (Paris: Tallandier, 1991); *Daru en ses temps (1767–1829)* (Lille: Atelier National de Reproduction des Thèses, 1983); B. Morand, *Pierre Daru, 1767–1829. Intendant général de la Grande Armée* (Villargoix: M.-F. Royer-Daru, 1993) is no more than a pamphlet and consists largely of extracts from letters and orders sent to Daru by the emperor and extracts from his correspondence; H. de La Barre de Nanteuil (preface by F. d. Langle), *Le Comte Daru ou l'Administration militaire sous la Revolution et l'Empire* (Paris: J. Peyronnet and Cie, 1966). B. Daru, *Le Comte Daru (1767–1829). Daru et Napoléon, une relation de confiance* (Boulogne-Billancourt: Éditions RJ, 2012).
9. Stendhal was much closer to Daru's younger brother, Martial, and, despite attempting to use Pierre's influence when it suited him, frequently antagonised and often mocked the latter. R. Alter and C. Cosman, *A Lion for Love. A Critical Biography of Stendhal* (Cambridge: Harvard University Press, 1986), 42–43, 82–83. On Daru's negotiation of the Bourbon restoration, and his relationship with Machiavelli, see X. Tabet, 'La "Venise nouvelle" de Pierre Daru', in *Histoire de la République de Venise*, ed. P. Daru (Paris: Robert Laffont, 2004), ix–xliv.

10 The key early editions of Daru are P. A. N. Daru, *Histoire de la République de Venise* (7 vols; Paris: Firmin Didot, 1819); *Histoire de la République de Venise* (8 vols; Paris: Firmin Didot, 1821); *Histoire de la République de Venise* (8 vols; Paris: Firmin Didot, 1826).
11 On the role of the Venetian archives for Ranke's views on the writing of history, see E. Muir, 'Leopold von Ranke, His Library, and the Shaping of Historical Evidence', *Syracuse University Library Associates Courier* 22, 1 (1987): 3–10. For a less positive view of Ranke's assessment of the Venetian archives, see U. Tucci, 'Ranke and the Venetian Document Market', *Syracuse University Library Associates Courier* 22, 1 (1987): 27–38.
12 'A Sonnet by Browning', *Century Magazine* 27, 4 (1884): 640.
13 Cited J. J. Norwich, *Paradise of Cities. Nineteenth-Century Venice Seen through Foreign Eyes* (London: Viking, 2003), 108.
14 S. Romanin, *Storia documentata di Venenzia* (10 vols; Venice: Naratovich, 1853–64).
15 H. Brown, *Life on the Lagoons* (London: Rivington, 1894), 296–97.
16 A. Symons, *Cities of Italy* (London: Dent, 1907), 71–112.
17 Ibid., 90.
18 Ibid., 109.
19 Ibid., 88.
20 Ibid., 73.
21 Ibid., 76.
22 C. Dickens, 'An Italian Dream', *Pictures from Italy* (London: Bradbury, 1846), 107–19 (119).

# Chapter Nine

# A TOWN CALLED ENTROPY: BOOM AND BUST IN ARNOLD BENNETT'S POTTERIES

## Gary F. Fisher

In the first days of January 2020 I decided to make a literary pilgrimage within the English Midlands. Given that this region has produced some of the most revered writers in English literature, I was somewhat spoilt for choice in terms of destination. Stratford-upon-Avon, the picture-perfect birthplace of William Shakespeare, stands out as the obvious choice for the bookish tourist. The city of Birmingham, erstwhile stomping ground and inspiration of a young J. R. R. Tolkien, compounds cosmopolitan cuisine with a profound literary heritage to make for another attractive destination. Perhaps even the rugged, industrial landscape of the Erewash Valley, backdrop to so many of D. H. Lawrence's rebellious and panoptic castigations of modernity, might serve to attract the literary pilgrim. Yet I chose a different, and altogether overlooked, destination. I went to the loose confederation of towns that comprise the Potteries, or Stoke-on-Trent as they are described on a map today. I went on the trail of an author who once ruled the literary world, but has long since departed from the popular imagination. I went in search of Arnold Bennett.

You may be forgiven if that name means little to you. It means little to most. Yet, during the early twentieth century, Arnold Bennett was perhaps the most frequently read, prodigious and recognisable authors in the English-speaking world. At the age of 21, Bennett left behind his humble origins and moved from the provincial Midlands to the bright lights of London in order to pursue a career as a writer. In 1898 he published his first novel, *A Man from the North*, which took inspiration from his experiences of moving southwards. By the end of the First World War, he had continued publishing novels at the rate of one per year, penned eight plays, worked as a wartime propagandist for His Majesty King George V, served as the editor of a popular women's magazine, and all the while maintained a lively career as a journalist publishing across numerous newspapers and periodicals.[1] Bennett's literary success thrust him into a world of international acclaim. Writing in 1925, fellow Midlander J. B. Priestley described Bennett as 'one of the most successful men of letters of his time'.[2] In that same year, an issue of the *Sewanee Review*, the oldest continuously published literary magazine in America, predicted that, upon his death, Bennett would enter the pantheon of the English language's greatest wordsmiths:

When he dies he will perforce fly for companionship to that heaven where the indignant shade that is Mr. Nicolson's Tennyson stalks forever across the gloomy moors.[3]

This prediction has evidently proved false. Bennett's name and works have all but entirely slipped from the popular consciousness, and few have even heard of him, let alone read one of his many works. In 2012 Bennett's surviving grandson agreed to unveil a plaque marking the location in which Bennett penned one of his masterworks, and even he confessed to never having read the work in question.[4]

If he is known at all, Bennett is typically known for one of two things: his tempestuous relationship with a now more revered literary rival, and his dining habits. Virginia Woolf, now one of the English language's most celebrated female writers, engaged Bennett in a very public rivalry over their differing conceptions of literary excellence. In their own time, Bennett drastically outsold Woolf, seeming to emerge the victor of their artistic sparring. But, as the decades has passed, Woolf has firmly embedded herself in the approved canon of English literature, while Bennett has all but slipped from memory. Woolf's public criticisms of Bennett, in which she outlines her own literary method, are now beginning and end of many a reader's experience of Bennett. As one literary critic has put it, Bennett now lives 'only as a reflection in his enemy's eye'.[5] Besides being Woolf's foil, there is one other avenue through which Bennett's memory lives on: his questionable culinary tastes. Raised on a simple Staffordshire diet of oatcakes and brown ale, as Bennett's wealth grew, his dining habits became opulent bordering on philistine. One of his favourite concoctions can still be ordered at the Savoy Hotel in London today: the 'Omelette Arnold Bennett', an epicurean combination of eggs, smoked haddock, heavy cream and copious amounts of cheese.[6] It goes without saying that Bennett was something of a portly gentleman.

In a sense, Bennett's diminished reputation is an apt parallel for the condition of Staffordshire's modern-day Potteries. Once the unquestionable centre of the global pottery trade, Stoke-on-Trent has become a byword for post-industrial decline in twenty-first-century Britain. The great pottery furnaces and workshops that once blackened the skyline have fallen silent. The few that survive mostly trade on their storied brand names, producing small quantities of ornate, artisanal crockery perfect for the front window of a charity shop, or as the last-minute wedding gift for a distant cousin. The town's principal function on the national stage seems to be less as a commercial centre and more as a political barometer during democratic exercises. Every election cycle the town plays host to a great northwards migration of pollsters, pundits and politicos who descend upon its hapless citizens before retreating back to the safety of the M25. The modern-day function was particularly pertinent during my own visit to the Potteries, occurring as it did in the wake of the 2019 general election, which saw the complete rout of the Labour party from the town amidst a wider political realignment of the nation's industrial and post-industrial heartlands.

But why am I telling you this? What does a long-forgotten, albeit colourful and prolific, Edwardian novelist have to do with the tradition of travel writing? And why, if he so keenly escaped the industrial drudgery of his hometown in order to ensconce himself in the dining rooms of London's finest hotels, would I visit the Potteries, rather than the Savoy Grill, in search of him? The answer to that lies in Bennett's subject matter and the manner in which he depicted it. He may have departed the Potteries as soon as his circumstances permitted, but few authors are as indelibly associated with a place as Bennett is with the Potteries, and even fewer can claim to have played such a foundational, if sometimes unsung, role in defining how an entire community is perceived by the outside world.

Bennett may have decamped from the Potteries early into adulthood, but he never disowned his birthplace. The vast majority of his works, especially his most celebrated, took a fictionalised version of his home town as their setting: the 'Five Towns'. This is in reference to the fact that the real-world Potteries were composed of multiple towns that, though initially distinct and separate communities, had expanded and overlapped to the point that, during Bennett's life, they ultimately amalgamated into a single unit: the modern-day town of Stoke-on-Trent. In actuality there were six towns that federated to form Stoke-on-Trent, but Bennett decided that 'Five Towns' was more euphonious than 'Six Towns' and so chose to omit the town of Fenton.[7] So important has Bennett been in defining the image of the Potteries that they are today sometimes referred to as the 'Five Towns', with the modern-day residents of Fenton still complaining that they are the 'forgotten town'.[8]

This ingrained connection between Bennett and the Potteries owes not just to the fact that Bennett chose to set so many of his novels in a fictionalised version of the town but the way in which he wrote them. Bennett was not primarily a travel writer. But his approach to writing fiction was so scrupulous in its evocation of place that his works not only exert the same effect upon readers as travel literature but also expose the fluid generic distinctions between fiction and – what purports to be – non-fiction. Eschewing the experimental and metaphysical approaches of his modernist contemporaries, Bennett adopted a social realist approach to literature. This profoundly influenced his choice of subject matter and the manner in which he chose to relate it. The novelist, Bennett believed, should avoid being tempted to take that which is exceptional or 'unusual' as their subject matter. Instead, true literary merit lay in taking subject matter that is 'fundamental and universal' and demonstrating the intense drama and beauty that was innate to even the most seemingly ordinary of settings and lives:[9]

> The great novelist is he who takes the common experience of ordinary people and so vitalizes and interprets it as to make us, for the moment at least, see it as the wealth it really is. [10]

To Bennett, life, all life, was more beautiful than any construction that might spring from an author's imagination. The goal of the novelist was merely to convey that beauty to his readers.

The foundation of success in this task? Observation. In Bennett's 1914 guide to novel writing, *The Author's Craft*, the first chapter outlining the path to authorial success was titled 'Seeing Life'. This is because, Bennett believed, the foundation of literary success lay not in the act of original creation on the part of the author but in the systematic observation and transmission of the beauty that already exists in the world:

> The novelist is he who, having seen life, and being so excited by it that he absolutely must transmit the vision to others, chooses narrative fiction as the liveliest vehicle for the relief of his feelings.[11]

This observation ought not be limited to the actions and mannerisms of the people themselves but also of the world in which they inhabit. The physical environment that a people build and inhabit is, according to Bennett, just as, if not more, an important window into their character:

> Every street is a mirror, an illustration, an exposition, an explanation, of the human beings who live in it. Nothing in it is to be neglected. Everything in it is valuable.[12]

As such, he even recommends the study of geography as essential for truly compelling literature. Calling geographical knowledge 'the mother of discernment', he proposes that 'the varying physical characteristics of the earth are the sole direct terrestrial influence determining the evolution of original vital energy'.[13] In his epic novel *Clayhanger* (1910), he opens his story with a long and loving description of the landscape of the Five Towns, the confluence of different canals, the sharp ridges and the grime-encrusted hedgerows. After much description, he explains to his reader why he has dedicated such effort to explaining these details: 'These interesting details have everything to do with the history of Edwin Clayhanger, as they have everything to do with the history of each of the two hundred thousand souls in the Five Towns.'[14] The physical environment is, for Bennett, part of its inhabitants' character.

Travel, Bennett argued, was a key tool the aspiring novelist might use to hone this observational ability. By stripping us of the familiar and transplanting us into the alien, travel 'makes observers of us all'. In noticing the alien way that a train in Paris organises its seating, or a cat in London roams the thoroughfares, the traveller may be awakened to the significance of such details in discerning the character of a locale and all the better prepared to see the beauty of life.[15] In essence, in order to effectively capture the beauty of the everyday, one must become a traveller within it.

This focus on the ordinary earned Bennett much celebration as well as some derision. The American journalist H. L. Mencken complained of Bennett that he was too objective and documentarian in his writing, that he dealt 'solely with precisely what is', rather than what may be.[16] It was joked of Bennett that, if he took an Atlantic cruise liner, he would spend his journey 'counting the rivets'.[17] Yet, for many, this unique aspect of Bennett's approach was what set his work apart. J. B. Priestley praised Bennett's status as the 'romancer of what had hitherto appeared the least romantic' and that his work comes as 'the result of observation rather than creation'.[18] Reviews of his work published in the United States praised the 'miraculous fashion' in which Bennett took seemingly mundane subject material and 'rubs these leaden surfaces of life until they shine with interestingness'.[19] Perhaps no text in Bennett's extensive corpus demonstrates his ability to identify and communicate the literary beauty of observed reality – as well as the fluid intersection of the roles of novelist and traveller – as the epic and deeply personal *Clayhanger* (1910).

A fictionalised alternate history of his own life, Bennett transposes himself onto the character of a young boy: the titular Edwin Clayhanger. He considers how his own life might have progressed had he not taken the impetuous step to abandon the family business and relocate to London to pursue his dream of being a writer. Instead of haddock omelettes and international acclaim at the Savoy, Clayhanger experiences an utterly unexceptional life of bland respectability in the town of Bursley (a fictionalised version of the real Potteries town of Burslem). He leaves school and is funnelled into a junior role in the family printing business. He develops an interest in architecture but lacks the courage to resist his father's wishes and pursue it at the expense of the family business. He falls in love with an intrepid young woman but misses his opportunity to solidify their relationship and loses her to another man. Inheriting the printing shop and a comfortable income, Edwin Clayhanger ultimately ages into a life of unexceptional lower-middle-class gentility, all against the backdrop of the equally unexceptional Potteries.[20]

Of all Bennett's novels, it is in this story that the connection between the methods of the traveller and of the novelist that Bennett proposes in his *Writer's Craft* is perhaps best demonstrated. In preparation for writing *Clayhanger*, Bennett made a rare return to his hometown to perform research on the people and places he intended to immortalise. Writing in his journal in 1909, he notes of this visit that 'I cannot read in Burslem. All I can do is go about and take notes. My mind is in a whirl all the time.' He describes how, while travelling around and observing the people, he 'had got into an extraordinary vein of "second sight"' and 'perceived whole chapters'.[21] More than simply approaching the Potteries as a traveller while researching *Clayhanger* and taking elements of the novel straight out of what he witnessed there, he even turned the principal character into a traveller of sorts. The novel is structured as a *bildungsroman*, a coming-of-age story. It follows a young man leaving behind the innocence of childhood and viewing the world through the foreign lens of adulthood. Edwin is presented almost as if experiencing the people and place for the first time, as if a traveller in an unknown land.

This positioning of the novel's protagonist as an alien in his native landscape is introduced when the reader first meets Edwin. It is his last day of school and his first day of adulthood. Looking out onto a narrowboat bringing in a shipment of clay to be fashioned into a crockery in one of the Potteries' many kilns, he realises how little his schooling has prepared him for adulthood, and how even something as mundane as his home's principal industry remains a mystery to him.

> 'Where does that there clay come from?' asked Edwin. For not merely was he honestly struck by a sudden new curiosity, but it was meet for him to behave like a man now, and to ask manly questions.[22]

The effect of this narrative element extends beyond Edwin investigating the mundanities of the crockery trade. Edwin's naivety serves as the conduit through which Bennett can express his findings from his traveller-like research into his birthplace. Presented to readers as an outsider, Edwin is able to view the Potteries through fresh eyes. As Edwin surveys the Potteries' industrious skyline, Bennett comments, 'Beauty was achieved, and none saw it.'[23]

There is one episode in which the novel's intrusion into travel writing, or perhaps travel writing's intrusion into the novel, becomes particularly apparent. Edwin, now a man and unconstrained by curfews, wanders around his town at night for the first time in his life:

> As a schoolboy it had been definitely forbidden to him to go out at night; and unless sent on a special and hurried errand, he had scarcely seen the physiognomy of the streets after eight o'clock. He had never seen the playground in the evening. And this evening the town did not seem like the same town; it had become a new and mysterious town of adventure. And yet Edwin was not fifty yards away from his own bedroom.[24]

It is here that Bennett's writing most seems to resemble that of a traveller's account. The utterly ordinary sight of a row of terraced houses dimly lit by gas lamps suddenly becomes alive with foreign sights and sounds. The dim glow of lights within the pubs becomes filled with the 'savage ecstasy of life'. The Bursley Town Hall is transformed from a dull civic building into a monument to the 'secret nobility' of the town. The remnant of the day's market, a few stalls selling 'vegetable, tripe, and gingerbread', is given an account that sounds more like the description of a Middle Eastern Souk at the foot of some grand Mosque that one might find in Robert Byron's *Road to Oxiana* (1939):

> These slatternly and picturesque groups, beneath their flickering yellow flares, were encamped at the gigantic foot of the Town Hall porch as at the foot of a precipice. The monstrous black walls of the Town Hall rose and were merged in gloom; and the spire of the Town Hall, on whose summit stood a gold angel holding a gold crown, rose right into the heavens and was there lost.[25]

Combine the novelty that the Potteries pose to his titular character with the fact that Bennett believed descriptions of the physical environment to be generative of character, and you are given a novel that is as much about the place in which it occurs as it is the characters that occur within it. You are given a novel that is so dedicated to evoking the character of the place in which it occurs that modern geographers use it as a means to understanding the human landscape of the region.[26] You are given a novel that infringes so heavily into the realm of travel writing that, for all intents and purposes, it can be used as such.

And that is precisely what I did. With Bennett's picture of the town in my mind, I made my way to modern-day Stoke-on-Trent. Growing up in nearby Birmingham and privy to the internecine bickering that characterises so much of the modern-day Midlands, my expectations were suitably managed. But, no managing of expectations would have prepared me for my experience on that grim January morning. I found a city that initially appeared as a twisted parody of the town presented in *Clayhanger*. As my journey progressed, however, I came to see modern-day Stoke not as inversion of Bennett's Potteries but rather as a grim fulfilment of its most notable ideals.

With no specific itinerary in mind, my intention was to imbibe the general atmosphere of the place. Being dropped off by my wife, who was frustrated that my jaunt was delaying her visit to the January sale at the Emma Bridgewater factory store, I gave my destination as 'Stoke, just Stoke'. Dutifully, she entered 'Stoke' into her phone and left it up to Google Maps to decide which particular location – within the centreless, sprawling, overlapping five (or rather six) towns that comprise Stoke-on-Trent – would be defined as 'Stoke'. To its credit, Google Maps, evidently aware of the multiplicity of settlements comprising the modern conurbation known as Stoke-on-Trent, deposited me well to the west of the modern city centre, on the historic high street of what was once the independent town of Stoke.

That Stoke's high street was not Stoke-on-Trent's high street was obvious. With hindsight, Stoke's high street was remarkably ahead of its time. In presenting me with a high street that felt so utterly empty and devoid of life, it aptly predicted the future that would befall so many of the world's high streets with the coming of global quarantine. Bennett described the glow of light from the windows of pubs as emanating a 'savage ecstasy of life' in *Clayhanger*.[27] I experienced a savage emptiness of it. The shopfronts – where not boarded – appeared invariably dark and lifeless. There was a stone market hall whose façade declared that it had been open since 1900. Even it was not open today.

One exception emerged as I paced the street: a shop with its lights turned on and attended by a living, human figure. Its sign proclaimed it to be a newsagent, declaring itself 'Centre News'. Its surroundings suggested anything but. The figure outside was a weathered gentleman of indeterminate old age. His clothing told the tale of a life lived. He wore a battered high-vis jacket that had lost any of its lustre, a greyed woollen hat whose fraying made it difficult to identify where hat ended and hair began, and rough, heavy boots whose leather had been worn down to reveal the bare steel guarding his toe caps. There was little on his person that was not due a repair or a replacement. By his actions, he soon revealed the shop's promise of light and life to be false. With his hands pressed against the closed door, he peered uncritically at the shop floor. The lights were on, but nobody was home.

Giving no reaction to my arrival, he allowed me to initiate conversation. 'No-one in?' I offered. Not allowing his attention to wander from the unattended shop, he answered without looking, 'Lights are on.' 'Is the door locked?' I asked. A low growl answered me in the affirmative. 'Maybe they've gone to the loo?' I charitably proposed, this time to no acknowledgement. After a pause in which he continued to survey the empty store, I made another attempt at conversation. 'Say, I was just passing through and thought I'd stop for a look around. I don't suppose you know if there are any shops, or markets, or anything, round here you'd recommend?' This question did, finally, lure his attention away from the empty newsagent though. Inspecting me up and down and reaching some secret judgement, he answered, 'Won't find anything like that round here. Y'want ter go up Hanley,' before returning his attention to shop window. Evidently irritated that his vigil was being disturbed, I limited myself to one further question, 'Ah, Hanley, wonderful. Thank you. Say, I don't suppose you know what would be the easiest way for me to get there from here?' He answered with a single word, 'Bus.' My welcome clearly overstayed, I thanked him once more, hopped on a bus and headed to the bright lights of Hanley.

In terms of initial impressions, a town more contrary to the spirit of that presented in *Clayhanger* could not be written. Rather than empty and lifeless, Bennett captured the Potteries at the height of their industrial energies.[28] The town is presented as an unceasing hive of activity, with columns of thick smoke emanating from the various pottery kilns being a constant feature of his descriptions of the landscape. Even a game of tennis in the back garden is accompanied by 'a column of thick smoke [rising] from a manufactory close behind the house'.[29] The inhabitants of the Five Towns, who fuel this industry, are variously described as a 'multitude' and a 'swarming mass of heads', the noise of whom is 'overwhelming' in its 'crashing force'.[30] Bennett explains the attitude to life and work embodied by the town's industrialists:

> Spend and gain! And, for a change, gain and spend! That was the method. Work till sheer exhaustion beat you. Plan, scheme, devise! Satisfy your curiosity and your other instincts! Experiment! Accept risks! Buy first, order first, pledge yourself first; and then split your head in order to pay and to redeem! When chance aids you to accumulate, let the pile grow, out of mere perversity, and then scatter royally! Play heartily! Play with the same intentness as you work! Live to the uttermost instant and to the last flicker of energy![31]

The Clayhanger's family business as the pre-eminent printers in town places Edwin right at the beating heart of a town at the forefront of a global industry. Surveying the great printing presses in his father's shop, Edwin observes the enormous vitality of the town that is reflected there:

> Darius Clayhanger's establishment was a channel through which the life of the town had somehow to pass. Auctions, meetings, concerts, sermons, improving lectures, miscellaneous entertainments, programmes, catalogues, deaths, births, marriages, specifications, municipal notices, summonses, demands, receipts, subscription-lists, accounts, rate-forms, lists of voters, jury-lists, inaugurations, closures, bill-heads, handbills, addresses, visiting-cards, society rules, bargain-sales, lost and found notices: traces of all these matters, and more, were to be found in that office; it was impregnated with the human interest; it was dusty with the human interest; its hot smell seemed to you to come off life itself, if the real sentiment and love of life were sufficiently in you. A grand, stuffy, living, seething place, with all its metallic immobility![32]

Taking place against the backdrop of this office, which 'clattered and thundered early and late', readers cannot help but get the impression of a town seizing its future with both hands, excitedly embracing the opportunities that it might bring.

Such was the attitude that characterised the Potteries in Bennett's day, an attitude that ought to leave no room for the utter absence of life that I found on that cold January morning. Walking down that desolate high street and past those unoccupied shopfronts, it was difficult to square Bennett's description of the place with my own experience. One could scarcely believe that these two towns – modern Stoke-on-Trent and Bennett's Potteries – even occupied the same space, let alone that many of these buildings and streets had stood almost unchanged since Bennett's day, so great was the apparent disparity between them.

After my adventure on Stoke's high street, I felt utterly disconnected from the world of Bennett. I duly did as advised and hopped on a bus to Hanley, one of the other six towns that conglomerated to form the modern city of Stoke-on-Trent. A quick Google search during the bus ride informed me that, since the confederation of the towns in 1925, Hanley had become the de facto centre of the newly formed city. This process seems to have come to a head in recent decades. City councillors, chiding the 'six towns mentality' and spirit of 'parochialism' that they believed was holding the city back, have attempted to eschew the civic pluralism underpinning the city's identity and focus all investment on unsuspecting Hanley.[33] When my bus deposited me there, I was able to see the fruits of their efforts.

I was met with a sight utterly ubiquitous to any British city: a shopping centre. Behind its sleek, glass-fronted exterior and shining red brickwork, it offered a Starbucks, a Chiquitos, a Cineworld and a whole assortment of other familiar brands that wouldn't challenge my sensibilities. Aisles and walkways crowded with masses of shoppers jostling to exploit the January sales. A choir of card readers pinged in tribute to the spirit of consumption that seized the place. Observing this intrusion of modernity into the city, I briefly calculated the number streets, shopfronts and market-stalls that must have been torn down to make way for this monument to crass commercialism. I couldn't help but feel a pang of sadness at the loss of Bennett's Potteries, even if I had yet to experience those Potteries for myself.

And yet, in experiencing that loss of past, it suddenly struck me that this shopping centre was, perhaps, as good a tribute to the spirit of Bennett's Potteries as could be imagined. One side-effect of this harsh, acquisitive spirit that Bennett assigns the Potteries in *Clayhanger* is an almost complete disregard for its past. Repurposing, redesigning and rebuilding any and all existing buildings and materials in pursuit of growth, the place and space inherited by the inhabitants of Bennett's Potteries is one destined to be unfeelingly consumed in the fires of progress. What rural idyll remains between the rapidly converging Five Towns is increasingly encroached upon by housing developments that spread with 'the rapidity of that plant which pushes out strangling branches more quickly than a man can run'.[34] Where fresh pasture cannot be found for such new developments, existing space finds itself being haphazardly stripped of its identity and converted to some new purpose:

> Ragged brickwork, walls finished anyhow with saggars and slag; narrow uneven alleys leading to higgledy-piggledy workshops and kilns; cottages transformed into factories and factories into cottages, clumsily, hastily, because nothing matters so long as 'it will do'; everywhere something forced to fulfil, badly, the function of something else; in brief, the reign of the slovenly makeshift, shameless, filthy, and picturesque.[35]

The Clayhanger print-shop becomes a prime example of this alienation of present from past. As the novel progresses and the business grows, it is decided that the space above the workshop in which the Clayhanger family resides would be better used as a workshop for further printing presses. The family decamps to a new home and, in Bennett's words, 'the rooms in which they had eaten and slept and lain awake, and learnt what life and what death was, were to be transformed into workshops and stores for an increasing business'.[36]

In this sense, although initially offensive in its gauche ostentation and demolition of past, the shopping centre seemed a rather fitting continuation of the spirit of industry found in Bennett's Potteries. In ruthlessly flattening the past in its pursuit of progress, Hanley's shopping centre perhaps offered me the closest experience to the spirit of Bennett's Potteries that the modern visitor might find. The appreciation that Hanley's pursuit of vulgar profit earned from me was, however, reluctant. Bennett's Potteries had overflowed with character. His novels took an utterly unexceptional part of the world and celebrated the specific and exclusive beauty and character that could be found there and only there. His descriptions of life in the Five Towns could not be stripped of their context and applied to anywhere else in the world. At every level, they are uniquely reflective of the specific social, cultural and geographic conditions that characterised life in the Potteries. Stoke's high street, likewise, had lain thick with character, even if it was not necessarily the same character as was presented in *Clayhanger*. There was nothing characterful, exceptional or specific about the experience found in Hanley's shopping centre. At that exact time, up and down the country, millions of shoppers in thousands of shops in hundreds of cities were engaging in the exact same act of ritual consumption, the only thing distinguishing them from each other being their postcode. It was an experience that was utterly universal.

A glance at the front page of the local newspaper interrupted this thought and reminded me that, despite appearance, this was not a town like any other. A week after Christmas, two days into the new year, *The Sentinel* offered its readers a grim reminder of the extreme post-industrial deprivation that continued to characterise the town:

> City Infant Death Rate 'The Worst in England'
> Shock figures more than double national average[37]

Bennett himself could not have written a more tragically poetic interplay of personal and physical environment. Beyond the bright lights of Hanley there was a city struggling to generate a future.

Leaving the comfort of Hanley's shopping centre, I set off in a random direction and found myself at the edge of a small park optimistically titled 'Central Forest Park'. As with Centre News on Stoke's high street, this name made promise that the location itself could not deliver, situated as it was in the centre of nothing in particular. The park oriented itself around a dirty brown pond picketed by a lone angler and a large hill blocking out what little light the winter sun could provide. The hill offered promise. In *Clayhanger*, Bennett had dedicated many a paragraph to loving descriptions of the Potteries' industrial skyline:

> To the east rose pitheads, chimneys, and kilns, tier above tier, dim in their own mists. [...] The sedate reddish browns and reds of the composition, all netted in flowing scarves of smoke, harmonized exquisitely with the chill blues of the chequered sky.[38]

There is one structure in particular that characterises the skyline of the Potteries as Bennett captures it: the Bottle Kiln. So named because their broad bases and narrow chimney resemble the top of a glass bottle, it is within these iconic buildings that the fruits of legions of potters' labours were turned from soft clay into hard crockery. Their presence in Bennett's works and period photographs of the town is inescapable. Even match-day photos of Stoke Football Club from the period feature their unmistakeable silhouette looming in the background behind the stands.

In search of this iconic skyline, I crested the hill. It is a fact of life that skylines change. Structures are built, extended, torn down and replaced as circumstances demand. The Potteries do not so much seem to have changed as they have dissembled. The iconic bottle kilns no longer litter the view as they once did. Yet, they haven't been removed. Nor have they been preserved. Rather, they have simply been left. Some have survived, most have fallen, the city has persisted around them regardless. One occasionally catches a glimpse of one edging out from behind a row of terraced houses, weeds infringing upon their otherwise iconic silhouette. More often though, one spies a vacant plot filled with rubble where one formerly stood. A quick Google search reveals that fewer than fifty bottle kilns now survive. There are no 'flowing scarves of smoke' to knit the whole view together. Instead the air, like the landscape itself, lies still. There is no spirit of industry to animate the place. Entropy is the order of the day.

Surveying the view, I couldn't help but think of another great writer of the British Isles, Oscar Wilde. In his *The Picture of Dorian Gray* (1890), the titular character kept a portrait in his attic that aged on his behalf. Looking at that skyline, it felt as though I was viewing such a portrait myself, one that Bennett's Potteries had hidden away to decay in their place. Bennett himself would likely have been horrified that such a fate befall his muse. It is a fact routinely commented on that Bennett consistently demonstrates a fervent disgust for the ageing process throughout his works set in the Five Towns. Comparing him to Dickens, one contemporary commentator wrote:

> The fact is that Mr. Bennett has always viewed age and disease and death with the eyes of a young man. Dickens sees age as potential vision; Bennett as physical decay. Dickens sees death as the meeting-place of time and eternity; Bennett as the breaking down of the life-cells.[39]

This is not unique to Bennett. Many of his contemporaries who examined life in the Potteries similarly identified that the towns' aggressive profit-seeking was accompanied by a cruel disregard for that which has exceeded its usefulness:

> The leisurely and gracious things of life are not the immediate or even the ultimate concerns of life in 'the Potteries', and old age is likely, in such places, to be harsh and acquisitive. When men and women, who have spent their activities entirely in money making, reach the age at which they possess much money but are no longer able to employ themselves in its acquisition, they become crabbed, unlovely, mean.[40]

Rather than being the result of authorial licence, this distaste for ageing evidence throughout Bennett's works seems instead to represent the lived reality that he experienced growing up in and observing life in the Potteries.

This unwillingness to see dignity in ageing is perhaps best demonstrated in *Clayhanger* by the character of Mr Shushions, a character that, try as I might, I found myself unable to expel from my thoughts when viewing the modern skyline. Mr Shushions was, in his prime, one of the foremost citizens of the Five Towns. He led churches, founded schools and, taking pity on a gifted but deeply impoverished young boy named Darius Clayhanger, elevated the Clayhanger family from working-class toil to middle-class gentility. All this is forgotten in Edwin's time though. When Edwin comes of age, Shushions is simply a 'doddering old fool' whose defining feature is that he is 'very old'.[41] Even Edwin is ignorant of the fact that it is to Mr Shushions that his family owe their present high standing and merely regards the veteran as an unfortunate old man.[42] Worse than simply being forgotten, Shushions is overtly disdained by many residents of the Five Towns. In one instance, he is set upon and berated by a group of youths. When a police officer intervenes, he mistakes Shushions's agitated senility for drunkenness and adds to the disrespect afforded the man. Observing the scene, Edwin considers Shushions's lot:

> The old man had lived too long; he had survived his dignity; he was now nothing but a bundle of capricious and obstinate instincts set in motion by ancient souvenirs remembered at hazard.[43]

Looking at the modern skyline and thinking of Mr Shushions, I couldn't help but reach a bleak conclusion. If Bennett believed that place reflected person and vice versa, a truer personification of the modern city could not have been written than Mr Shushions' account. Stoke-on-Trent has lived too long; it has survived its dignity; it is now nothing but a bundle of capricious and obstinate instincts set in motion by ancient souvenirs remembered at hazard. It has become the very thing that Bennett loathed, a twisted inversion of the spirit of vigorous entrepreneurship that once animated the town.

Disheartened by this conclusion, I sought consolation. Resolved to end my visit on a more optimistic note, I headed to a site that sought to capture the spirit of the Potteries as they were in Bennett's time. The Gladstone Pottery Museum was founded in 1974 by a group of volunteers disheartened by the disappearance of the iconic bottle ovens from their landscape. Gaining control of a relatively intact pottery works, they have sought to preserve it for future generations. As an industrial heritage project, it is a positive example of its sort. One can wander in the footsteps on the works' potters, read accounts of their lives, be shocked at their young age and poor conditions, observe a piece of lumpen clay be transformed into a plate by a friendly volunteer and finish the day with a cappuccino in the café. Shielded from the post-industrial poverty being experienced by many of the modern residents, one is free to safely revel in the historical squalor and exploitation suffered in pursuit of profit by their ancestors.

One thing stood out in my memory from my visit to the Pottery Museum, and it concerned the pottery kilns themselves. Looking at the bottle ovens up close, I couldn't help but notice a set of curious iron belts placed at various, seemingly random, heights around the kilns. Some ovens had a single belt, others several. Some were rusted and worn with age, others shone with black enamel. A guide explained their purpose to me. Apparently, the unique shape of the kilns means that their weight lies in an unusual way. As they age and the mortar erodes, rather than tumbling to one side or collapsing at their foundations, they swell. The weight of their narrow top presses down through the centre of the structure and causes them to bulge at their wide middles. Ultimately, this pressure becomes too great for the structure to bear, and the bulge bursts, bringing the oven down under its own weight. These iron girdles, strapped around these sagging middles, sought to delay this process by containing this bulge. As the ovens continued to swell in spite of their belts, more belts were added to further delay the inevitable. When I asked my guide the long-term plan to prevent this seemingly interminable collapse, I was told simply to 'keep adding belts'.

More than anything else from my visit, this statement aptly contained the condition and fate of the modern-day Potteries. In *Clayhanger*, Bennett caught the town at the height of its advancement. Yet, he was also pensive about this attitude of growth at any cost. When Edwin sees the aged Mr Shushions being bullied and berated by the younger men, he is disquieted by their short-sightedness, attacking the fate that they themselves were one day destined to enjoy:

> Edwin was revolted by the spectacle of the younger men baiting him. He was astonished that they were so shortsighted as not to be able to see the image of themselves in the old man, so imprudent as not to think of their own future, so utterly brutalized.[44]

Rather than inverting the spirit of harsh, unfeeling profit-seeking that characterised Bennett's Five Towns, the modern city of Stoke-on-Trent seems instead to have fulfilled it. Once so narrowly obsessed with the furtherance of its industry, with the loss of this industry, it has become a city without a purpose. Observing the forlorn efforts to prop up the sagging pottery kilns and delay the inevitable erasure of what relics survived of the town's industrial past, I was treated to a very physical representation of the spirit of entropy that penetrates the place. Bennett, in his belief that physical spaces reflect personal characteristics, could not have written a better representation of the place.

Blending travel writing and fiction, Bennett crafted stories that were as much about place as they were the people within it. During my own visit, I experienced the Potteries through both my own eyes and the eyes of Edwin Clayhanger. This lens coloured everything I saw, whether I realised it or not. This lens first meant that I saw in Stoke's empty high street a cruel antithesis to the vision of the Potteries presented in Bennett, a dreary, sullen wasteland completely bereft of the spirit of industry that had animated the place in *Clayhanger*. Then, viewing the utterly ordinary sight of a shopping centre through this lens, this verdict was paused and this hub of conspicuous consumption appeared, briefly, as a survival of the commercial spirit that Bennett had so perfectly captured. This hive of activity was soon revealed, however, to be but a single oasis of industry amidst a desert, and a shallow, characterless oasis at that. It was in seeking higher ground and surveying the skyline of the city, before going in for a closer inspection at one of its surviving iconic bottle kilns, that I was finally able to reconcile my own experience of the Potteries with that given by Bennett. Stoke-on-Trent has neither continued nor abandoned the spirit of harsh, acquisitive industrialism that Bennett immortalised. Rather, it has fulfilled it. The Potteries, in seeming to have outlived their economic usefulness and been consigned to a state of post-industrial poverty, have suffered exactly the same fate experienced by those poor souls living within Bennett's Potteries that had exceeded their value. Like Mr Shushions being berated for his senility, all former glories and honours have been forgotten. Like Mr Shushions, they have 'lived too long' and 'survived [their] dignity'.[45] Like Mr Shushions, they have 'forgotten to die'.[46]

That final line is, perhaps, a little too strong. This chapter was intended as a love letter to the Potteries and one of its most famous sons. Instead, in writing, it seems to have turned into a *fatwa* calling for its destruction. I'm sure many a proud Stokie reading this will feel outrage at the short shrift I have given their town. They may feel I have done their storied and distinctive city a disservice. They may question what, other than empty streets and a grey atmosphere, I expected to find when visiting during the grip of winter. The eagle-eyed may even notice one or two details that don't quite add up and, perhaps, call into question the veracity of my account. I would ask any wronged readers to hold off on their judgement, briefly delay their outrage and think back to the purpose of this volume. Taking advantage of our unique global condition, this volume seeks to pick apart the conceit that underpins travel writing: that the writer is presenting a documentary account of their visit to a place. I would also ask any offended readers to further consider the points raised at the beginning of this chapter concerning Bennett's own fluid relationship to the travel writing tradition. This account has inverted Bennett's social realist approach to literature. Where Bennett used travel and observation to inform his fiction, I have used Bennett's fiction to inform my travel and observation. As such, this account has been placed in a blended space. Being exclusively a product of memory, both literary and personal, it occupies an intersection between fact and fiction. The question should not be which elements of my account are fact and which fiction but, rather, what's the difference?

## Notes

1 Bennett's prolific output and popularity is discussed in C. d. Stasio, 'Arnold Bennett and Late-Victorian "Woman"', *Victorian Periodicals Review* 28 (1999): 40–53; G. G. Fromm, 'Remythologizing Arnold Bennett', *NOVEL: A Forum on Fiction* 16 (1982): 19–34 (21); S. Hynes, 'The Whole Contention between Mr. Bennett and Mrs. Woolf', *NOVEL: A Forum on Fiction* 1 (1967): 34–44 (34).
2 J. B. Priestley, 'Modern English Novelists: Arnold Bennett', *English Journal* 14 (1925): 261–68 (268).
3 G. B. Dutton, 'Arnold Bennett, Showman', *Sewanee Review* 33 (1925): 64–72 (72).
4 D. Moggach, 'Arnold Bennett', *Great Lives*, 29 April 2014, https://www.bbc.co.uk/sounds/play/b041xdgm.
5 Hynes, 'The Whole Contention', 34.
6 R. Saloman, 'Arnold Bennett's Hotels', *Twentieth Century Literature* 58 (2012): 1–25 (6).

7  As Bennett himself explained, 'The sound of the phrase "Six Towns" is not so good as the phrase "Five Towns". "I" in "Five" is an open vowel. "I" in "Six" is a closed vowel, and is not nearly so striking. To my mind a broad sounding phrase for the district was very important.' This quotation is reprinted in the *New York Times Book Review*, 20 April 1930, 7.
8  Instances of the residents of Fenton making this complaint can be found throughout the local newspaper record. Examples include: R. Ault, '"Some People Believe This City Has Five Towns" – Families Question if Fenton Has Been "forgotten"', *StokeonTrent Live*, 4 February 2019, https://www.stokesentinel.co.uk/news/stoke-on-trent-news/some-people-believe-city-five-2492949; J. Burn, '"It's Victimisation!" Does This Stoke-on-Trent Town Always Get the Short End of the Stick?', StrokeonTrent Live, 10 February 2020, https://www.stokesentinel.co.uk/news/stoke-on-trent-news/its-victimisation-stoke-trent-town-3798803.
9  A. Bennett, *The Writer's Craft* (New York: George H. Doran, 1914), 17.
10  'Review: Clayhanger', *North American Review* 192 (1910): 849–51 (849).
11  Bennett, *The Writer's Craft*, 39.
12  Ibid., 26–27.
13  Ibid., 24. The intersection between fiction and geography in Bennett's works is discussed in B. J. Hudson, 'The Geographical Imagination of Arnold Bennett', *Transactions of the Institute of British Geographers* 7 (1982): 365–79; 'Arnold Bennett, Transport and Urban Development', *Geography* 101 (2016): 85–92.
14  A. Bennett, *Clayhanger* (London: Methuen, 1954), 3–4.
15  Bennett, *The Writer's Craft*, 16–17.
16  J. Potter, 'H. L. Mencken and Arnold Bennett', *Menckenmania* 130 (1994): 1–5 (2).
17  St. J. Ervine, 'Some Impressions of My Elders: Arnold Bennett', *North American Review* 214 (1921): 371–85 (374).
18  Priestley, 'Modern English Novelists', 264.
19  Dutton, 'Arnold Bennett, Showman', 64.
20  The intersection between autobiography and fiction in *Clayhanger* is discussed in N. H. Bukowski, 'Mr. Bennett and Mrs. Woolf', in *A Voice Still Heard*, ed. N. Howe (London: Yale University Press, 2014), 335–40 (339); M. Drabble, *Arnold Bennett* (Aylesbury: Hazel Watson and Viney, 1974) 174–76; Hudson, 'The Geographical Imagination', 367, 372–73; 'Arnold Bennett', 88; E. E. Irvine, 'The Clayhangers: Father and Son', *British Journal of Social Work* 12 (1982): 365–79 (83, 85, 88–89).
21  Drabble, *Arnold Bennett*, 171.
22  Bennett, *Clayhanger*, 7.
23  Ibid., 8–9.
24  Ibid., 69.
25  Ibid., 74.
26  As recently as 2016, the Geography Association's journal *Geography* has featured articles using Bennett's novels as a means to understand the industrial landscape of the early twentieth-century Potteries, Hudson, 'Arnold Bennett', 356–79.
27  Bennett, *Clayhanger*, 74.
28  The industrial might of the Potteries during their boom is discussed in J. Matson, 'Staffordshire and the American Trade', *Metropolitan Museum of Art Bulletin, New Series* 4 (1945): 81–83 (81); J. Stobart, 'Identity, Competition and Place Promotion in the Five Towns', *Urban History* 30 (2003): 163–82 (163).
29  Bennett, *Clayhanger*, 402.
30  Ibid., 241–42, 245, 303.
31  Ibid., 199.
32  Ibid., 101–2.
33  The controversy arising from the city council's decision to focus investment on Hanley is discussed in articles such as 'Is Stoke-on-Trent's "Six Towns Mentality" Holding It Back?',

*BBC News*, 25 July 2013, https://www.bbc.com/news/uk-england-stoke-staffordshire-23163683#:~:text=%22This%20is%20not%20about%20us,over%20the%20past%20 20%20years.
34 Bennett, *Clayhanger*, 169.
35 Ibid., 16.
36 Ibid., 256.
37 *The Sentinel*, 2 January 2020, 1.
38 Bennett, *Clayhanger*, 3–8.
39 Dutton, 'Arnold Bennett, Showman', 70.
40 Ervine, 'Some Impressions of My Elders', 382–83.
41 Bennett, *Clayhanger*, 22, 249, 252.
42 Mr Shushions' role in rescuing Darius Clayhanger from the workhouse is discussed in ibid., 34–38.
43 Ibid., 249.
44 Ibid., 250.
45 Ibid., 249.
46 Ibid., 252.

Chapter Ten

# TRAVELLING TOWARDS TRANSCULTURALISM? STATUES, REMEMBRANCE AND MOURNING IN BLOEMFONTEIN, SOUTH AFRICA

Kate Law

Bloemfontein is a complex place. An American might call it 'flyover country' – a space which you pass 'over' or 'through' on your way from Johannesburg to Cape Town. For those visiting the country on holiday, their time is more likely to be spent looking for the 'big five' at Kruger National Park, marvelling at Table Mountain in Cape Town, making the solemn pilgrimage to Robben Island or sipping pinotage in the winelands around Stellenbosch. In short, Bloemfontein is rarely thought of as a *destination*. As one former resident has put it, 'The isolation of this rural province from the big cities, the desolation of the endless spread of dry, brown, open veld, the general lack of cosmopolitan entertainment and the rigid conservatism of the place will test your spirit.'[1] Yet in January 2013 – one-way ticket in hand – I found myself moving there. With my suitcase and a sense of trepidation for company, I was on my way to take up a postdoctoral fellowship at the University of the Free State (UFS) in the newly formed International Studies Group.

Although I'd spent time in Cape Town, Bloemfontein – I was told – was *quite* a different proposition. If the mood in (White) Cape Town is generally one of confident exceptionalism (try finding anyone who admits to voting for the NP – the political party that instituted and maintained apartheid), then I'd got the sense that the idea of the 'rainbow nation' – a metaphor coined by Archbishop Desmond Tutu to promote racial reconciliation in the post-apartheid period – didn't have the same resonance in a city that was feted as the home of Afrikanerdom.[2] After I had accepted the job and was trying to make sense of the unending loop of Kafkaesque bureaucracy that getting a visa entailed, I set about some half-hearted research, attempting to get a sense of the university and city – some 6,000 miles away – that I was moving to. My sofa sleuthing yielded a series of peculiar if not particularly exciting titbits: J. R. R Tolkien, author of *The Hobbit* and *Lord of the Rings*, was born in Bloemfontein in 1892; it was where the English football team had been knocked out of the 2010 World Cup; shops were prohibited from selling alcohol on Sunday; and there was a zoo/big cat park, the ominously titled 'Cheetah Experience'. Rather more worrying, however, was the first news item that cropped up concerning UFS: that of the so-called 'Reitz scandal'.

In 2007, four White Afrikaner male students, Danie Grobler, R. C. Malherbe, Schalk van der Merwe and Johnny Roberts, who lived in the Reitz (hall of) residence, were filmed forcing five elderly Black cleaning workers – Rebecca Adams, Laukaziemma Koko, Noom Phoro, Nitta Ntseng and David Molete – to take part in a series of degrading 'challenges', including a running race and an eating and drinking contest, in which the workers were made to eat food which appeared to have been urinated on. This hazing, as one of the Reitz Four explained, was simply part of the 'selection process' that other Black South Africans should expect if the university carried out its plans to desegregate campus accommodation.[3] Astonishingly, the video had apparently been made as Grobler et al.'s entry into an annual residence competition, the Reitz cultural evening. Shockingly, it won. It was only when the video was later leaked on YouTube in February 2008 that 'all hell broke loose and a little-known university in the rural heartland of South Africa would make headlines across the world for all the wrong reasons'.[4] The actions of the 'Reitz Four' were abhorrent on many levels. The bald racism was clear to see; the fact that these young men – not quite 'born frees' but close enough – felt comfortable in humiliating elderly Black workers who cleaned their dorm rooms was a stark reminder of the limits of 'rainbowism' in the supposedly *new* South Africa.[5]

That the video had won a competition – and had thus been sanctioned as acceptable by their peers – was also deeply troubling. Those who sought to defend the Reitz *boitjies* claimed that it was harmless fun that had perhaps got a bit out of hand.[6] They maintained that the film was a reasonable vehicle through which the young men were expressing their anger at plans to desegregate campus accommodation, a process which they believed would junk their dorm traditions and rituals.[7] Conversely, criticism and anger from both inside and outside of the country dismissed the facile defence that 'boys will be boys' and rather focused on the fact that this video was symptomatic of a broader problem; that racism was alive and well and was part of the country's 'ugly present'.[8] UFS's immediate response to this very public embarrassment was to expel all four students and grant the five workers paid leave. In July 2008, the Reitz residence was closed, and two months later the vice chancellor Frederick Fourie resigned.

By March 2009, under the 'crushing weight of history and culture, race and class, memory and identity', the charismatic education scholar Jonathan Jansen was appointed as UFS's new vice chancellor.[9] The first Black vice chancellor in the institution's history, Jansen's platform was one of 'reconciliation', and he earnestly set about bridging the racial divide. A powerful orator, in his inaugural address, Jansen apologised to the Black workers, took responsibility for the actions of the Reitz Four and pardoned them as 'his children'. Going further, he welcomed Grobler et al. back to campus to resume their studies (an invitation they declined) and apologised 'to every decent white citizen' of the university who felt 'shamed by the Reitz incident'.[10] During his seven-year tenure, Jansen's transformation project enjoyed many significant victories; he established an institute for reconciliation and social justice, improved the university's academic reputation, pushed the institution further towards financial stability and, crucially, spearheaded programmes that championed equity for both staff and students.

Although Jansen was very much a community figure – he sometimes dragged his desk outside his office building so students could informally speak to him; he had a regular column in *Die Volksblad*, the local Afrikaans newspaper, and was a prolific user of social media – I often wondered how far his message *actually* travelled. Things seemed better at UFS, and once again students took pride in being 'Kovsies', but how representative was the atmosphere on campus? What significance – if any – did the rhetoric of reconciliation play in private spaces? Did the topography of the city act as an impediment to integration? This chapter investigates these questions by analysing monuments and memorials in two different heritage sites across the city – *Die Nasionale Vrouemonument* (The National Women's Monument) at the War Museum of the Boer Republics, and the Nelson Mandela Statue at Naval Hill – before finally returning to the UFS campus to examine the ways in which the #RhodesMustFall debate became localised through the statue of M. T. Steyn – the last president of the Orange Free State. Following on from Ndletyana and Webb, I examine whether Bloemfontein's monuments are 'social divisions carved in stone', or if they can be 'cenotaphs to a new identity'.[11] I ask whether 'multiplicative commemoration' is possible in Bloemfontein, or whether the city's statuary highlights a more 'monologic' process in which separate and 'singular historical narrative[s] of national identity' and memorialisation exist awkwardly alongside one another.[12]

## 'They Suffered Courageously and Patiently': Afrikaner Nationalism at *Die Nasionale Vrouemonument*

Arriving in Bloemfontein as a Brit or – as I acquiesced to – as an Englishwoman, I was asked on multiple occasions what I knew about Emily Hobhouse, the 'Angel of Love' from Cornwall who had been the heroine of the Afrikaner people since the turn of the twentieth century.[13] Until her father's death in 1895, Hobhouse fulfilled the duties expected of her as a maiden aunt.[14] As the century drew to a close, however, Hobhouse took significant strides outside of the private sphere, moving to Minnesota to minister to Cornish miners.

Despite a recent attempt to provide a more expansive overview of her political activism, Hobhouse is most well known for her humanitarian work among Boer women and children interned in the concentration camps of the second South African War.[15] A committed pacifist, Hobhouse became involved in the war through her role as secretary of the South African Conciliation Committee, a British anti-war organisation.[16] As the conflict progressed, Hobhouse learned of the existence of so-called 'Refugee camps' in which increasingly large number of Boer women and children were being kept by the British.[17] As one contemporary account read: 'We were taken out of our house and the house was burnt [...] we were not allowed to take anything with us but clothes [...] We are half an hour from Bloemfontein in a camp; they call it the Refugee Camp. There are 13 families in the camp. We are placed 12 in one tent.'[18] Having founded the South African Women and Children Distress Fund to raise funds and material aid for those interned, in 1900, Hobhouse travelled to South Africa 'for purposes of relief'.[19] Arriving in Cape Town on 27 December, Hobhouse planned to make her way north up through the Orange River Colony and finally on to the Transvaal, assessing the condition of the camps as she went. As martial law had recently been declared, however, her plans were contingent on the support of the commander of the British, Kitchener. Refusing her request, Kitchener acquiesced to Hobhouse travelling as far north as Bloemfontein, and she first reached the city on 24 January 1901. In possession of a pass which allowed her permanent access to the camps, Hobhouse quickly realised that 'the barest necessities of life were lacking or inadequately supplied [...] shelter was totally insufficient [...] there was *no soap* provided [...] the water supply would not go around'.[20] The longer Hobhouse spent in Bloemfontein, the more she saw the conditions in the camps deteriorate. As she wrote, 'I called repeated attention to the insufficient sanitary accommodation, and still more to the negligence of the camp authorities in attending to the latrines.'[21] Going further, she noted that 'sickness was increasing [...] [and] disease and death were stamped upon' the faces of those in the camps.[22] The deleterious conditions left a lasting impression on Hobhouse, and she set about educating the British public about 'the miserable scene'.[23] In reporting 'the wholesale cruelty'[24] of the (White) camps, Hobhouse was vilified by Britain's press and political elite with the Secretary of State for the Colonies, Joseph Chamberlain, scornfully labelling her a 'hysterical spinster of mature age'.[25]

If Hobhouse was reviled in Britain, in South Africa she was revered as the heroine of the Afrikaner people, and she maintained a strong attachment to South Africa for the rest of her life. A 'symbol of the accompanying affection of far-off South African friends', in 1921, Rachel Isabella 'Tibbie' Steyn, wife of M. T. Steyn, raised £2,300 through a half-crown collection list so Hobhouse could buy a house for her retirement.[26] Although she died in Britain in 1926, Hobhouse's ashes are ensconced in *Die Vrouemonument* in Bloemfontein, an act which signified her literal incorporation into a narrative of the war that emphasised Afrikaner suffering and loss.

Erected some 13 years earlier, *Die Vrouemonument* was the brainchild of M. T. and Tibbie Steyn. Conceived 'to commemorate the self-sacrificing love displayed by the women and children for their nation and their fatherland during the Anglo-Boer War', it sits approximately three miles south of the centre of Bloemfontein, in an area that is now mostly populated by factories and second-hand car dealerships.[27] A prominent 'site of memory', *Die Vrouemonument* is a particularly important 'site of mourning' for the country's approximately 2.7 million White Afrikaans speakers, a place in which the British atrocities of the second South African War have been indelibly inscribed on the White Afrikaner psyche.[28]

From a distance – to the jet-lagged traveller at least – *Die Vrouemonument* appears as a maquette of the Washington monument, with the obelisk dominating the surrounding landscape. At its base sits a bronze sculpture of two forlorn-looking women, one holding a dying child in her arms, while the other looks on into the distance. Flanked by two bas-relief panels which depict women being forced into concentration camps, *Die Vrouemonument* sits in a circular enclosure, and from its unveiling in December 1913, it has carried a 'directly ethnic political message',[29] becoming increasingly 'enveloped in the swirl of Afrikaner nationalism'.[30] Although ill health prevented Hobhouse from attending the unveiling, extracts of a speech she had prepared to 'commemorate those who suffered bravely and died nobly' were read at the ceremony.[31] Cultivating a particularly gendered narrative of war that (over)emphasises female docility and helplessness, *Die Vrouemonument* sits as a paean to patriarchy and, as Anne McClintock has observed, 'in portraying the Afrikaner nation symbolically as a weeping woman, the mighty male embarrassment of military defeat could be over-looked'.³² Alongside this obfuscation the monument also continues to perpetrate the 'myth of a white man's war'.³³ The erasure of Black South Africans as 'agents as well as victims' of the conflict astounded me when I first visited it in early 2013.³⁴ Considering its genealogy this is not wholly surprising, and as Elsie Cloete has so plainly put it: 'it (*Die Vrouemonument*) was intended for whites only'.³⁵ In the post-apartheid period, the monument continues to be a heuristic device and totem through which Afrikaner sorrow and loss is emphasised. Despite the conflict having taken place well over a hundred years ago, I was surprised at what a cultural touchstone it still was for many Afrikaners. Temporally, apartheid – the legally mandated system of White supremacy – was much 'closer', but as Afrikaners were the antagonists and not the victims of this arrangement, the retreat into history is perhaps not surprising. By looking into the past, Afrikaners therefore make a discursive leap which unites their current 'affliction' of 'being a minority in a multicultural environment' to their suffering at the hands of the British over a hundred years earlier.³⁶ In continuing to uncritically venerate the – admittedly sorrowful – experiences of White women and children at *Die Vrouemonument*, Afrikaner nationalists are thereby choosing to see themselves as an 'embattled and systematically oppressed' people, wilfully ignoring and refusing to accept the brutality of and enduring legacies of apartheid.³⁷

## 'A Source of Inspiration to all South Africans and Indeed to All of Humanity': The Nelson Mandela Statue, Naval Hill

Some seven kilometres away on the northern side of the city, on the incongruously named Naval Hill, sits the largest statue in the world of liberation struggle leader, former president and global icon Nelson Mandela. In the post-apartheid period, the commemoration of 'struggle heroes' such as Mandela is central to a new project of identity formation. In 'celebrating new heroes', as Sabine Marschall argues, South Africans are able to create an ideological rather than a biological genealogy, 'a chosen ancestry' that fosters a sense of shared community.³⁸ Cast in bronze by sculptor Kobus Hattingh, the statue was donated to the city by prominent local businessman Freddy Kenny.³⁹ As Kenny explained: 'Madiba [Mandela's isiXhosa clan name] always watched over us when he lived […] now he will watch over us for eternity.'⁴⁰ At its official unveiling on 7 December 2012, former president Jacob Zuma opined that the statue was 'a symbol of the country's reconciliation and tolerance as a nation'.⁴¹ As Marschall has cogently observed, 'the link or ideological ancestry between the immortalised likeness of the past hero and members of the present elite is aptly illustrated when high political officials have themselves photographed next to the statue at the occasion of the official unveiling'.⁴² At a time when his premiership – and by extension the fortunes of the ruling party – in the African National Congress (ANC) was being rocked by a series of increasingly lurid scandals, Zuma took the opportunity to remind South Africans how far they had come. As he observed, 'It reminds us of our journey from the birth of the African National Congress here in Mangaung [Sesotho name for Bloemfontein] in 1912, to the democratic elections in 1994, and now, this year, the centenary of the ANC, the oldest liberation movement in Africa.'⁴³

From my first visit in January 2013, I was a regular visitor to Naval Hill, the site upon which the Mandela statue sits. I'd been warned by well-meaning *tannies* never to go there after dark because of the 'satanic groups' who met there – shorthand for either Black South Africans or, even more disturbingly in their minds, counter-cultural Whites who rejected the *braai* and *Boer* approach to life so commonplace in the city.[44] From my house in Langenhoven Park – a suburb named for the poet whose most famous work, *Die Stem*, became the national anthem during apartheid – it was an easy 20-minute drive to Waverley, one of the most exclusive suburbs in the city, and to the foot of Naval Hill. To the romantically inclined, Bloemfontein fits Kipling's bill of being a place 'washed with sun'.[45] For those with less baroque tastes, settler writer Leonard Fleming's mordant observation that 'you can see more land and less scenery in the Free State [the province which the city is in] than in any other country in the world' is likely to ring true.[46] Apart from going to see the statue, Naval Hill had two other draws. First – and unbelievably – atop the hill there was a nature reserve home to giraffes, blue wildebeest, zebra, eland and springboks. It was quite something to be driving a temperamental Fiat Punto to then find your path blocked by two languid giraffes that had no intention of moving. Secondly – and as its name conveys – it was one of the few places where you could actually get a view of the city. After British troops captured the city in the South African War, they set up base there, and the Wiltshire Regiment laid out a white horse on the eastern slope as a landmark for riders coming in from across the veld.

In my visits I was not on the lookout for *Bittereinders* coming across the plains, but the ability to see and make sense of – literally and metaphorically – what stretched out in front of me.[47] A statue instead of a monument, at eight metres high, the bronze Mandela towers over the city. Sculpted to imply movement, Mandela's right arm is aloft in a clenched fist, echoing the pose he struck when he was finally released from prison in February 1990 following the conclusion of his 27-year internment. On 25 February 1990, just two weeks after his release, Mandela visited Bloemfontein and addressed a large ANC rally, where he reaffirmed the party's commitment to the overthrow of the apartheid state. As he put it, 'The Free State is seen by our people as a bastion of white conservatism. We serve notice that this state of affairs must be remedied.'[48]

Although the statue at Naval Hill certainly nods to his revolutionary past – he was the founder of the ANC's armed wing, uMkhonto we Sizwe (MK), and in his blistering speech at the Rivonia Treason trial, he declared that democracy was an 'ideal' for which he was 'prepared to die' – his memory and legacy have been deployed in two distinct ways since the end of apartheid.[49] First, in the service of the nation, and particularly in an attempt to promote racial reconciliation in the immediate post-apartheid *dénouement*, his revolutionary legacy was blunted and softened. This was the Mandela that embraced rugby and, by extension, White South Africans, the man who cavorted with the Spice Girls and who took tea with Betsie Verwoerd. In this sense then, Mandela was 'a metonym of the wider "miracle" [...] of breaking the political mold [*sic*] of the past to enact the impossible, and to do so with captivating charism and charm'.[50] Visiting Bloemfontein in September 1994, five months into his presidency, Mandela gave a speech in which he 'impressed upon the nation the need for reconciliation'.[51] Indeed it was this aspect of his legacy that was invoked at the unveiling of the statue on Naval Hill in 2012. As former executive mayor Thabo Manyoni put it: 'The statue symbolises social cohesion among the citizens of Manguang and South Africa as a whole, and acts as a representation of a better future we envisage for the city.'[52] Stretching the metaphor even further, the ANC then released 94 doves (one for each of Mandela's years) shortly after the official unveiling took place. Secondly, and as was particularly visible during the ANC's 2014 election campaign, voters were encouraged to 'do it for Mandela'. In doing so, and as Litheko Modisane has written, 'the significance of Mandela has become more important than the man'.[53] In claiming that the party had a 'good story to tell', the ANC's election slogan encouraged voters to seek refuge in the past, as the present – state corruption exemplified through the audacious 'Nkandlagate' scandal – was certainly less appealing.[54] Through invoking his legacy – rhetorically or in bronze – the Mandela statue is therefore imagined as a site of renewal and 'symbolic healing' for the city.[55] Yet, despite this, the time I saw the most White South Africans near the statue was in preparation for the Saturday morning parkrun. So perhaps in Bloemfontein at least, there's still a way to travel on the path towards reconciliation.

The latest development in the city's heritage legacy is the removal and relocation of the M. T. Steyn statue from the UFS campus to the Anglo-Boer War museum next to *Die Vrouemonument*. Despite being something of a backwater, Bloemfontein has not been immune to the highly politicised statue debates that were reignited in the wake of the successful #RhodesMustFall (RMF) campaign at the University of Cape Town in 2015. Although its potential relocation had been mooted as early as 2003, since the #RMF campaign, the university expended considerable energy trying to decide precisely what to do with the statue of the Boer leader. Immediately in front of the vice chancellor's office, the Steyn statue was hard to miss, and in 2014, it was the focal point of a public art project, Cigdem Aydemir's 'plastic histories'.[56] Attempting to give voice to 'alternative histories', Aydemir shrink-wrapped the statue of Steyn and then sprayed it shocking pink. In doing so, the statue underwent a (temporary) metamorphosis from bronze to bright pink. Therefore, in queering it and creating a palimpsest, Aydemir was able to subvert – albeit temporarily – the dominant colonial iconography of the piece.

Although the university's transformation journey had been accelerated since the arrival of Jansen, for his critics on the left, the journey wasn't progressing quickly enough, something that was brought into particularly sharp relief in the wake of the #FeesMustFall protests when in February 2016 the statue of C. R. Swart – one of apartheid's most staunch henchmen – was toppled by student protesters and members of the Economic Freedom Front (EFF) outside of the law building.[57] Three months later, Jansen announced he was stepping down as vice chancellor, and in April 2017, Francis Petersen was appointed as his replacement. One of Petersen's first inheritances was the university's 'Integrated Transformation Plan', a framework to 'widen the scope and radically accelerate transformation in the University', whereby UFS committed itself to taking 'a comprehensive and critical look' at the statues on campus.[58] In what followed, the Steyn statue remained at the forefront of the university's plans to 'identify symbols and spaces that need transformation, and ensure that any changes promote a socially just institution which celebrates freedom of expression and provides a sense of solidarity and belonging for all', with the institution embarking on an extensive period of public deliberation to decide if the Steyn statue should stay on campus.[59] The polarised nature of the debate regarding the removal of public statues – broadly speaking that of iconoclasm – and the 'erasure' of history versus questions of decoloniality and social justice are at the heart of a global culture war, with the debates in South Africa being part of this broader contestation regarding public understandings of history and monumenture.

In the context of the heritage impact assessment that was carried out, members of Afriforum, a right-wing pressure group that 'focuses on the rights of Afrikaners as a community', co-opted the language of reconciliation and argued that the removal of Steyn was an attack on Afrikaner 'cultural freedom', suggesting that the relocation of the statue would not promote a 'culture of inclusivity' on campus.[60] Going further with their casuistry, Afriforum attempted to portray Steyn as an anti-colonial 'liberation hero' who resisted the perfidious forces of British imperialism, while those calling for Steyn's removal argued that 'the truth of the matter is this: inanimate objects have power – to define, to teach, to disrupt and to keep alive ideals. The power that is perpetuated by the statue forces everyone around it to agree with the violent history that necessitated it.'[61] Notwithstanding appeals from groups such as Afriforum and the far-right political group Freedom Front Plus, and following the conclusion of the public consultation, UFS decided to remove and relocate Steyn to the Anglo-Boer War Museum. In doing so, UFS argued that this 'spatial re-interpretation' would 'promote inclusivity and meaning of space in a sustainable manner that balance[d] the intricacies of the past, the present, and the future'.[62]

In 2020, Bloemfontein's 'heritage transformation' is far from over.[63] The city's monuments – redolent of its residents – sit in a state of 'juxtaposition', whereby they exist somewhat uneasily alongside one another.[64] Although the Mandela statue and *Die Vrouemonument* are far from being frozen tableaus, they speak to and serve very different constituencies in the city. If the statue of Mandela is 'probably the main symbol of post-apartheid nationalism in the city', then *Die Vrouemonument* is equally important to the Afrikaner imaginary.[65] Ostensibly serving different constituencies, only time will tell if 'multiplicative commemoration' is possible, or even desirable, in Bloemfontein. One thing's for sure; the city still has a considerable way to travel on its journey of reconciliation, with its public monumenture continuing to play an opaque role in the process.

## Notes

1 J. D. Jansen, *Leading for Change: Race, Intimacy and Leadership on Divided University Campuses* (London: Routledge, 2015), 41.
2 X. Mangcu, 'The State of Race Relations in Post-Apartheid South Africa', in *State of the Nation: South Africa 2003–2004*, ed. J. Daniel, A. Habib and R. Southall (Cape Town: HSRC Press, 2003), 105–17 (105).
3 C. Soudien, 'Who Takes Responsibility for the "Reitz Four"? Puzzling Our Way through Higher Education Transformation in South Africa', *South African Journal of Science* 106, 9–10 (2010): 1–4 (1).
4 Jansen, *Leading for Change*, 18.

5 The idea of those who are 'born free' is often understood in two ways. Those who were born after Nelson Mandela became president were literally 'born free'; it is also applied to those who politically came of age after 1994. See V. Malila and A. Garman, 'Listening to the "Born Frees": Politics and Disillusionment in South Africa', *African Journalism Studies* 37, 1 (2016): 64–80.
6 *Boitjie*, literally 'boy', is an Afrikaans term of affection, and '*kom boitjies!*' (come on boys!) is often shouted by spectators at rugby matches. In a phone interview with the *Sunday Times*, Johnny Roberts' father, James, was reported as saying: 'Why should our sons be punished for fooling around? We were all students once, we all got into trouble. But when race is involved, their lives have to be ruined. For what? We all make mistakes.' Cited in J. Smith, 'Vexed Varsity's New Broom', *Saturday Star*, 17 October 2009.
7 For an excellent piece which historically situates the Reitz Scandal and the broader problems of segregated campus accommodation, see E. Fairbanks, 'A House Divided', *Slate*, 24 June 2013, https://slate.com/news-and-politics/2013/06/university-of-the-free-state-in-bloemfonteins-segregation-how-the-legacy-of-racism-lingers-in-post-apartheid-south-africa.html.
8 S. Jacobs, 'South Africa's Ugly Present', *The Guardian*, 28 February 2008, https://www.theguardian.com/commentisfree/2008/feb/28/southafricasuglypresent. See also Y. Malan, 'Reconciliation Means Never Having to Say You're Sorry', *Huffington Post*, 3 March 2010, https://www.huffpost.com/entry/reconciliation-means-neve_b_365323?guccounter=1&guce_referrer=aHR0cHM6Ly93d3cuYmVsZmVyY2VudGVyLm 9yZy9wdWJsaWNhdGlvbi9yZWNvbmNpbGlhdGlvbi1tZWFucy1uZXZlci1oYXZpbmct c2F5LXlvdXJlLXNvcnJ5&guce_referrer_sig=AQAAAETIjmBT9QxsWgAOLzfRKmR_ 1zKU7PnU-0hRIqwFyGPZBTuGn92KR74XNfQgKdLZOA9_ lE4KFBc7cRlX57c5eCgFPz3B3G0ogArwDl_v5Pflf5yXRNlEPAOGquBhcYrVOE6_ SsGxqolevLXE5fzJdvRtLFqYiFvDGoO0j6D1tLHT.
9 Jansen, *Leading for Change*, 17.
10 J. D. Jansen, 'Why We're Withdrawing Charges against Reitz Four', *Politicsweb*, 18 October 2009, https://www.politicsweb.co.za/news-and-analysis/why-were-withdrawing-charges-against-reitz-four--j. For a faithful telling of the Reitz story (including timeline) and outcome, see J. Taylor, 'A Qualitative Exploration of the Reitz Reconciliation Process as an Exercise in Restorative Justice' (University of the Free State, MA dissertation, 2014).
11 M. Ndletyana and D. A. Webb, 'Social Divisions Carved in Stone or Cenotaphs to a New Identity? Policy for Memorials, Monuments and Statues in a Democratic South Africa', *International Journal of Heritage Studies* 23, 2 (2017): 97–110.
12 C. E. Holmes and M. Loehwing, 'Icons of the Old Regime: Challenging South African Public Memory Strategies in #RhodesMustFall', *Journal of Southern African Studies* 42, 6 (2016): 1207–23 (1207).
13 F. H. Beer, *Emily Hobhouse: The Angel of Love* (London: Charaton Books, 2002).
14 For more on Hobhouse's early life, see E. Brits, *Emily Hobhouse: Beloved Traitor* (Cape Town: Tafelberg, 2016). For more on the expectations/confines within which Vicwardian 'spinsters' were expected to live, see K. Holden, ' "Showing Them How": The Cultural Reproduction of Ideas about Spinsterhood in Interwar England', *Women's History Review* 20, 4 (2011): 663–72.
15 See, for instance, R. Gill and C. Muller, 'The Limits of Agency: Emily Hobhouse's International Activism and the Politics of Suffering', *Safundi* 19, 1 (2018): 16–35.
16 The second South African War, or – as it is still generally referred to by Afrikaners – the Second Boer War, was fought from October 1899 to May 1902 between the two Boer republics of the Transvaal and the Orange Free State against the combined forces of the British Empire. For more on British women who campaigned against the war, see E. Riedi, 'The Women Pro-Boers: Gender, Peace and the Critique of Empire in the South African War', *Historical Research* 86, 231 (2013): 92–115.

17 The British calculated that the internment of Boer women and children – essentially in concentration camps – would weaken the resolve of the Boer guerrillas and would bring them to terms. Alongside this, the British made widespread use of the 'scorched earth' policy, a military tactic that seeks to destroy anything of value – homes, livestock, crops – that would sustain insurgent fighters. Despite the fact that by September 1900 the British had captured both the capital cities of the Boer Republics, the war continued for a further two years due to the guerrilla tactics employed by the Boer armies.
18 Unknown writer (female) as cited in E. Hobhouse, *The Brunt of the War and Where It Fell* (Essex: Methuen, 1902), 62.
19 Ibid., 114.
20 Ibid., 116.
21 Ibid., 119.
22 Ibid., 122.
23 E. Hobhouse, *Report of a Visit to the Camps of Women and Children in the Cape and Orange River Colonies to the Committee of the South African Distress Fund* (London: Friars Printing Association, 1901), 4. Naturally, in a piece of this brevity I am painting in broad brush strokes, for more on Hobhouse's own understanding and representation of the camps, see her book, *The Brunt of the War and Where It Fell* (Essex: Methuen, 1902).
24 Hobhouse, *Report of a Visit to the Camps*, 4.
25 V. Ware, 'All the Rage: Decolonizing the History of the British Women's Suffrage Movement', *Cultural Studies* 34, 4 (2020): 521–45.
26 J. Hobhouse-Balme, *Living the Love: Emily Hobhouse Post-War (1918–1926)* (British Columbia: Friesen Press, 2016), 89.
27 N. J. v. d. Merwe, *The National Women's Monument* (n.p., 1926), 17.
28 J. Winter, *Sites of Memory, Sites of Mourning: The Great War in European Cultural History* (Cambridge: Cambridge University Press, 1995). The figures from the 2011 census are the most up-to-date account of the country's population and are disaggregated by ethnicity, language and household income. White Afrikaners number 2.7 million and make up approximately 5 per cent of the country's population of 51 million. P. Lehola, *Census 2011: Census in Brief* (Pretoria: Statistics South Africa, 2012), report no. 03-01-41.
29 A. Grundlingh, 'The National Women's Monument: The Making and Mutation of Meaning in Afrikaner Memory of the South African War', in *Writing a Wider War: Rethinking Gender, Race, and Identity in the South African War, 1899–1902*, ed. G. Cuthbertson, A. Grundlingh and M.-L. Suttie (Ohio: Ohio University Press, 2002), 18–36 (26).
30 Grundlingh, 'The National Women's Monument', 31.
31 As cited in N. J. v. d. Merwe, *The National Women's Monument*, 48.
32 A. McClintock, '"No Longer in a Future Heaven": Women and Nationalism in South Africa', *Transition* 51 (1991): 104–23 (110).
33 For more on the experiences and involvement of Black South Africans, see P. Warwick, *Black People and the South African War 1899–1902* (Cambridge: Cambridge University Press, 1983).
34 B. Nasson, 'Warriors without Spears: Africans in the South African War, 1899–1902', *Social Dynamics* 9, 1 (1983): 91–95 (91). According to Albert Grundlingh, approximately 14,000 Black people died in separate concentration camps. Grundlingh, *The National Women's Monument*, 33.
35 E. Cloete, 'Writing of(f) the Women of the National Women's Monument', *Literator* 20, 3 (1999), 35–50 (38). Throughout this piece I have purposely referred to it as *Die Vrouemonument* rather than using its full title *Die Nasionale Vrouemonument* precisely because of this fact.
36 J. Boje and F. Pretorius, 'Kent gij dat volk: The Anglo-Bower War and Afrikaner Identity in Postmodern Perspective', *Historia* 56, 2 (2011), 59–72 (71).
37 C. Verwey and M. Quayle, 'Whiteness, Racism and Afrikaner Identity in Post-Apartheid South Africa', *African Affairs* 111, 445 (2012): 551–75 (551).

38 S. Marschall, 'Commemorating "Struggle Heroes": Constructing a Genealogy for the New South Africa', *International Journal of Heritage Studies* 12, 2 (2006): 176–93 (176).
39 As Marschall notes, in post-apartheid South Africa, 'the socialist model' of monuments has been rejected, with the country still being 'deeply influenced by Western monumental traditions'. Hattingh's Mandela, therefore, falls into the latter aesthetic camp. See S. Marschall, 'Transforming the Landscape of Memory: The South African Commemorative Effort in International Perspective', *South African Historical Journal* 55, 1 (2006): 165–85 (166).
40 L. Polgreen and M. Mabry, 'In Nation Remade by Mandela, Social Equality Remains Elusive', *New York Times*, 7 December 2013.
41 News24, 'Mandela Statue a "Symbol of Tolerance"', 13 December 2012, https://www.news24.com/News24/Mandela-statue-a-symbol-of-tolerance-20121213.
42 Marschall, 'Commemorating "Struggle Heroes"', 187.
43 News24, 'Mandela Statue'.
44 For more on satanism, 'race' and moral panics, see N. Falkof, '"Satan Has Come to Rietfontein"': Race in South Africa's Satanic Panic', *Journal of Southern African Studies* 38, 4 (2012): 753–67.
45 Kipling, 'The Burial', 1902. Kipling wrote this poem to be read at the funeral of Cecil Rhodes.
46 As cited in Jansen, *Leading for Change*.
47 *Bittereinders* were Boer fighters who fought on until the 'bitter end'.
48 N. R. Mandela, 'Nelson Mandela's Address to Rally in Bloemfontein', 25 February 1990, http://webcache.googleusercontent.com/search?q=cache:I1ex_qlkJ5YJ:https://archive.nelsonmandela.org/index.php/za-com-mr-s-21&client=firefox-b-d&hl=en&gl=uk&strip=1&vwsrc=0.
49 N. R. Mandela, 'I Am Prepared to Die', 20 April 1964, http://db.nelsonmandela.org/speeches/pub_view.asp?pg=item&ItemID=NMS010&txtstr=prepared%20to%20die.
50 D. Posel '"Madiba Magic": Politics as Enchantment', in *The Cambridge Companion to Nelson Mandela*, ed. R. Barnard (Cambridge: Cambridge University Press, 2014), 70–91 (71). Betsie Verwoerd was the widow of Hendrick Verwoerd, former prime minister (1958–1966), who is often referred to as the 'architect' of apartheid.
51 N. R. Mandela, 'Address by President Nelson Mandela before Free State Leaders, 17 September 1994', accessed 23 September 2020, http://www.mandela.gov.za/mandela_speeches/1994/940917_freestate.htm.
52 B. Ndaba and M. Moloto, 'Biggest Statue Ever of Madiba on Naval Hill', *The Star*, 13 December 2012, https://www.iol.co.za/the-star.
53 L. Modisane, 'Mandela in Film and Television', in *The Cambridge Companion to Nelson Mandela*, ed. R. Barnard (Cambridge: Cambridge University Press, 2014), 224–43 (224).
54 For more on Nkandla, see S. Tisdall, 'Public Discontent Rises as Jacob Zuma's Ship Sinks in South Africa', *The Guardian*, 5 April 2016.
55 J. D. Giblin, 'Post-Conflict Heritage: Symbolic Healing and Cultural Renewal', *International Journal of Heritage Studies* 20, 5 (2014): 500–18 (504).
56 C. Aydemir, 'Plastic Histories 2014', *Cigdem Aydemir*, accessed 21 September 2020, http://cigdemaydemir.com/plastic_histories.html.
57 For more on 'Fees Must Fall', see R. Hodes, 'Questioning "Fees Must Fall"', *African Affairs* 116, 462 (2017): 140–50; M. W. Ndlovu, *#FeesMustFall and Youth Mobilisation in South Africa: Reform or Revolution?* (London: Routledge, 2017).
58 'Integrated Transformation Plan', University of the Free State, 13, accessed 21 September 2020, https://www.ufs.ac.za/docs/default-source/all-documents/the-ufs-integrated-transformation-plan.
59 Ibid.

60 Chantelle du Preez, chairperson of Afriforum Youth's Kovsies branch, cited in 'Afriforum Youth's Kovsies Branch Opposes Removal of Steyn Statue', *Afriforum*, 10 April 2018, https://www.afriforum.co.za/en/afriforum-youths-kovsies-branch-opposes-removal-steyn-statue/.
61 T. Rossouw, 'This Is Why Steyn Must Fall', *Mail & Guardian*, 23 March 2018, https://mg.co.za/article/2018-03-23-00-this-is-why-steyn-must-fall/.
62 M. Serekoane and F. Petersen, 'As Statues Fall Globally, the University of the Free State Chose a Different Path', *Daily Maverick*, 9 July 2020.
63 S. Marschall, 'The Long Shadow of Apartheid: A Critical Assessment of Heritage Transformation in South Africa 25 Years On', *International Journal of Heritage Studies* 25, 10 (2019): 1088–102 (1088).
64 Ibid., 1091.
65 L. Marais and C. Twala, 'Bloemfontein: The Rise and Fall of South Africa's Judicial Capital', *African Geographical Review* 39, 1 (2020): 11.

# Chapter Eleven

# RECOLLECTIONS OF THE KING'S HOUSE

## David Robinson

The door bangs continually. A portal conducting the well-equipped and the shoddy alike between the warm haven of the bar and the Biblical deluge beyond. Orderly Dutch and German hikers stand tall and proficient in expensive, pristine kit. Reluctant British teenagers hump unkempt backpacks, complaining at their parents to the accompaniment of clattering, colliding walking poles. They bump against frowning disapproval from chisel-faced and heavily biceped fanatics, practically born outdoors, impervious, for whom a little rain is the least of climatic dramas.

Jack and I hear the clatter more than see it. We are both distracted: he, an errant spaniel focused on mind control techniques, willing the bar staff to throw him yet another sausage; me, one hand wrapped around a coffee mug, the other marking my place in Dorothy Wordsworth's account of her own journey to this place.

Dorothy and her brother, the better-known Romantic poet William Wordsworth, together with fellow poet Samuel Taylor Coleridge, travelled nearly 700 miles through Scotland, in 1803, on a six-week tour. According to John Campbell Shairp, editor of the first published account of the journey, 'poor Coleridge' was 'ill at ease, and in the dumps all the way, stretched asleep on the car [carriage] cushions'.[1] Dorothy records how Coleridge, having been unwell for many of the 15 days he endured, and being unwilling to continue travelling in an open car through regular downpours, eventually left their party at Loch Lomond to make his own way to Edinburgh and thence home.[2] Dorothy and William continued on together for the full six-week tour. Dorothy recorded her observations for her friends rather than public consumption. It was common practice to circulate such private journals among interested friends and acquaintances. That said, it is likely that she did indeed intend for her 'private' journal to be published at some point. C. K. Walker, the editor of the 1997 edition of *Recollections of a Tour Made in Scotland – A.D. 1803*, describes Dorothy's writing up, which she did back home over a period of 20 months, as 'crafting' her account. The very fact that her writing was interrupted and that, despite finding the task arduous, she worked assiduously on it until complete suggests it was more than a simple journal for friends and family.[3] *Recollections* was eventually published in 1874, nearly 20 years after Dorothy's death in 1855. The account won immediate acclaim and was quickly republished in a second British edition, one for readers in the United States, with third and fourth British editions produced by 1897. A fifth edition appeared in 1941 and yet another in 1997.[4] Although less famous than her brother, Dorothy was a poet in her own right. Indeed, in his editorial introduction, Dorothy's editor, John Shairp, asks 'whether the prose of the sister is not as truly poetic and as memorable as her brother's verse'.[5] Certainly, as its regular reprinting would imply, *Recollections* was one of the most popular early travel accounts of Scotland.

As Shairp has pointed out, the Wordsworths came 'at a time before the flood of English interest and "tourism" had set in across the Border'. Much of Scotland was little known to English readers, lending Dorothy's account a 'historic value [...] it marks the state of Scotland, and the feeling with which the most finely gifted English men came to it'.[6] Of course, it was a highly subjective 'state of Scotland', not a vision of the country in which the Scots were given any say. Nineteenth-century travel accounts were not only particularly popular during the period discussed but also garnered considerably more academic and cultural respect, and carried more authority, than does the genre today. As Carl Thompson notes, rather than 'read principally for personal amusement', travel writing was 'a vital medium for debate and dissemination across a broad range of disciplines and discourses'.[7] Indeed, the act of travel itself constituted what Thompson has called 'a conspicuous claim of, and bid for, cultural and intellectual authority'.[8] This idea was hardly new, as Yaël Schlick describes; from Socrates onwards, 'travel and wisdom' were inextricably bound together.[9] Travel writing was a particularly important vehicle for women to stake a claim for greater cultural and political inclusion. Thompson highlights the 'public influence and agency that women might garner from travel writing', in a bid for wider recognition as 'intellectuals' and 'cultural commentators', a process he describes as 'a journey to authority'.[10]

The cacophony of walking poles is insufficient to distract me from the realisation that I sit in the very place in which Dorothy and William had rested overnight on Saturday, 3 September 1803 – the King's House hotel in Glencoe. Perhaps they had sat in this very same spot, warming themselves at the fire after journeying from Ballachulish that day, through 'a mountain waste, mountain beyond mountain'.[11] As they emerged from the glen in their horse-drawn 'jaunting car',

> our guide pointed out King's House to us, our resting-place for the night. We could just distinguish the house at the bottom of the moorish hollow or basin – I call it so, for it was nearly as broad as long – lying before us, with three miles of naked road winding through it.[12]

The lodging must have been a welcome sight. Their day had not lacked drama, and they had found the final push 'the longest three miles we had yet travelled'.[13] Dorothy and William had risen at 6 a.m. and the sun, she wrote, was now setting, suggesting it was around 6:30 p.m.[14] Shortly after leaving their night's lodging at Ballachulish, their horse had backed up,

> frightened by the upright shafts of a roller rising from behind the wall of a field adjoining the road. William pulled, whipped, and struggled in vain; we both leapt upon the ground, and the horse dragged the car [light two-wheeled carriage] after him, he going backwards down the bank of the loch, and it was turned over, half in the water, the horse lying on his back, struggling in the harness, a frightful sight![15]

Fearing their car destroyed, Dorothy was relieved to find help at hand when, 'luckily, a man came up in the same moment, and assisted William in extricating the horse'. After an hour's delay, the two men, 'with the help of strings and pocket-handkerchiefs',

> mended the harness and set forward again, William leading the poor animal all the way, for the regular beating of the waves frightened him, and any little gushing stream that crossed the road would have sent him off.[16]

Strings and handkerchiefs! Rather different to modern road-side assistance and the convoys of minivans today, transporting hikers' luggage between comfortable overnight stops, while their owners walk the next section of the West Highland Way. The muted chatter of the search-and-rescue helicopter from somewhere in the near distance pulls me back from the nineteenth century. The *chop chop chop* reinforces the absence of emergency facilities available to travellers like Dorothy and William Wordsworth, should their horse and car mishap have proved more serious. Some modern travellers only appreciate this point when, having attempted a summit with no water, or in flip-flops, they are recovered, from the mountain and their own stupidity, by the unpaid heroes of the mountain rescue teams.

Dorothy and William's accident might have been sufficient excitement for one day, but in the style of the true no-nonsense nineteenth-century traveller, Dorothy ploughed on. After leaving the carriage to be fixed by the local blacksmith, she took refreshments with his wife and then with the wife of the English manager of a nearby slate mine. The latter, Mrs Rose, offered Dorothy both red and white wine as a morning restorative.[17] Reinforced, Dorothy rejoined her brother for the onward journey but, 'being afraid that if the horse backed or took fright we might be thrown down some precipice', they thought it best to engage a local to guide them through Glencoe.[18] En route, they were drawn to a particularly picturesque mountain and they 'could not resist [their] inclination' to climb it.[19]

Travellers who have spent any time around the mountains of Glencoe know there are none whose ascent is not a serious physical endeavour, and Dorothy's initial underestimation of the required effort will chime with many who have since followed in her footsteps. As she and William 'climbed steep after steep', she realised that the mountains were 'far higher than they appeared to us' from the valley below. Thinking they had perhaps taken on more than they ought,

> I was going to give up the accomplishment of our aim, when a glorious sight on the mountain before us made me forget my fatigue. A slight shower had come on, its skirts falling upon us, and half the opposite side of the mountain was wrapped up in rainbow light, covered as by a veil with one dilated rainbow: so it continued for some minutes; and the shower and rainy clouds passed away as suddenly as they had come, and the sun shone again upon the tops of all the hills. In the meantime we reached the wished-for point, and saw to the head of the loch.[20]

Dorothy conformed to no stereotype of the acquiescent nineteenth-century female traveller, seeking approval from their menfolk for every move. A few decades earlier or later, readers might have debated the appropriateness with which she threw herself into climbing up a mountainside in poor weather. In the mid-eighteenth century, before the Wordsworths' Scottish trip, mountain climbing and walking for the simple purpose of physical and emotional experience was frowned upon, considered dangerous and irresponsible. Early mountaineers used scientific research as an excuse to explore these regions, taking with them primitive equipment to measure temperature and pressure. Mountains were traditionally sites of primeval fear, to be avoided. In the eighteenth century, Enlightenment science and rationalism pushed back against superstition and undisciplined emotional responses. Later travellers subverted the Enlightenment desire for scientific knowledge, the readings from their rickety science projects justifying their exertions while also forming the basis of the science of geology.[21] By the time Dorothy travelled to Scotland, Romantics were countering an Enlightenment narrative that they considered ignored the importance of human emotional responses. William was at the very centre of this movement.

In the decades after Dorothy's journey through Scotland, reviewers in popular periodicals were increasingly critical of the travel writings of women who dared to challenge propriety through displays of independence, or were daring to offer social and political commentary. In a famous 1845 review of 'lady travellers', Elizabeth Rigby, in the popular and influential *Quarterly Review*, wrote that she had no intention of considering 'that more systematic set of [lady] travellers who regularly make a tour in order to make a book'.[22] Instead, the main advantages that women brought to travel accounts were, claimed Rigby, abilities 'created by nature', those 'very habits of order and regularity that make her domestic'. Essentially, the eye for detail and organisation that made Englishwomen such good wives and mothers and 'all that best fits her to live in her own country' were also, wrote Rigby, 'what best fits her to visit others'.[23] This is a subject to which I shall return, but suffice to say that, by mid-century, the reading middle classes linked women's ability to record interesting details of their travels to their domestic responsibilities, to which they were 'naturally' suited. It is also worth noting that women regularly ignored what Rigby and others claimed were the appropriate activities for female travellers and subverted expectations by using their accounts to debate and critique social and domestic norms back home.[24] In 1803, though, Dorothy obviously felt free to explore the mountains and did so entirely for the human physical and emotional experience of the act itself.

Dorothy was captivated by the mountains of Glencoe, which 'we could see the whole of [...] to their very summits'. They appeared, Dorothy wrote,

> more majestic in their own nakedness than our imaginations could have conceived them to be, had they been half hidden by clouds, yet showing some of their highest pinnacles. They were such forms as Milton might be supposed to have had in his mind when he applied to Satan that sublime expression – 'His stature reached the sky.'[25]

Dorothy noted the water cascading down one mountain, 'a rivulet, which came tumbling down as white as snow from the very top of the mountain'.[26] I know, almost certainly, Dorothy was referring to the water coursing down between Gearr Aonach (Short Ridge) and Aonach Dubh (Black Ridge), two of the 'Three Sisters' of Glencoe.[27] Dorothy and I might have shared in watching the valley floor chaffinches picking off midges on their low strafing runs, all zip and chippy earnest across the heather. Following the water course upwards, she may not have caught glimpses of the hooded crows, as *their* behaviour today has been influenced by the changing nature of Glencoe's visitors. With one wing dipped, the crows soar on their reconnaissance circuits. Highly intelligent animals, the crows wait not just for the abandoned remnants of a hiker's snacks but also for backpacks left unattended, having learned the art of burglary, undaunted by the range of fastenings and zips in their way. Crows have been known to manoeuvre backpacks over the edges of precipices, to burst open on the rocks below. Travellers shape not only the landscapes and economies of the places they visit and record but also the very rhythms of life on the mountain.

In 1803, Dorothy would probably not have seen so many crows, drawn as they are now by scavenging opportunism. Climbing these mountains would have been difficult even for someone who was brave and hardy. It was much easier for Jack and me: we had been able to follow Dorothy's tumbling water course along a well-cut trail. It had rained. Highland rain takes as many forms as Inuit snow. That day's came in long, vertical, rods, drifting with the wind, attacking us like sticks of paratroopers defending their mountain retreat.

As we approached the top, the paras gave up and we found what Dorothy had not seen, the source of her 'rivulet', the plateau of Stob Coire nan Lochan, where water gathers in a connected network of small lochans before pouring over the edge. The plateau brings the heads of Gearr Aonach and Aonach Dubh together, the water falling in the separating divide we had climbed, some kind of umbilical between two of the conjoined Sisters.

The path makes the modern ascent to nan Lochan an exercise in physical exertion, rather than the nineteenth-century climb of exploration across the surface of a mountain untamed. Modern mountain clothing mitigates random blasts of foul weather which must have been deeply unpleasant for Dorothy. But my privileged access to the hidden parts of the mountain comes at a price. These mountains have been commoditised, tamed by path and signpost and navigational satellite coverage, promoted by the local tourist board as sites of interest for the modern traveller. What would have been an expedition into a potentially dangerous and unknown wilderness for Dorothy, in tweeds and a bonnet, has been reduced to a few words in a guidebook: 'a stout hike; sensible footwear required'. Having said that, it is interesting to see the degree to which, in the late nineteenth century, the editor of Dorothy's first edition, John Shairp, felt the same problem already existed. Remarking on the increasing numbers of tourists clambering over the glens, 'air and exercise are well', wrote Shairp, 'but the relish and benefit of these would not be lessened, but enhanced, if heart and imagination were being fed at the same time'.[28]

Of course, Dorothy and I are as guilty as each other of projecting our own romantic fantasies onto an innocent landscape. These Scottish mountains were once various land masses which, 400 million years ago, travelled from the southern hemisphere to collide and coalesce into formations as high as the current alps. Their present lower and relatively rounded peaks are the result of half a billion years of erosion. What conceit to concern ourselves with the changes in human activity over time, given the Highlands were already almost unimaginably ancient when the first bipedal hominids left Africa. Dorothy looked up at the same Three Sisters from which Jack and I looked out across Scotland. These old ladies have born stoic witness to the innumerable foibles and violence of humankind. As Dorothy briefly recognised, in 1692, the MacDonalds fled the Glencoe massacre, under the skirts of the eastern Sister, Beinn Fhada. They bore the same rocky visage looking down on the very first travellers fifty thousand years ago. Of course, the Sisters do not care. It is testament to our own vanities that we think they might even notice.

I would like to think that Dorothy's exhilaration on the mountain softened her dawning realisation that their last three miles to the King's House was to be on foot. The previous 12 hours, from dawn to dusk, had seen their carriage overturned and repaired, 13 miles walked and ridden and a mountain climbed. Even an expensively equipped modern hiker might welcome the sight of the King's House after such an exhausting day. Dorothy found the King's House busy and her first impression boded ill, coming face to face 'on entering the door', with two sheep carcasses, 'hung up, as if just killed from the barren moor, their bones hardly sheathed in flesh'. She and her brother waited just inside, impatient to be seated among the 'crowds of men [who] were in the house – drovers, carriers, horsemen, travellers', all seeking to be fed. Eventually, 'a woman, seemingly about forty years old', the only hostess in the place,

> came to us in a great bustle, screaming in Erse [Gaelic], with the most horrible guinea-hen or peacock voice I ever heard, first to one person, then another.[29]

Matters did not improve. The rooms were large but with shabby décor, empty of furniture or furnishings. The fire was inadequate, fuelled by wet peat. Victuals were in short supply, and the Wordsworth siblings were advised by a fellow traveller to order as soon as they could. When supper finally arrived, it consisted of a

> shoulder of mutton so hard that it was impossible to chew the little flesh that might be scraped off the bones, and some sorry soup made of barley and water, for it had no other taste.[30]

Having been initially offered blankets on which to sleep, Dorothy was eventually given some sheets although her hostess, known throughout only as 'the woman', said she'd be obliged if Dorothy might first dry them out by the fire, although its meagre heat was barely sufficient for the task.

It is fortunate for the commercial success of the King's House that Dorothy's review never graced TripAdvisor: 'never did I see', she complained, 'such a miserable, such a wretched place'. It was, wrote Dorothy, in a brilliant turn of phrase, 'as dirty as a house after a sale on a rainy day'; and with its empty rooms, 'looked as if more than half the goods had been sold out'.[31] Of course, large numbers of visitors, with feet wet and dirty from the boggy moor, could hardly avoid spreading their muck, but cue the ubiquitous refrain of English travellers complaining about 'foreign' food, inadequate hotels and poor service. And foreign the Highlands certainly were to Dorothy, almost *other worldly*. She wrote,

> She ['the woman'] and the house, upon that desolate and extensive Wild, and everything we saw, made us think of one of those places of rendezvous which we read of in novels – Ferdinand Count Fathom, or Gil Blas, – where there is one woman to receive the booty, and prepare the supper at night.[32]

Dorothy drew on fiction to make sense of her experiences, for herself and her readers, so alien did it feel to the English, bourgeois, leisured traveller. Through reference to novels well known to her readers, Dorothy conjured images of men of ill-repute and women of dubious moral character, up to no good in scenes of Gothic wilderness.

Dorothy's narrative is driven, mostly, through the dialogue between herself and the women she met around the fireplace and on whom she prevailed to provide her with refreshments and social intercourse. This is somewhat at odds with Dorothy's editor, John Shairp, who discusses *Recollections* and its author very much within the context of her life-long support for her brother, William. Although he offers a biographical sketch of Dorothy, it is William about whom Shairp wanted to talk.[33] This contrasts with the account itself, at the centre of which is Dorothy's confident voice, which speaks little of William, or men in general. Indeed, William's involvement is often reduced to that of groom, leading the horses, attending to their welfare, sourcing local assistance, while Dorothy dealt with the business of the traveller, engaging with and critiquing local society, visiting sites of interest and so forth. Shairp notes how few of the conversations between William and Coleridge are recorded. Other than a poor joke from Coleridge, 'they don't say a noticeable thing'.[34] Despite Shairp's best efforts, this is Dorothy's voice. A good example of women's travel writing that Carl Thompson has called a 'journey to authority', or women seizing the opportunity to demonstrate their ability to insert themselves into public cultural debates from which, by convention, they were largely excluded.[35]

Dorothy depicted these local women as firmly in charge of their environments, and their domestic activities formed the backdrop around which the men quietly carry and mend and attend to their duties in the background. Within their own environment, they are described as strong characters. At the King's House, for example, 'the woman was civil, in her fierce, wild way'. Yet, there was some ambivalence in Dorothy's projection of these empowered women. Dorothy was not ungrateful or overtly unkind but, in their various ways, the women she described inevitably failed. The blacksmith's wife, who was good enough to entertain and refresh Dorothy, was 'slovenly and lazy'.[36] Elsewhere, the inn at Inveroran promised much by appearances, but the food was of poor quality.[37] The waiting times to be served or attended were interminable. At Douglas Mill, supposedly one of the best inns in Scotland, they pulled up outside, only to be ignored. 'At an English inn of this size,' complained Dorothy,

> a waiter, or the master or mistress, would have been at the door immediately, but we remained some time before anybody came; then a barefooted lass made her appearance, but she only looked at us and went away.[38]

At the King's House, to their annoyance, they were left to stand inside the door for a lengthy period. Dorothy had to prevail on 'the woman' to send a boy to fetch breakfast the following morning, only for him to return to with just a solitary egg.[39] Everywhere was dirty and the kitchens not organised to best advantage. It was in these details, Dorothy wrote, that 'we felt the difference' between England and Scotland.[40]

Dorothy's choice of domesticity as a marker of cultural virtue (or lack of it) was no accident. In 1803, the importance of their family structures was increasingly claimed by the middle classes as characteristic of their virtue generally, in a contestation with aristocratic birth as the determinant of social, cultural and political authority.[41] Through novels, poems, plays, academic histories, political speeches and newspaper and periodical articles, as well as travel accounts, Britain's apparently stable constitutionality at home and increasing global dominance was held a product of middle-class values of sobriety, morality, industriousness and thrift. At the heart of this was the middle-class family, where wives and mothers created domestic stability, providing comfort and succour for their husbands, from the rough and tumble of business and politics, and education to their children, to grow up and understand their moral and civic duties. Stability at home justified imperial intervention abroad, as the British brought their civilising 'benefits' to the broader world. Travellers' accounts of the absence of domestic virtue, in the Highlands and beyond, were not innocent or casual observations. Dorothy offers us a microcosm of how travellers create and configure the places from which they report, at the intersection of race, class and gender, where Scotland, England and its imperial territories all sat within a single frame of analysis. Ironically, the kind of domestic discourse Dorothy deployed in 1803 was quickly turned against women, who would shortly be expected to restrict their talents, in theory anyway, to the home and family environment. By the time John Shairp wrote his introduction to Dorothy's first published edition, the gendered vocabulary of travel had shifted. In 1803, Dorothy had asserted her independence in the Highland mountains. By the middle of the century, imperial men were busy 'penetrating virgin territory' and 'pushing into the interior' in Africa and India.

Dorothy's account, which appears to be relatively innocent, if slightly snobby and insensitive, is actually layered with meaning. The differences between England and Scotland were not merely those of idle bourgeois sensibility; they were differences of progressive modernity. Dorothy's were middle-class English standards of domesticity, understood as markers of an advanced civilisation. Dorothy had a hint of the imperial about her. Her conduct had the ring of a colonial administrator or visiting memsahib, plied with refreshment and constant attention, the centre of 'fifty', sometimes a 'hundred questions'.[42] She did not simply observe; she surveilled, recorded, categorised, accumulated, analysed and anthropologised the 'objective' evidence to show, definitively, what the Highlands *were like*. Hers was a reconnaissance mission to help those south of the border to quantify and understand the differences encountered. Written from a position of apparent cultural superiority, and with the authorising characteristic of the writer having *been there* to see things in person, such accounts become empowered and empowering. Dorothy's narrative of cultural superiority and inferiority was the rehearsal of a strategy put to devastating use in the decades to come in Britain's Imperial dominions, where travel writing facilitated, even valorised empire. It turned out to be a short step from observing 'inferior' societies to justifying intervention and control of them, on the basis of the 'civilising mission'. Of course, the imperial mission was also one in which Scots played an important and enthusiastic part. And many lowland Scots also found the Highlands as 'barbarous' as the English described them. As Silke Stroh remarks, there were 'existing Lowland traditions of representing Highlanders as inferior and potentially hostile Others'.[43]

In another colonial rehearsal, Dorothy's fantasy of cultural supremacy had been slightly disrupted by her meeting, earlier in the day, with Mrs Rose, the wife of the English mining manager. Everywhere, Mrs Rose was locally deferred to, treated as 'greatly superior' and 'as a chief in this secluded place, a Madam of the village'.[44] Perhaps jealous of the stolen limelight she assumed due to her, Dorothy noted Mrs Rose 'dressed like one of our country lasses' and 'certainly had no better education' than they.[45]

Dorothy's social and cultural position vis-à-vis the local population of the Highlands is interesting. Relative wealth allowed her to self-fashion as a social and cultural elite in the Highlands, to an extent which her modest financial means would not allow back home. In this, she mirrored colonial narratives that often lamented how many lower-class Britons were able to live abroad, in a fashion considerably beyond their means back home. Such circumstances blurred the lines so clearly demarcated in Britain, of class, prestige and social position, a framework around which the social elite draped their mantle of authority. Dorothy had already set out from deep within cultural and geographical border country. Hailing from Cumberland, she occupied what her editor hints at as a liminal civilisational space between England-proper and Scotland. Between 'the north-country English', he wrote, and 'the Lowland Scots there was less difference of fibre and of feeling than there generally is between Cumbrians and Londoners'.[46] The landscape was set out in gradations of civilisation, from the south of England to its north, into the Scottish Border lowlands and, finally, the wild and unknown Highlands. The Borders acted as the acceptable cultural interface between England and Scotland. As John Shairp notes, Robert Burns and Walter Scott, both lowlanders, 'seemed to call across the Borders on Wordsworth to come and look on their land'.[47] It was, therefore, from an unstable position of social authority that Dorothy proceeded across Scotland. Insecurity, perhaps, bred irritation when the poorly dressed and ill-educated Mrs Rose seemed to usurp Dorothy's superiority in the estimation of the local population.

Parallels between Scotland and Britain's emerging empire are also apparent in John Shairp's introductory comments. He makes the point that, to Boswell and Samuel Johnson, their visit to the Hebrides, a generation earlier, was akin to 'a journey to the heart of Africa [...] a world as strange as any which Livingstone could now report of'.[48] How much things had changed in Dorothy's time was debatable. When their local Highlands guide was able to pick out their path 'where often no track was visible to us', it reminded Dorothy 'of what we read of the Hottentots and other savages'.[49] Dorothy's account is peppered with an assortment of comments in which she assumes a position of authority over a Scotland which, apparently, lacked the same civilised modernity as England. Her party had, she wrote, 'frequent reason to regret the want of English hedgerows and English culture'.[50] At the village of Crawfordjohn, they met 'a well-informed man' whose company they enjoyed, although he was 'somewhat pedantic in his manners', an observation explained by 'the difference between Scotch and English'.[51] Dorothy was 'annoyed by carts and dirt' which impeded their progress, while 'the road was full of people, who all noticed our car in one way or other'.[52] How irritating! Such an attitude might explain why 'the children often sent a hooting after us'.[53] Between Johnson and Boswell's journey, that of the Wordsworths' and John Shairp's comments on Dorothy's journey, Scotland was little changed as the traveller's inferior mirror image of English cultural superiority.

At the King's House, late into the night, Dorothy and William sat while the sheets dried by the guttering fire. They discussed the days' adventures and 'looked out of the window towards a huge pyramidal mountain at the entrance of Glen Coe', a mountain Jack and I had walked that very day, the Buachaille Etive Mòr. Between her window and the mountain, 'the dreary waste was clear, almost, as sky, the moon shining full upon it'. As rain ran down the pane, wrote Dorothy, 'I could have fancied that there was nothing else, in that extensive circuit over which we looked, that had the power of motion.'[54] Glencoe, at night, was not just *other*-worldly; it was an *un*-world, an absence of existence. As I looked out of my own window towards that same Buachaille, what had changed there in two hundred years? Sometimes, travellers move in time rather than geographical space.

Dorothy's Glencoe was an accumulation of experiences far away, a projection of her own fantasies, as much as an accurate depiction of what she encountered. She and William, although captivated by the mountains, were disappointed in the wild emptiness of much of Glencoe and Rannoch Moor. As Dorothy admitted, 'we had been prepared for images of terror, had expected a deep, den-like valley with overhanging rocks'.[55] Her expectations were that of the *sublime*, a literary device that would become associated with her brother's poetry, the excitement of the human emotions through the majesty and the terrifying power of nature. She followed these comments with some lines from William's description of the Alps:

> Black drizzling crags that spake by the way-side
> As if a voice were in them; the sick sight
> And giddy prospect of the raving stream;
> The unfetter'd clouds, and region of the heavens,
> Tumult and peace, the darkness and the light[56]

To mitigate her disappointment, Dorothy substituted William's Romantic imagery for her own unfulfilled fantasies.

The nineteenth-century route between the King's House and Fort William is, today, crowded beyond anything that Dorothy or her brother might have imagined. The military road to Fort William was constructed by Major William Caulfield and his more-famous predecessor, General Wade. Between them, they built the roads which carried the troops needed to supress the Jacobite Highlands in the first half of the eighteenth century. After crossing the dark and remote Rannoch Moor, the 'road' rises up to ascend a ridge in a series of great switchbacks known as the Devil's Staircase, before dropping down to Kinlochleven and on to Crianlarich and then Fort William. The route now facilitates a different type of invasion, as the popular hiking path, the West Highland Way, starting just north of Glasgow and finishing at Fort William. Literally, hundreds of hikers and runners can be seen at any one time on the Way, many stopping at the

King's House for a warm drink or an overnight stay, some to dry out from the rain or take refuge from the legendarily voracious Scottish midges, before the lung-busting climb up the Devil's Staircase. This is why the King's House is frenetically busy today, as Jack and I munch on sausages and drink coffee, respectively. The needs of its modern visitors, hikers and climbers, are little different to those of British soldiers or Dorothy and William Wordsworth in the eighteenth and nineteenth centuries: respite from the climate and the sapping environment; rest and sustenance for the onward journey.

If some of Dorothy's comments were in a tradition of critical English travellers, it was an attitude to which, I admit, I am equally susceptible. I, too, found myself dissatisfied with the King's House. The establishment, today, is sparkling clean, with menus full and prices to match. My problem is not cultural difference; it is the *lack* of it. The King's House menu is the same transnational homogeneity found everywhere. Panini and pizza, £5 for a bacon bap consisting of two slices of bacon on a lightly buttered white roll which tastes of cotton wool, and one tiny sachet of ketchup. From Glencoe to Göttingen, the same anti-cuisine is served up by the regiments of liveried staff that have replaced the soldiers. And like soldiers, the staff are mostly from places somewhat remote, from Ireland, Liverpool, Poland, Romania, rarely – judging by those I spoke to – from Scotland. So hard has the management found it to secure local staff, they have built accommodation to house those they recruit from the world over. There are other problems too. Outside the hotel every morning, staff feed tame deer by hand to the 'oohs and aahs' of iPhone-equipped guests, despite the repeated requests from the police and those who manage deer stocks not to do so. Deer are tempted down from the hills, across the main road, presenting danger to themselves and motorists alike. The deer become accustomed to being fed and come to rely on such food sources. I hear a story about a member of staff who lives in a cottage, on whose door a particular animal would knock with its antler every morning for its breakfast. When the staff member went on holiday, she canvassed among her colleagues for someone to provide continuity of service. The building itself, or rather the original eighteenth-century part of it, has had its character expunged. It has been whitewashed away, like the dust of ages, covered up with coats of 'lilac bland' or whatever non-colour a corporate interior designer has deemed sufficient to remove any possibility of difference between here and a motel chain anywhere. In recent years, prior to a redevelopment in 2018, the King's House was known as a climber's bar, with mountaineering memorabilia around its walls. Even that has gone. I want Dorothy's virgin wilderness and her thrill of outdoor discovery; a bit of that nineteenth-century dirt; to see the drovers; to feel the presence of 'the woman' and hear her Gaelic 'peacock voice'.

Of course, this is my own projected fantasy of what I expect Glencoe to be. I can hardly expect the local population to return to 'quaint' nineteenth-century poverty for my amusement. Nor come to the King's House to do the jobs they have *chosen* not to do. Nor deny young people from elsewhere the opportunity to live here and do the jobs they *have* chosen to do. Were the footpaths, markers and maps removed, I would have no better chance than Dorothy of accessing those high places. I am a reasonably fit 50-something, an experienced hiker and a fairly competent climber at low grades of technical difficulty. The commoditisation of the mountains is the only reason I am able to be here to complain of it. On the face of it, where Dorothy highlighted difference, I bemoan the lack of it.

The truth is, we both seek to justify our senses of cultural superiority. For Dorothy, that of England over Scotland; for me, the idea that I am a *traveller*, not a tourist. We manufacture difference, or at least interpret it in ways that legitimise the projection of our own fantasies onto space and place. In one sense, Dorothy and I revel in our disappointment. It is our dissatisfaction that marks, for us, our superiority. As I muse on these points, to my shame, I reflect that Dorothy interacted with the local people far more than I have tried to do.

The British state came to Glencoe in force and deadly earnest, driving their military roads deep in Scotland's heart. Later, along those same roads, Dorothy and William came as part of another wave, the English leisured classes, curious to see what time had made – as her editor put it – of the 'northern savages' since the Jacobite uprisings of 1745. A little later, Sir Walter Scott supervised the 1822 visit of George IV, its montage of pageantry still largely responsible for the enduring images of 'Scottishness' for the English. As Dorothy's editor put it, Scott is accredited 'with whatever enchantment invests Scotland in the eyes of the English, and of foreigners'.[57] The kilts and tartans of Scott's stage management turned Scotland, in the eyes of the English, from a nation that the historian Macaulay, in 1848, called 'rude and martial' into one he described as bound to England by 'indissoluble ties of interest and affection'.[58] Once-dangerous symbols of Highlands rebellion and savagery were tamed and emasculated, made safe to the English gaze. As well as constitutional incorporation, England reinvented Scotland aesthetically, a 'safe' version they felt they had 'civilised' and dragged into the modern world.

Now I come to the King's House along that same road, the conduit for different travellers. The King's House, the ski centre across the road, the various business in and around the local villages, the more substantial town of Fort William some 16 miles away, even the positioning of the numerous laybys, for coaches to rapidly disgorge and reingest their camera-bearing contents, have all been substantially shaped by the various incursions along Major Caulfield's road. The tourists, the hikers and climbers, the skiers and mountain bikers come to experience the 'real' Scottish Highlands, although it is a space visited, created even, in their imaginations first, and understood by what they have read of it. Glencoe has been invented by travellers of one type or another since the early eighteenth century.

On the Buachaille that morning, I had met travellers of numerous nationalities. One was an American woman who asked me, 'Where are all the Scottish people?' I wasn't sure. 'As it's mid-morning on a Wednesday, they're probably at work,' I replied. She shrugged, accepting but strangely dissatisfied. Perhaps she expected hordes of kilted and sinewy Highlanders roaming the gloaming. I could have asked the queue of locals at the chippy that evening in Glencoe village, who looked, to me, somehow incongruous, out of place without backpacks or yellow and orange ponchos. But I don't know. I am ashamed to say that I didn't speak to them.

## Notes

1  D. Wordsworth, *Recollections of a Tour Made in Scotland – A.D. 1803* (Edinburgh, 1875), xxxviii.
2  Ibid., 117. Carol Kyros Walker, editor of the 1997 edition of *Recollections*, suggests that Coleridge's poor health may have been attributable to his opium addiction, or rather his

attempts to use the Scottish journey to withdraw from the drug: D. Wordsworth, *Recollections of a Tour Made in Scotland – A.D. 1803*, ed. C. K. Walker (Yale: Yale University Press, 1997), 15.
3   Wordsworth, *Recollections*, 1997, 18–19.
4   For publishing history of *Recollections*, see ibid., 23–26.
5   Wordsworth, *Recollections*, 1875, ix.
6   Ibid., xxxv.
7   C. Thompson, 'Journeys to Authority: Reassessing Women's Travel Writing, 1763–1862', *Women's Writing* 24 (2017): 131–50 (135).
8   Ibid., 136. Elsewhere Thompson notes that 'travel was strongly invested with epistemological prestige and civic responsibility': *Women's Travel Writings in India, 1777–1845*, vol. 1 (Abingdon: Routledge, 2020), ix.
9   Y. Schlick, *Feminism and the Politics of Travel after the Enlightenment* (Lewisburg: Bucknell University Press, 2012), 16, my emphasis.
10  Thompson, 'Journeys to Authority', 133.
11  Wordsworth, *Recollections*, 1875, 174.
12  Ibid., 175.
13  Ibid.
14  According to modern data tables: 'Glen Coe, Scotland, United Kingdom – Sunrise, Sunset, and Daylength, September 1803', accessed 10 October 2020, https://www.timeanddate.com/sun/@2652652?month=9&year=1803.
15  Wordsworth, *Recollections*, 1875, 166.
16  Ibid.
17  Ibid., 167–70.
18  Ibid., 171.
19  Ibid., 170–71.
20  Ibid., 171.
21  For the combined history of science and ascending mountains in Europe, see F. Fleming, *Killing Dragons: The Conquest of the Alps* (London: Granta Books, 2000). Romanticism and the 'sublime' view of mountainous regions also coincided with the development of the science of geology: see R. MacFarlane, *Mountains of the Mind* (London: Granta Books, 2003). See also S. Bainbridge, *Mountaineering and British Romanticism: The Literary Cultures of Climbing, 1770–1836* (Oxford: Oxford University Press, 2020); W. Bainbridge, *Topographic Memory and Victorian Travellers in the Dolomite Mountains: Peaks of Venice* (Amsterdam: Amsterdam University Press, 2020).
22  E. Rigby, 'Lady Travellers', *Quarterly Review* 76 (1845): 98–137 (55).
23  Ibid.
24  Katheryn Walchester, for example, explores how 'women writers both manipulate the discourse of the domestic sphere and transgress its boundaries to offer various perspectives on European politics': *Our Own Fair Italy* (Bern: Verlag Peter Lang, 2007), 7.
25  Wordsworth, *Recollections*, 1875, 174.
26  Ibid.
27  The third being Beinn Fhada (Long Hill).
28  Wordsworth, *Recollections*, 1875, xlviii.
29  Ibid., 176.
30  Ibid., 177.
31  Ibid., 176.
32  Ibid., 177.
33  The first 34 pages of Shairp's introduction are devoted mostly to William's life and career. Dorothy is mostly mentioned only in as much as she supported her brother.
34  Wordsworth, *Recollections*, 1875, xlvi.
35  As discussed above, in Thompson, 'Journeys to Authority', 133.
36  Wordsworth, *Recollections*, 1875, 167.

37 Ibid., 182–83.
38 Ibid., 29.
39 Ibid., 180.
40 Ibid., 29.
41 For an account of the rise of domestic discourse from within the nascent middle classes in the early nineteenth century, see L. Davidoff and C. Hall, *Family Fortunes: Men and Women of the English Middle Class* (London: Routledge, 2019).
42 Wordsworth, *Recollections*, 1875, 147, 167.
43 S. Stroh, *Gaelic Scotland in the Colonial Imagination: Anglophone Writing from 1600 to 1900* (Evanston: Northwestern University Press, 2017), 33. See also A. MacLeod and E. Baigent, 'Cultural Perceptions of the Scottish Highlands in Eighteenth-Century Maps', *Imago Mundi* 59 (2007): 126–28.
44 Wordsworth, *Recollections*, 1875, 170.
45 Ibid.
46 Ibid., xxxv.
47 Ibid., xxxvi.
48 Ibid.
49 Ibid., 228.
50 Ibid., 133.
51 Ibid., 27.
52 Ibid., 52.
53 Ibid.
54 Ibid., 178.
55 Ibid.
56 Ibid. These lines offer an early glimpse of The Simplon Pass, a section of William Wordsworth's poem, 'The Prelude', eventually in 14 books and only seen by the public on its publication after his death in 1850.
57 Ibid., xxxvii.
58 T. B. Macaulay, *History of England from the Accession of James II*, vol. 1 (London: J. M. Dent, 1953), 70.

# Chapter Twelve

# OCCUPYING HER TIME: GINETTE EBOUÉ, FRANCE, 1940–42

## Sarah Frank

In June 1940, as the German army advanced through France, Ginette Eboué, a Guyanese philosophy student, found herself in Paris, a city I do not love. Eboué came from an important family. Her brothers Robert and Henry were soldiers at the front, and her parents, Eugénie Eboué-Tell and Felix Eboué, were in the colonies. Unable to flee France in time, Eboué stayed with a distant relation, while she looked for a way to leave and for something to do in the meantime.[1] French historians love Paris. On social media during the Covid lockdown, they regularly lamented about missing their annual research trips and access to patisseries and cheese. My feeling was unending gratitude and relief that I was not stuck in the two-bed flat in a Parisian suburb that had been my home for almost ten years. Instead, I was in a two-bed flat in a village outside of St Andrews, Scotland. Despite having a view of the Eiffel Tower (in winter, when the trees are bare, and only if you lean precariously over the balcony and angle your head to the left), Paris has always left me feeling suffocated. Paris has vast boulevards, world-class architecture and beautiful, curated walks along the Seine, some of which we will visit with Eboué. However, it is in Scotland where one can breathe. Fife has space and colour: fields full of wheat or sheep, dramatic clouds span the horizon and the wind blusters off the North Sea. So, it is from the east coast of Scotland, in the drizzly rain, that we travel from Paris, to the south of France, over the Pyrenees, through Spain and onto Brazzaville with Ginette Eboué. We will experience the German invasion of France, the defeat, the implications of the armistice agreement and the emergence of two different 'Frances' – one under Phillippe Pétain in the metropole and one under Charles de Gaulle in the colonies. As we travel with Eboué, we are comforted with how this new reality contrasted with an imagined ideal of Paris and the French Republic while examining how our personal experiences of place and space engage with our historical understandings.

Ginette Eboué's narrative reveals the movement of a wealthy, young, Black woman through the highly regulated space of German-occupied France. Her father Felix Eboué was governor of Chad, later governor-general of French Equatorial Africa, and the highest-ranking Black man in the French colonial administration. Her mother Eugénie Eboué-Tell was celebrated for her participation in the resistance, and after the war representing Guadeloupe, she brought her feminist and anti-colonial politics to the French Assembly.[2] Yet, despite Eboué's importance, her voice and the voice of other Black

French women are rarely represented in historical literature, which prefers to imagine the French resistance as White and male. Early scholarship on France during the Second World War emphasised the distinctive and regrettable breach of traditional French ideals and Republicanism that the Vichy regime represented. Using mainly French sources, it concentrated on conspiracy, collaborators and resistance fighters while avoiding the darker aspects of the occupation.[3] Until the 1960s French scholarship continued to focus on the French resistance, highlighting the valour of the French who fought back against the German occupation. While the scholarship has changed considerably since Robert Paxton's famous 1972 publication *Vichy France* demonstrated that France had collaborated with Germany out of self-interest, histories of the Second World War are overwhelmingly written about White men.[4] Luckily, recent scholarship has sought to overcome that false divide between metropole and colony and engage with questions of race and racism.[5] Historians Annette K. Joseph-Gabriel, Keisha Blaine, B. Jules-Rosette and T. Denean Sharpley-Whiting have demonstrated the central, defining, transnational roles Black women played in the mid-twentieth-century feminist and anti-colonial politics.[6] It is due to their substantial scholarship that we can understand Ginette Eboué's experiences within the wider history of race and resistance.

In many ways, Eboué's report is not a travel account in the traditional understanding of the term. She is not a tourist visiting foreign lands; she is Guyanese and French living and studying in Paris. However, under German occupation and a reactionary French government, much of France felt like a foreign country. Indeed, many of her comments and recollections describe the discrepancy between Paris, as she previously experienced, and Paris under German occupation. Despite the restrictions, Eboué's background and status allowed her a greater freedom of movement than many experiencing the same occupation. We see this in Eboué's ability to travel across France, including to areas out of reach to the average French man or woman. She goes to visit her brother, a soldier captured by the German army and held in a POW camp in eastern France, as well as crosses the demarcation line, a closed frontier between the unoccupied northern zone and the unoccupied 'Vichy' zone in the south. Her father's early engagement with the external resistance in Brazzaville, Congo, ensured that Eboué would eventually need to leave France. As Covid-bound non-travellers, we follow Eboué across internal and external borders engaging with the imagined and physical landscapes, a changing vocabulary and a sense of movement during a time of both inertia and great change.

Having mobilised the empire and the metropole for war, and after a mere six weeks of fighting, France fell to the advancing German army.[7] While France's ally, Great Britain, led a daring retreat at Dunkirk, the French too retreated into older habits in an attempt to understand the magnitude and meaning of such a defeat. We meet Eboué in the chaotic days of May 1940 just before everything changed. A school student in a prestigious lycee, Eboué and her classmates had spent much of the Phony War in a secluded Fleury-Merogis, 'in magnificent surroundings'.[8] As the news of the war worsened, the school decided to send the children home. Eboué's report conveys a sense of panic and angst as the Germans approached, and she attempted to gather the necessary papers to fly out of France. At the last minute, Eboué's flight from Bourget, a small airport outside Paris, to join her parents in Brazzaville, capital of the French Congo, was cancelled. Devastated,

Eboué's only option was to stay with a distant cousin in Paris and wait as the German army drew ever closer.

One of the difficulties for Eboué and those who lived through the defeat was how quickly the familiar became alien and the future felt unknowable and terrifying. On 10 May 1940, Paris was declared an open city, and the last French government of the Third Republic fled to Tours and then to Bordeaux. Eboué recalled feeling alone, demoralised and worried as the lights and gas were cut off. Gathering with neighbours, these women stayed awake for hours listening to the cannonade, which eventually transformed into the deafening noise of trucks as the Germans made their entrance into Paris. As Eboué described,

> it was a parade without end. Hours passed. Day arrived. We rushed to the window. Just then we received a violent shock; we had just seen the *Boche* flag on the Eiffel Tower. So they are here. Terrible reality. Where are our people? Dead? Prisoner? When will I get news of my parents?[9]

Despite the dramatic change in landscape, daily life and its requirements pushed through, and Eboué went out to buy food for lunch. She quickly abandoned that task when faced with two German soldiers 'with guns on their shoulders and helmets giving them cruel expressions' outside her apartment block.[10] Over the next few days, everything changed. The Germans took Paris on 14 June 1940, and Paul Reynaud, the centre-right Premier, resigned two days later. The extremely popular hero of Verdun, Phillippe Pétain, replaced Reynaud and announced his intention to request an armistice. France had been defeated, and most believed that the United Kingdom would fall equally soon. Charles de Gaulle's now-famous, then-relatively-unheard radio address of 18 June 1940 argued that France could fight on with the empire. Until Eboué's father Felix rallied Chad to de Gaulle two months later, few in the metropole or colonies believed resistance was possible or logical. By 10 July, Pétain was given full constitutional powers in a legal vote. His government became known as the Vichy regime, as this spa town in the southern zone became the seat of his new government. Pétain sought a return to a 'traditional' French lifestyle: agriculture, large families, Catholicism and repentance for the 'decadence' of the Third Republic which had allegedly 'weakened' the nation and caused its defeat.[11] Eboué's place – as a Black woman, a member of the elite and the daughter of a resistance leader – within this new France, built on the symbolic importance of an empire configured on notions of racial supremacy, was complicated, to say the least.[12] Yet, her narrative remains optimistic, insightful and detailed as Eboué takes us on a journey from Paris to Brazzaville from 1940 to 1942.

While researching for my PhD, and what would become my first book, I set out to find the traces of 85,000 colonial soldiers who became POWs in 1940. They were captured with approximately 1.5 million White French soldiers in May and June 1940, the period with which Eboué opens her report. Unlike the White POWs who were taken to Germany, soldiers from across the French Empire – including Black French citizens like Eboué's brothers Henry and Robert, or Leopold Senghor, Eboué's first husband – were interned in camps in occupied France. This zone included eastern cities like Epinal and

Vesoul, to Orleans and Poitiers, over to Britany, and south along the coast to Bordeaux and the Landes. Following the archival trace of these prisons set me on a path which echoed that taken by Eboué 70 years early. I started in Paris at the National Archives and Vincennes for the military archives. In search of more individualised information, I visited 17 departmental archives looking for their experiences in the occupied zone of France. Unfortunately, my limited funding rarely stretched to include such luxuries as rooms with a private shower! In order to save on hotel costs, I often found myself in one of the Paris train stations waiting for the first train to Caen, Vesoul or Charleville. It was always freezing and full of characters you hoped would not come to talk to you. It is through this lens that I read how Eboué and a friend waited for a 6 a.m. train at Gare de l'Est in February 1941. They were going to try to visit Eboué's brother Henry at a POW camp in Charleville in eastern France. I can picture them freezing in the station waiting for the track number to be announced, but my image is of a much more modern Gare de l'Est. As Eboué's train moved east, it was stopped in Rethel, at the limit between the occupied and forbidden zones of France. Armed German guards forced everyone without official travel papers, including Eboué and her friend, off the train. The two women wandered into a local restaurant where they were greeted warmly, while they figured out how to cover the final 30 miles of their trip. In reading this part of the text, my mind's eye remembers the armed guards in the train station and other public spaces, but for me they are obviously not German, but French. Paris has long had heavily armed police officers patrolling public spaces; but since I arrived for my junior year abroad in a few days before 11 September 2001, their presence has imprinted on my vision of the capital. The increased policing in the months following the beginning of the US invasion of Iraq was so striking that it overshadows and blurs memories of travel from different years. Unlike the guards Eboué met, the French police were ostensibly there to protect the locals, travellers and tourists, which, if you are White, you could almost believe. In this way, my images and experiences intertwine with Eboué's descriptions.

Imagining France under German occupation and the Vichy regime can be quite challenging. The dramatic shift in the political landscape accompanied the sights of German soldiers and Nazi flags. A closed border appeared separating occupied and unoccupied zones. Yet, Paris is a city that immediately evokes an image in the minds of the reader, regardless if they have travelled to the city of lights or not. Frequent tourists will recall small bistros they found among the labyrinthine streets of Montmartre, or in the still relatively quiet Buttes aux Cailles, shunning those who queue for the dizzy heights of the Eiffel Tower or crowd around the Mona Lisa's deceptively small frame. Few would know or even recognise Eboué's Paris, which changed almost overnight as the French government fled the capital, accompanied by many of its citizens. She wrote: 'Paris is now deserted and mute. The last few days have seen an incredible parade of cars full to the brim, chariots pushed by those hoping to flee, cats and dogs abandoned and wandering sadly in the capital.'[13] Even as the news worsened and fear took hold, Eboué and her distant cousin did what so many tourists and travellers have done: they went for an after-dinner walk on the Esplanade des Invalides, in the seventh arrondissement. There, among the Hausmannian buildings and overcrowded cars heading south, Eboué was overcome by a desire to flee, but as a nearby policeman advised it was already too late, 'they' had reached Pantin, a northern suburb of Paris.[14] With nothing else to do, the two women returned home and waited. Ginette Eboué's account of the German occupation of France between 1940 and 1942 shows us how daily life was reshaped by a new reality and what efforts were made to create a new normalcy under the strange new circumstances. In searching for that new normalcy, Eboué takes us on a long voyage across time and place.

Travel narratives bring us to different physical spaces; they take us on holiday or walking up hills or taking the train. The passage of time is also different. When on holiday or travelling, time goes by at its own pace, while we ignore the responsibilities of our normal daily lives. As we read travel narratives, we are drawn through each day, as our guides describe delicious breakfasts or dinners in small cafes with copious amounts of red wine. These are the details that we expect in travel writing, to bring us the flavour of a place through the minutia. While Eboué is not on holiday, much of her regular life is suspended until a new political and administrative structure can be put in place, with schools and the economy reopening. Together, we travel not only through different physical spaces, we are shown how the passage of time sped up and slowed down during the first two years of German occupation – an experience which will feel more familiar to us now. March 2020 seemed impossibly long, with new information and rumours of a new disease from around the world researched us in our homes. Many of us experienced a shift in our understanding of time, of our experiences of movement through the days and the weeks, which can perhaps help us understand how Eboué wrote about the summer of 1940. She recalled a sort of frantic energy, the rumours flying (the Germans have reached Nantes, school is closed, millions of people fleeing south, flights are cancelled and, finally, 'the Germans are here'[15]). This quickly shifted into a sense of disbelief, causing the momentum to stop, while the magnitude of the defeat became real. Once the Germans arrived, or national lockdowns were announced, the only thing left to do was wait for instructions on how to live with the new reality.

While not wanting to draw exaggerated comparisons between Eboué's experience of the Second World War and our experience of Covid-19, our sense of normality has changed, perhaps permanently, over the past few months. This comes across most clearly in our sense of time. The news about Covid trickled in: In January we learnt about a new virus in China, but we were reassured that it did not seem to affect children, and only those with 'pre-existing' conditions were at risk. Already conceptions of 'acceptable losses' were being drawn, along lines of age, race and socio-economic status. The world watched as Wuhan locked down, built hospitals, and we started paying closer attention to statistics. Still assuming coronavirus was far away, we condemned 'wet markets'.[16] Mardi Gras celebrations in New Orleans drew almost 400,000 people together to celebrate, drink, dance and watch a parade.[17] That seems inconceivable now. In March, everything changed, and the month felt like it lasted for years. We remained glued to the news, checking in with family in other countries, terrified that the schools would close and worried that they had not yet closed. On 11 March 2020, the World Health Organisation declared Covid-19 to be a pandemic. We watched Tiger King, downloaded Zoom and Teams, went outside for an hour and met our students online. We learnt a new vocabulary of lockdown, social distancing, quarantine, shielding. We saw world leaders divide quickly into the competent and the dangerous. For lucky people, their experiences of food shortages were limited to the difficulty of finding flour. For everyone else, the pandemic continues to exacerbate existing inequalities. Our concept of time and ability to plan for the future remains stalled, and no one knows how it will resolve. As the semester begins again, and we think back on the past few months, those early days of lockdown seem like a lifetime ago. We can go to the supermarket or the pub. In August, Scottish children returned to school. Our normal routines have resumed with masks and hand sanitiser. At the same time, we long for a return to normalcy; the west coast of the United States is on fire; police continue to kill Black men, women and children; and Covid numbers are increasing. The pull between 'normalcy' and pandemic remains political, as workers are told to 'reopen the economy' and to stay home to stay safe. As I continue to abuse the metaphor, one can see (limited) connections to Eboué's France during the summer of 1940. The French Third Republic, under which colonial occupation expanded and the First World War was won, had inconceivably fallen. The decisions made in the aftermath of the devastating defeat were complicated by how quickly the situation changed over three short months. The events of June, July and August 1940 are crucial for understanding the political decisions, military choices and means by which men and women settled into new lives. Indeed, the length of Eboué's narrative reflects the importance of this period, with most details concentrating on these early months, when everything was in flux.

The use of military language by political leaders has created a connection in the public's mind between the pandemic and the world wars. When Americans received their one-time stimulus payment, the enclosed letter from Donald Trump declared, 'As we wage total war on this invisible enemy, we are also working around the clock to protect hardworking Americans like you from the consequences of the economic shutdown.'[18] The front page of *The Guardian* on 24 March quoted British prime minister Boris Johnson telling people to 'stay at home, this is a national emergency'. The emergency being, coincidently, how Ireland referred to the Second World War. Declarations of solidarity, a sense of national pride, nationhood and celebration of heroes were meant to assuage fears of lockdown and school closings and help us through mourning and death. Irish Taoiseach Leo Varadkar expressed pride in the medical community, stating during an 18 March update that 'not all superheroes wear capes … some wear scrubs and gowns [...] we are asking people to come together as a nation by staying apart'.[19] The same day, in France, President Emmanuel Macron declared, 'We are at war,' as he outlined further restrictions to movement. His speech told the French public that 'France has never had to make such [difficult] decisions [...] during peacetime'.[20] So we stayed home; we tried to educate our children while working full-time; we reassured our students that they would be alright while wondering if we would emerge unscathed at the other end. We went for walks around our neighbourhoods, had drinks over Zoom and checked in with friends who were alone. We worried, we baked, we worked, we cried and we stayed home, as summer travel plans evaporated and more and more people got sick and died. It feels important to note how, in the midst of great tragedy, daily life continues whether we are ready or not. When faced with a grave and devastating new reality, Eboué's solution was to pass her baccalaureate exams and prepare for the next step of her studies.

This edited collection gives a unique opportunity not only to travel while in lockdown but also to engage with the question of subjectivity, something which many of us historians find to be uncomfortable. We rarely write in the first person, as it seems to diminish our expertise. In becoming experts in our field of history, we mastered methodology and scholarship, foreign languages, gained insight into reading illegible handwriting and noted which libraries had good tea (the National Library of Ireland) and those which required a thermos (all the others). Less often do we engage with how and why that knowledge was acquired. We all made intellectual choices to study a time period, or region, certain people or cultures. I have been learning French since I was 12, after a much-disliked teacher recommended I take Spanish because it would be easier. Stubbornness did not improve my language-learning skills. My first trip to Paris was during the summer before my senior year of high school. I joined a Canadian study-abroad programme, and we stayed in the Maison Belge in the Cite Universitaire, across from the Parc Montsouris. Years later, this would be a regular running route for me, where I could reminisce about the time we got stuck on an RER (Regional Express Rail) bound for the shed. Eventually an angry conductor found us and led us down a ladder and back along the tracks, while he yelled at us incomprehensible French. More recently, I have wondered why exactly Ivanka Trump had also joined that programme. This was the year France won the World Cup, and we watched match after match on a giant TV in the Stade Charlety next door to our dorms. Nearly four years later, I returned as a Hamilton College Junior Year abroad student. Leaving our small campus housing 1,600 students in beautiful upstate New York for the busy, noisy, crowded streets of Paris was a bit of a shock. Even more challenging was the move from a small liberal arts college, where classes rarely had over fifteen students, to large French lecture halls where the professors actually had to ask the students to stop talking. Still, this was the year I mastered the language and travelled most weekends armed with a 'borrowed' copy of *Europe on a Shoestring*. I also realised, with excitement, that there was more to French literature and culture than Moliere and Balzac. There was also Duras, Malraux. I went to the opera at Bastille – having bought myself a ticket for my 21st birthday – with friends to see M. C. Solaar in concert at the Zenith. With a class, we saw *Et Prends bien garde auz Zeppelins*, a play taken from Guillaume Appollinaire's *First World War Poems*, with little dialogue but including sounds and smells. A few years older than Eboué was, I too left Paris bound for Francophone Africa. My trip was a direct flight from Paris to Dakar for three months of studying and exploring: different people, different contexts, different goals. In this way, the historian layers her knowledge of the past with her engagement with travel writing and own memories of travel within these different spheres, which entangles the different pasts with the present. In my case, I am intimately familiar with much of the landscape Eboué describes. I lived in Paris for over eleven years at different points in my life: as a student in high school and university, then as a postgraduate, first following the footsteps of colonial POWs captured in 1940, and later as a parent to two French children while finishing my dissertation and writing my book in the Bibliothèque nationale de France (BNF). My own path is completely different to the one Eboué travelled during the Second World War. Still, my own travels and intellectual journey provide a sense of familiarity with Eboué's narrative. This volume offers a chance to explore the personal roots of those intellectual choices and to engage with how our own experiences inform our scholarship. Rather than writing with a distance which can sometimes be forced, this exercise encourages, extolls us to explore the value of the subjective and to conceive of travel as something beyond the corporeal experience. By addressing the invisible 'I' in our own research, we can engage in a meaningful way with our subjects' own subjectivity.

Ginnette Eboué's experiences in France during the occupation were as exceptional as she was, and they force us to confront many preconceived ideas on travel, wartime experience and on life under occupation. As a social historian, I am fundamentally interested in the day-to-day experiences: how people lived and travelled through war and occupation. With Eboué's text, we see how these lived experiences can intersect with travel narratives as we move through different cities and spaces. As Michel de Certeau argued, the way we visualise space or cities is often disconnected from the experiences of those who live and walk through it.[21] For example, we can easily imagine picture postcards of Paris centred on Notre Dame or Sacre Coeur, showing tourists milling about. However, those images do not reflect my experiences of desperately trying to push through the crowds to catch the last 47 bus home to the suburbs. For many people, Eboué might be an 'unfamiliar' walker in these spaces – she was wealthy, young, Black, educated, privileged, with extremely important parents and an unwavering sense of bravery. Yet, as Gabriel-Joseph demonstrates, in her masterful *Reimagining Liberation*, Black women, including Eboué's mother, were central in redefining French identity with their transnational, feminist and anti-colonial politics.[22] As Eboué walks across the Franco-Spanish border, her narrative pushes us to challenge our concepts of spatial history, memoir and travel narratives. Leaving Perpignan in the south of France, Eboué met up with one of her friends in a tiny village near the border. At 11 p.m., with three guides, Eboué, her friend and a Spanish woman who had escaped from a French detainment camp began walking across fields, climbing over barriers and crossing streams.[23] They walked for hours in the cold and dark, only stopping to rest at 4 a.m. After a few hours of rest, and later a cold lunch provided by the guides, they resumed their walk through the afternoon and into the night. The paths were treacherous, with the constant risk of falling into an unseen crevasse. Eventually, they arrived at a small village where they slept for three hours. The next day they boarded a train bound for Barcelona.[24] Unlike a holiday narrative, Eboué's travel is full of danger. Indeed, they narrowly escaped arrest by flirting with the military policeman who was checking papers on the train to Barcelona. As Eboué recalled, 'If we had been caught we would have been sent back to France, moved from prison to prison, or simply incarcerated for an indeterminate amount of time.'[25] A few lines later, safely installed with a kind Spanish woman, Eboué returns to more traditional topics for travel narratives: the sights and food of Barcelona – hairdressers, shops, bakeries, ice-cream shops. The next day they reported to the British Consulate for visas and passage to Brazzaville.

As other contributions to this volume have done, Eboué's writing allows us to engage with the definition of travel writing, the utility of a limited or broad definition, and examine who gets to define the genre: literacy scholars, historians or the writers themselves. Eboué would not consider her report to be 'travel writing': but would she have considered this a military report? A memoir? An important contribution to her father's legacy? Or the beginning of her own story? The document is an unpublished one, housed in the Felix Eboué file at the Archives de l'Ordre de la liberation in Paris, along with two reports written by her brothers Henry and Robert. Travellers and readers are shaped by their experiences in new and unfamiliar places. Their writing reveals as much about themselves as people as it does about the locations we read about. People recount carefully chosen anecdotes, revealing a mix of fact and fiction; and historians, aware that the lines can blur, build arguments from a number of different sources. We depend on our expertise as historians of the French empire and the Second World War to allow us to unpick the details in Eboué's writing and be able to contextualise her information so we can declare if her experiences were atypical or meaningful. Students often think that good academic writing based on archival research is objective. However, archives and historians are subjective and often reflect hierarchies of history that determine whose experiences are important, or what history must be learnt first. This is why many French students will know of Jean Moulin, and not Felix Eboué, even though both coordinated resistance activities during the war and were later interned in the Pantheon with the other 'Great Men of France'. How many know the story of Ginette Eboué or other Black women in the resistance? Furthermore, Eboué's experiences diversify our understanding of who the important actors of the Second World War were while pushing back against a binary division between metropole and colony, which Ann Stolar and Fred Cooper identified 20 years ago.[26] As Eboué's report demonstrates, the exchanges between France and its overseas empire, between metropole and periphery, did not just flow outwards from Europe towards the territories overseas. Rather, movement was dynamic, entangled and shaped by a racial and gendered hierarchy. Eboué's and her family – including her first husband Leopold Senghor, who would become a deputy and later first president of independent Senegal – played an important role in shaping mid-twentieth-century France and Empire. Their marriage was politicised and publicised as a symbol of political unity between Africa and the Antilles, much to the Eboué's disadvantage, as she was 'flatten[ed] into symbols of transatlantic agreement or discord in the collective imaginary'.[27] However, first Eboué travelled alone, away from the media and societal expectations, following a complicated path to find her brothers in Spain and her parents in Congo-Brazzaville.

The long (exciting?) narratives on my travels around the francophone world serve several purposes for this book chapter. First, as an excuse to remember a time when I had less grey hair, and travel was an important part of my life and research. Secondly, to show how the subjective is intertwined with the historical. My love of Dakar, which turned into three years of living, working and travelling in West Africa, has fundamentally shaped my scholarship. It was through my interactions and friendships with students and families in Guinea and Senegal that I began to understand the different and complex ways 'former French colonies' lived their experiences of colonialisation and post/neo-colonialism. It has given me a personal connection to the places I study and write about. When researching, we read hundreds, if not thousands, of documents in the archives. We take notes and reflect on the secondary literature we have read, and then we make choices on which examples to use, on how to connect the different threads to shape a compelling and coherent argument. In choosing what to include, whose stories to tell, the historian inserts a part of herself into the scholarship. This is why historiography can be fascinating (if only my students believed that). Importantly, local knowledge can also help push back against the overwhelming tendency of colonial archives to generalise, group and categorise the different peoples subject to colonial rule in ways that made sense to the coloniser. However, it is important to remember that my position and experiences were inherently privileged, and I need to check any assumptions and ideas regularly. Finally, the more I learnt as a historian, and the more postcolonial literature I read, the more I was able to reflect on the problematic nature of my role as a Peace Corps volunteer or a recruiter of students from across West Africa for an American university which would offer very little in funding to students hoping for an American Dream. Even my ability to travel safely in different spaces was due to my incredible privilege as a White person with 'good' passports. This volume, in allowing us to centre the interactions between travel and lockdown, scholar and traveller, Eboué and Frank, should also push us to question whose voices are accepted as authorities.

## Notes

1. G. Eboué, 'Report, Dossier "Félix Eboué"', *Archives de l'Ordre de la Libération* (Paris), 1.
2. A. K. Joseph-Gabriel, *Reimagining Liberation: How Black Women Transformed Citizenship in the French Empire* (Chicago: University of Illinois Press, 2020), 84.
3. J.-P. Azéma, 'Vichy et la mémoire savante: 45 ans d'historiographie', in *Le Régime de Vichy et les Français*, ed. J.-P. Azéma and F. Bédarida (Paris: Fayard, 1992), 26; A. Sigfriend, *Du IIIe au Ve Republique* (Paris: Editions Grasset, 1956).
4. R. O. Paxton, *Vichy France: Old Guard and New Order 1940–1944* (New York: Columbia University Press, 2001).
5. For histories of colonial soldiers, see N. E. Lawler, *Soldiers of Misfortune, Ivoirian Tirailleurs of World War II* (Ohio: Ohio University Press, 1992); M. Michel, *Les Africains et la grande guerre, l'appel à l'Afrique 1914–1918* (Paris: Karthala, 2003); R. S. Fogarty, *Race & War in France: Colonial Subjects in the French Army, 1914–1918* (Baltimore: Johns Hopkins University Press, 2008); A. S. Fell and N. Wardleworth, 'The Colour of War Memory: Cultural Representations of Tirailleurs Sénégalais', *Journal of War & Culture Studies* 9, 4 (2016): 319–34; D. Hasset, *Mobilizing Memory: The Great War and the Language of Politics in Colonial Algeria, 1918–39* (Oxford: Oxford University Press, 2019).
6. Joseph-Gabriel, *Reimagining Liberation*; K. N. Blain, *Set the World on Fire: Black Nationalist Women and the Global Struggle for Freedom* (Philadelphia: University of Pennsylvania Press, 2018); J.-R. Bennetta, *Black Paris: The African Writers' Landscape* (Chicago: University of Illinois Press, 1998); T. D. Sharpley-Whiting, *Negritude Women* (Minneapolis: University of Minnesota Press, 2002); R. Mitchell, *Vénus Noire: Black Women and Colonial Fantasies in Nineteenth-Century France*, vol. 34 (Athens: University of Georgia Press, 2020); M.-F. Niang, *Identités françaises: banlieues, féminités et universalisme* (London: Brill, 2019).
7. Martin Thomas argues that 197,300 troops came from sub-Saharan Africa, 300,000 from North Africa and 116,000 from Indochina; see M. Thomas, *The French Empire at War 1940–1945* (Manchester: Manchester University Press, 1998), 12.
8. Eboué, 'Report', 1.
9. Ibid., 2.
10. Ibid.
11. M. R. Marrus and R. O. Paxton, *Vichy France and the Jews* (Redwood: Stanford University Press, 1995), 30.

12 For a discussion on race, empire and the Vichy regime, see S. Frank, *Hostages of Empire and Vichy France* (Lincoln: University of Nebraska Press, forthcoming). For an excellent discussion on race and empire in France, see S. Peabody and T. Stovall, *The Color of Liberty, Histories of Race in France* (Durham: Duke University Press 2003).
13 Eboué, 'Report', 1.
14 Ibid., 1–2.
15 Ibid., 1.
16 P. Beech, 'What We've Got Wrong about China's "Wet Markets" and Their Link to Covid-19', *World Economic Forum*, 18 April 2020, https://www.weforum.org/agenda/2020/04/china-wet-markets-covid19-coronavirus-explained/.
17 'Mardi Gras 2020 Photos', *New Orleans Advocate*, 25 February 2020. See H. B. Grant, 'Covering Covid-19: How Headlines Evolved as the Virus Spread', *Journalism Institute: National Press Club*, 5 May 2020, https://www.pressclubinstitute.org/coronavirus-coverage-timeline/.
18 Notice from The White House, Washington DC, 'Your Economic Impact Payment Has Arrived', signed Donald Trump, 1 May 2020.
19 'Covid-19 Emergency to Continue beyond March – Varadkar', *RTE*, 18 March 2020, https://www.rte.ie/news/2020/0317/1123774-taoiseach-to-broadcast-to-country-on-covid-19-at-9pm/.
20 '"Nous sommes en guerre": le verbatim du discours d'Emmanuel Macron', *Le Monde*, 16 March 2020, https://www.lemonde.fr/politique/article/2020/03/16/nous-sommes-en-guerre-retrouvez-le-discours-de-macron-pour-lutter-contre-le-coronavirus_6033314_823448.html.
21 M. d. Certeau, *The Practice of Everyday Life*, trans. S. Rendall (Berkeley: University of California Press, 1984), 92–93.
22 Joseph-Gabriel, *Reimagining Liberation*, 17.
23 Eboué, 'Report', 11–12.
24 Ibid., 12.
25 Ibid.
26 A. L. Stoler and F. Cooper, 'Between Metropole and Colony: Rethinking a Research Agenda', in *Tensions of Empire: Colonial Cultures in a Bourgeois World*, ed. F. Cooper and A. L. Stoler (Berkeley: University of California Press, 1997), 1–58.
27 Joseph-Gabriel, *Reimaging Liberation*, 21.

# EPILOGUE

## David Robinson and Gary F. Fisher

When this volume was proposed during the spring of 2020, we, as editors, considered the various obstacles that might emerge during its production. During those early days of the global pandemic, one such obstacle that we anticipated might emerge concerned the very impetus for the project: the Covid-19 pandemic. We, rather naively, questioned whether the effects of this pandemic were likely to be as significant or long-lasting as many predicted. Remembering the outbreaks of bird flu in 2005 and swine flu in 2009 that had dominated the headlines for months before being swiftly forgotten, we wondered whether the Covid-19 outbreak would likewise prove something of a 'flash in the pan'. The thought occurred to us that, by the time of the volume's publication, the global pandemic that inspired its production would have slipped from the popular consciousness and our project lost its relevance. This, evidently, has not been the case.

The production of this volume began in earnest just as the United Kingdom entered its first national lockdown on 16 March 2020. It was as the United Kingdom entered its second national lockdown on 5 November of the same year that we prepared to submit a first copy of the manuscript to our publishers. Besides the hundreds of thousands who have died globally as a result of this virus, the knock-on effects of lockdowns and social isolation have irrevocably changed the lives of almost every human being on this planet. It remains unclear how things will develop in the run-up to this volume's publication. There is increasing hope that vaccines may offer the solution to the world's ills, although many remain sceptical we will ever return to what we once considered normality. One thing is certain, though: our initial suggestion that this virus might end up as little more than a 'flash in the pan' was most definitely wrong.

What *is* certain is that this pandemic has unequivocally changed how we think about travel and travel writing. Worldwide travel has ground to a crashing halt. Here in the United Kingdom, those who might ordinarily jet off to Spain or the Seychelles for a summer jaunt have instead fixed their sights on the likes of Somerset, Salcombe and Skegness. Even short breaks within one's own county have become perilous, with the constant threat of sudden cancellation hanging over every booking. There seems little indication that this will change anytime soon.

With foreign travel unattainable for most, our ability to experience foreign locales will be increasingly mediated through the accounts of other travellers. The cultural memory generated by these historical accounts will be increasingly foundational in generating our expectations of different places. An entire generation of travellers, unable to directly access these places, will have to satisfy themselves with accounts from days gone by. They will have to read Augustus Hare's walks through Rome, W. H. Auden's adventures in Wuhan and Freya Stark's journeys with the Bedouin without being able to experience these places and peoples for themselves.

This volume, in inviting contributors to write accounts of places they are unable to visit, offers an experimental approach to exploring how this affects the literature of travel. By overlaying our own memories with those of our historical predecessors – or perhaps it is the other way around – this volume has called into question the extent to which one can ever truly independently experience a place. Rather, it has demonstrated the significant and inescapable role that cultural memory plays in mediating one's experience of a place. In doing so, it has, hopefully, not only proved an interesting and enjoyable read but also laid some original groundwork for thinking about a future in which we may all have to travel in isolation.

# CONTRIBUTORS

**Ross Balzaretti** is a recent head of history at the University of Nottingham, a historian specialising in Italy, the author of two monographs and over 60 articles and chapters for leading journals. He has visited the quiet market town of Varese Ligure in north-western Italy, almost every year since 1995, usually accompanied by a bustle of busy undergraduates. Ross is familiar with local archives and has interviewed many residents during this field work, but won't be doing so in 2020, because of Covid-19.

**Will Buckingham** is a novelist, nonfiction writer and philosopher. His education includes a master's degree in anthropology from Durham (1997) and a PhD in philosophy from Staffordshire University (2007). He has held various academic posts, including reader in writing and creativity at De Montfort University, visiting associate professor at Sichuan University and visiting professor of global cultures at the Parami Institute, Yangon. Will's novels often incorporate elements of his academic interests in philosophy and anthropology. The theme of 'otherness' is ever-present. This is explored in his book *Stealing with the Eyes* about his experience doing anthropological research in the Tanimbar Islands, Indonesia (also the setting of the novel *Cargo Fever*). An interest in the I-Ching led him to learn Chinese, travel to China and write a novel, *64 Pieces*, that consisted of 64 short stories inspired by the 64 hexagrams. His fiction has been translated into many languages. The children's book *The Snorgh and the Sailor* was shortlisted for the Coventry Inspiration Book Awards 2013. Will's new novel, *Hello Stranger*, is to be published in 2021.

**Jonathan Chatwin** is a writer and journalist, and author of *Long Peace Street: A Walk in Modern China*, which fuses travel and history to tell the story of modern China. His essays and articles have been published by CNN, the *South China Morning Post*, the British Film Institute, the *Los Angeles Review of Books* and Caixin, among other publications. Jonathan is also the author of *Anywhere Out of the World*, a study of the work of traveller and writer Bruce Chatwin, acclaimed in the *Times Literary Supplement* as offering 'the best account yet of the origins of [Bruce] Chatwin's restless mania'. He has discussed his work at international literary festivals, the Royal Geographical Society and on radio and podcast. He holds a PhD in English Literature and has spent the past 10 years studying, living in and traveling through modern China. He speaks and reads Chinese and now writes regularly on the country's history and culture for a range of publications.

# CONTRIBUTORS

**David Civil** is a scholar of postwar British politics. He was recently awarded his doctorate, following on from an award-winning MA thesis shortlisted for a national prize. He co-authored a special edition of the *Political Quarterly*, to commemorate the 60th anniversary of the publication of Michael Young's *The Rise of the Meritocracy*, and co-founded the *Midlands Historical Review*, a journal for showcasing postgraduate research. He is a fellow at the Young Foundation.

**EmmaLucy Cole** is a UK-based speaker, writer, explorer and biker. She is a fellow of the Royal Geographical Society, lectures as an associate fellow of the Higher Education Academy and co-director of the Vicarious Festival, an immersive celebration of cultural diversity through travel literature and photography. Emma has developed the concept of Downward Exploration: rather than traveling long distances and seeing many places superficially, she prefers spending time in static situations, getting to know people and building connections, learning dialects and customs rather than physically covering ground. Downward Exploration is the idea that small details matter: inflections of speech, ways of seasoning tahini, hand gestures, subtleties of gender interactions, how to eat with your hand, even the relative value of TV soap operas! Emma explores, but in one place!

**Gary F. Fisher** has recently been awarded his doctorate for his research on the reception of classical antiquity in eighteenth- and early nineteenth-century America. He has published various articles, chapters and book reviews on the subject of the ancient world's reception in early America, as well as various pieces on literature, history and criminal justice reform, in various newspapers and magazines. He also has several upcoming publications covering subjects ranging from digital learning techniques in modern higher education to Latin American engagement with the classics. In addition to having spent several years as a teaching associate at the University of Nottingham, Gary has held a research fellowship at the Library of Congress and been a research advocate at the Shakespeare Birthplace Trust and the library manager at a category C prison. Building on these experiences, he has recently joined Lincoln College, researching the integration of digital technology into vocational pedagogy.

**Sarah Frank** is a social and military historian specialising in the French Empire during the twentieth century. Before joining St. Andrews, she held a three-year postdoctoral research fellowship with the International Studies Group at the University of the Free State in Bloemfontein, South Africa. She is particularly interested in the everyday experiences of soldiers and their families under colonial rule. Her first monograph, *Hostages of Empire, Colonial Prisoners of War and Vichy France*, explores the experiences of war captivity of the 85,000 colonial prisoners of war who were captured by the German army in May and June 1940. *Hostages of Empire* examines questions of race and gender among a group of racialised colonial subjects (and some citizens!) in exile in the colonial metropole. It is based on her doctoral research, funded by the Irish Research Council, completed at Trinity College, Dublin, in 2015.

# CONTRIBUTORS

**Tim Hannigan** is the author of three books of narrative history set in Asia: *Murder in the Hindu Kush* (2011), which was shortlisted for the Boardman Tasker Prize; *Raffles and the British Invasion of Java* (2012), which won the 2013 John Brooks Award; and *A Brief History of Indonesia* (2015). He also edited and expanded *A Brief History of Bali* (2016) and wrote *A Geek in Indonesia* (2018). Tim has written travel features for newspapers and magazines in Asia, the Middle East, North America and the United Kingdom. He has also contributed to various radio and television documentaries on Asian history and worked on guidebooks to destinations including Bali, Nepal, Myanmar, India and Cornwall.

**Tory Hayward** is a science fiction writer, a publically funded visual artist and a professional science communicator. Before graduating with an MA in history from the University of Nottingham in 2011, Tory studied in Seoul, Cairo and Sofia. She spent a number of years working as a policy advisor in Brussels and Westminster, including a quirky stint as head of electric vehicles for a ministerial department. She is also a wildlife rehabilitator and custodian of a Victorian allotment garden.

**David Laven** is associate professor in history at the University of Nottingham. His principal interests lie in the field of Italian history from the late eighteenth century to Fascism, with a particular interest in nineteenth-century Venice and its mainland. In addition to authoring a number of monographs, chapters for edited collections and academic articles, David has a regular British and Italian media presence, including his appearances on BBC Radio 3 and Radio 4 (*Night Waves* in 2003 and 2007). He was a regular contributor on *Making History* between 2006 and 2010 and featured on Misha Glenny's *The Alps* in 2010 and *The Invention of Italy*. In addition, he was involved in *Turner in Venice* for Channel 5 in 2003 and *Venice* for the BBC Learning Zone in 2001.

**Kate Law** is a feminist historian of the British Empire who specialises in modern South African and Zimbabwean history. Prior to joining Nottingham in October 2018, Kate was a senior lecturer at the University of Chichester, where she taught widely on the modern history program, and a lecturer in gender studies at the University of the Free State, South Africa, before that. Kate's research has examined the relationship among transnational networks, settler colonialism and women's colonial histories, principally focusing on White women and the ambiguities of race and gender in the Southern African region. Her first monograph, *Gendering the Settler State: White Women, Race, Liberalism and Empire in Rhodesia c. 1950–1980* (2016), began the long overdue task of 'gendering' the history of British decolonization through examining how 'liberal' women responded to Unione Donne Italiane (Union of Italian Women), guerrilla insurgency and the coming of independence in colonial Zimbabwe.

**David Robinson** is an early-career researcher and has recently been awarded his doctorate for research into eighteenth- and nineteenth-century British travellers to India and Italy. He is currently a honorary postdoctoral fellow in the Department of History at the University of Nottingham. David has published articles for *The Conversation* and the

*Journal of British Identities* before starting the project to produce this current volume. He was also a co-founder of the *Midlands Historical Review*, a journal to which he has recently returned as editor-in-chief. David is at the start of a new assignment, as the director of a project to stage an academic conference based on the documentary films of Adam Curtis, from which he will produce a book in 2022.

# WORKS CITED

'1851 – Transcript of Piece HO107/1919 (Part 1)', Cornwall Online Census Project, accessed 17 September 2020, http://freepages.rootsweb.com/~kayhin/genealogy/51919.html.
Abu-lughod, L., *Veiled Sentiments: Honor and Poetry in a Bedouin Society* (London: University of California Press, 1988).
Ackroyd, P., *Wilkie Collins* (London: Vintage, 2013).
Addison, P., *The Road to 1945: British Politics and the Second World War* (London: Quarter Books, 1977).
'Afriforum Youth's Kovsies Branch Opposes Removal of Steyn Statue', *Afriforum*, 10 April 2018, https://www.afriforum.co.za/en/afriforum-youths-kovsies-branch-opposes-removal-steyn-statue/.
Ahmad, A., *In Theory: Classes, Nations, Literatures* (London: Verso, 1992).
Albergo Ristorante Amici, 'Albergo Ristorante Amici, Varese Ligure', accessed 16 October 2020, http://www.albergoamici.it/.
Alter, R., and C. Cosman, *A Lion for Love. A Critical Biography of Stendhal* (Cambridge, MA: Harvard University Press, 1986).
Amato, J. A., *On Foot. A History of Walking* (New York: New York University Press, 2004).
Arnold, F., *A Practical Guide to Health, and to the Home Treatment of the Common Ailments of Life, etc.* (London: Kempster, 1874).
Auden, W. H., '"Hankow", W H Auden's Early Drafts for *Journey to a War*', Add MS 61838, Western Manuscripts, British Library.
Auden, W. H., and C. Isherwood, *Journey to a War* (London: Faber and Faber, 1973).
Ault, R., '"Some People Believe This City Has Five Towns" – Families Question if Fenton Has Been "forgotten"', *StokeonTrent Live*, 4 February 2019, https://www.stokesentinel.co.uk/news/stoke-on-trent-news/some-people-believe-city-five-2492949.
Aydemir, C., 'Plastic Histories 2014', *Cigdem Aydemir*, accessed 21 September 2020, http://cigdemaydemir.com/plastic_histories.html.
Azéma, J.-P., 'Vichy et la mémoire savante: 45 ans d'historiographie', in *Le Régime de Vichy et les Français*, ed. J.-P. Azéma and F. Bédarida (Paris: Fayard, 1992), 23–43.
Azienda Agricola Pino Gino, accessed 18 October 2020, http://www.pinogino.it/.
Bagioli, G., *Guida d'Italia. Liguria* (Milan: Touring Club Italiano, 1982).
Bainbridge, B., *English Journey: Or, The Road to Milton Keynes* (New York: Duckworth, 1984).
Bainbridge, S., *Mountaineering and British Romanticism: The Literary Cultures of Climbing, 1770–1836* (Oxford: Oxford University Press, 2020).
Bainbridge, W., *Topographic Memory and Victorian Travellers in the Dolomite Mountains: Peaks of Venice* (Amsterdam: Amsterdam University Press, 2020).
Baker, T., 'A Tale of Twin Cities: How Coventry and Stalingrad Invented the Concept', *The Guardian*, 4 March 2016, https://www.theguardian.com/cities/2016/mar/04/twin-cities-coventry-stalingrad-war.
Baker, A. R. H., and M. Billinge, *Geographies of England: The North-South Divide, Imagined and Material* (Cambridge: Cambridge University Press, 2004).
Balzaretti, R., *Dark Age Liguria. Regional Identity and Local Power, c. 400–1020* (London: Bloomsbury, 2013).
———, 'Fieschi', in *Medieval Italy: An Encyclopedia*, vol. 1, ed. C. Kleinhenz (New York: Routledge, 2004), 336–37.

———, 'The History of the Countryside in Sixteenth-Century Varese Ligure', in *Ligurian Landscapes*, ed. R. Balzaretti, M. Pearce and C. Watkins (London: Accordia, 2004), 123–38.

———, 'Victorian Travellers, Apennine Landscapes and the Development of Cultural Heritage in Eastern Liguria, c.1875–1914', *History* 96, 4 (2011): 436–58.

Balzaretti, R., R. Hearn and C. Watkins, 'The Cultural and Land Use Implications of the Reappearance of the Wild Noar in North West Italy: A Case Study of the Val di Vara', *Journal of Rural Studies* 36 (2014): 52–63.

Balzaretti, R., P. Piana, D. Moreno and C. Watkins, 'Topographical Art and Landscape History: Elizabeth Fanshawe (1779–1856) in Early Nineteenth-Century Liguria', *Landscape History* 33, 2 (2012): 65–81.

Balzaretti, R., and C. Watkins, 'The Landscape History of Liguria Field Courses of the University of Nottingham', in *La natura della montagna. Scritti in ricordo di Giuseppina Poggi*, ed. R. Cevasco (Genoa: Oltre Edizioni, 2013), 204–10.

Baxendale, J., '"I Had Seen a Lot of Englands": J. B. Priestley, Englishness and the People', *History Workshop Journal* 51 (2001): 87–111.

———, 'Priestley and the Highbrows', in *Middlebrow Literary Cultures: The Battle of the Brows, 1920–1960*, ed. E. Brown and M. Grover (Basingstoke: Palgrave Macmillan, 2012), 69–81.

———, *Priestley's England: J. B. Priestley and English Culture* (Manchester: Manchester University Press, 2007).

Beeby, W. T., and E. Reynolds-Ball, *The Levantine Riviera. A Practical Guide to All the Winter Resorts from GENOA to PISA* (London: Reynolds-Ball's Guides, 1908).

Beech, P., 'What We've Got Wrong about China's "Wet Markets" and Their Link to Covid-19', *World Economic Forum*, 18 April 2020, https://www.weforum.org/agenda/2020/04/china-wet-markets-covid19-coronavirus-explained/.

Beer, F. H., *Emily Hobhouse: The Angel of Love* (London: Charaton Books, 2002).

Beers, L., *Red Ellen: The Life of Ellen Wilkinson, Socialist, Feminist, Internationalist* (London: Harvard University Press, 2016).

Bennett, A., *Clayhanger* (London: Methuen, 1954).

———, *The Writer's Craft* (New York: George H. Doran, 1914).

Bennetta, J.-R., *Black Paris: The African Writers' Landscape* (Chicago: University of Illinois Press, 1998).

Bergerot, B., *Daru, intendant général de la Grande Armée* (Paris: Tallandier, 1991).

———, *Daru en ses temps (1767–1829)* (Lille: Atelier National de Reproduction des Thèses, 1983).

Biodistretto Val di Vara, 'Biodistretto Val di Vara, Valle del Biologico', accessed 16 October 2020, https://www.biodistrettovaldivara.it/.

Black, C. B., *The Riviera* (London: A. and C. Black, 1898).

Blain, K. N., *Set the World on Fire: Black Nationalist Women and the Global Struggle for Freedom* (Philadelphia: University of Pennsylvania Press, 2018).

Blake, A. M., *How New York Became American, 1890–1924* (Baltimore: Johns Hopkins University Press, 2006).

Blanton, C., *Travel Writing: The Self and the World* (New York: Routledge, 2002).

Bluemel, K., 'Ordinary Places, Intermodern Genres: Documentary, Travel and Literature', in *British Literature in Transition, 1920–1940: Futility and Anarchy*, ed. C. Ferrall and D. McNeill (Cambridge: Cambridge University Press, 2018), 182–98.

Bohls, E. A., 'Picturesque Travel: The Aesthetics and Politics of Landscape', in *The Routledge Companion to Travel Writing*, ed. C. Thompson (Abingdon: Routledge, 2016), 246–57.

Boje, J., and F. Pretorius, 'Kent gij dat volk: The Anglo-Bower War and Afrikaner Identity in Postmodern Perspective', *Historia* 56, 2 (2011): 59–72.

Borm, J., 'Defining Travel: On the Travel Book, Travel Writing and Terminology', in *Perspectives on Travel Writing*, ed. G. Hooper and T. Youngs (London: Routledge, 2004), 13–26.

Bosworth, R. J. B., *Italy and the Wider World: 1860–1960* (London: Taylor and Francis, 1996).

Bowles, P., *The Sheltering Sky* (Hopewell, NJ: Ecco Press, 1977).

Bracewell, W., 'The Travellees' Eye: Reading European Travel Writing, 1750–1850', in *New Directions in Travel Writing Studies*, ed. J. Kuehn and P. Smethurst (Basingstoke: Palgrave Macmillan, 2015), 215–27.
Breckinridge, C. A., and P. v. d. Veer, *Orientalism and the Postcolonial Predicament: Perspectives on South East Asia* (Philadelphia: University of Pennsylvania Press, 1993).
Brits, E., *Emily Hobhouse: Beloved Traitor* (Cape Town: Tafelberg, 2016).
Broers, M., *Napoleon. Soldier of Destiny* (London: Faber and Faber, 2014).
———, *Napoleon. Spirit of the Age* (London: Faber and Faber, 2018).
Brome, V., *J. B. Priestley* (London: Hamish Hamilton, 1988).
Brown, H., *Life on the Lagoons* (London: Rivington, 1894).
Buckingham, W., *Stealing with the Eyes: Imaginings and Incantations in Indonesia* (London: Haus, 2018).
Bukowski, N. H., 'Mr. Bennett and Mrs. Woolf', in *A Voice Still Heard*, ed. N. Howe (London: Yale University Press, 2014), 335–40.
Burn, J., '"It's Victimisation!" Does this Stoke-on-Trent Town Always Get the Short End of the Stick?', *StrokeonTrent Live*, 10 February 2020, https://www.stokesentinel.co.uk/news/stoke-on-trent-news/its-victimisation-stoke-trent-town-3798803.
Burton I., in J. Robinson, *Unsuitable for Ladies: An Anthology of Women Travellers* (Oxford: Oxford University Press, 2001).
Buzard, J., *The Beaten Track: European Tourism, Literature and the Ways to Culture* (Oxford: Clarendon Press, 1993).
Campbell, L., *Coventry Cathedral: Art and Architecture in Post-War Britain* (London: Clarendon Press, 1996).
Campbell, M. B., 'Travel Writing and Its Theory', in *The Cambridge Companion to Travel Writing*, ed. P. Hulme and T. Youngs (Cambridge: Cambridge University Press, 2002), 261–78.
Carr, H., 'Modernism and Travel (1880–1940)', in *The Cambridge Companion to Travel Writing*, ed. P. Hulme and T. Youngs (Cambridge: Cambridge University Press, 2002), 70–86.
Caschetta, A. J., 'Review: Defending the West: A Critique of Edward Said's Orientalism', *Middle East Quarterly* 16 (2009): 77–79.
———, 'Review: Reading Orientalism: Said and the Unsaid', *Middle East Quarterly* 7 (2010): 78–80.
Casey, C., *Riviera Nature Notes*, ed. R. Cassy (Oxford: Signal Books, 2003).
Casillo, R., *The Empire of Stereotypes: Germain de Staël and the idea of Italy* (New York: Palgrave Macmillan, 2006).
'The Centrepiece of the Eternal City', *Rocco Forte Hotels*, accessed 4 October 2020, https://www.roccofortehotels.com/nl/hotels-and-resorts/hotel-de-russie/.
Certeau, M. d., *The Practice of Everyday Life*, trans. S. Rendall (Berkeley: University of California Press, 1984).
Cesena, A., *Relatione dell'origine et successi della terra di Varese descritta dal rev. prete Antonio Cesena l'anno 1558*, ed. S. Lagomarsini (La Spezia: Accademia Lunigianese di Scienze 'Giovanni Capellini', 1993).
Chaturvedi, V., *Mapping Subaltern Studies and the Postcolonial* (London: Verso, 2000).
"City Infant Death Rate 'The Worst in England,'" *The Sentinel*, 2 January 2020.
Claridge, A., *Rome: An Oxford Archaeological Guide* (Oxford: Oxford University Press, 1998).
Cloete, E., 'Writing Of(f) the Women of the National Women's Monument', *Literator* 20, 3 (1999): 35–50.
Collins, W., *Rambles beyond Railways* (London: Richard Bentley, 1851).
Conrad, J., *Heart of Darkness* (New York: Dover, 1990).
Courtney, C., *The Nature of Disaster in China: The 1931 Yangzi River Flood* (Cambridge: Cambridge University Press, 2018).
'Covid-19 Emergency to Continue beyond March – Varadkar', *RTE*, 18 March 2020, https://www.rte.ie/news/2020/0317/1123774-taoiseach-to-broadcast-to-country-on-covid-19-at-9pm/.

Crapsey, E., *The Nether Side of New York; or, The Vice, Crime and Poverty of the Great Metropolis* (New York: Sheldon, 1872).
Darley, G., 'Going to Coventry', *London Review of Books*, 26 August 2020, https://www.lrb.co.uk/blog/2020/august/going-to-coventry.
Daru, B., *Le Comte Daru (1767–1829). Daru et Napoléon, une relation de confiance* (Boulogne-Billancourt: Éditions RJ, 2012).
Daru, P. A. N., *Histoire de la République de Venise* (Paris: Firmin Didot, 1819).
———, *Histoire de la République de Venise* (Paris: Firmin Didot, 1821).
———, *Histoire de la République de Venise* (Paris: Firmin Didot, 1826).
Das N., and T. Youngs, *The Cambridge History of Travel Writing* (Cambridge: Cambridge University Press, 2019).
Davenport-Hines, R., *Auden* (London: Vintage, 2003).
Davidoff, L., and C. Hall, *Family Fortunes: Men and Women of the English Middle Class* (London: Routledge, 2019).
Deacon, B., *Cornwall: A Concise History* (Cardiff: University of Wales Press, 2007).
———, '"The Hollow Jarring of the Distant Steam Engines": Images of Cornwall between West Barbary and Delectable Duchy', in *Cornwall: The Cultural Construction of Place*, ed. E. Westland (Newmill: Patten Press, 1997), 7–25.
Defoe, D., *The Compleat English Gentleman* (London: D. Nutt, 1890).
———, *A Tour Thro' the Whole Island of Great Britain* (London: J. M. Dent, 1724).
———, *A Tour thro' the Whole Island of Great Britain* (London: Penguin, 2005).
Dickens, C., 'An Italian Dream', *Pictures from Italy* (London: Bradbury, 1846), 107–19.
Doren, J. B. J. v., 'De Tenimber-eilanden, ten zuid-westen van de Keij-eilanden', *Bijdragentot de Taal-, Land- en Volkenkunde van Nederlandsch-Indië* 12 (1864): 67–101.
Drabble, M., *Arnold Bennett* (Aylesbury: Hazel Watson and Viney, 1974).
Dursteler, E., 'Introduction: A Brief Survey of Histories of Venice', in *A Companion to Venetian History*, ed. E. Dursteler (Leiden: Brill, 2014), 1–24.
Dutton, G. B., 'Arnold Bennett, Showman', *Sewanee Review* 33 (1925): 64–72.
Dwyer, P., *Citizen Emperor: Napoleon in Power* (London: Bloomsbury, 2013).
———, *Napoleon: Passion, Death, and Resurrection, 1815–1840* (London: Bloomsbury, 2018).
———, *Napoleon: The Path to Power, 1769–1799* (London: Bloomsbury, 2008).
eBay Italia, accessed 18 October 2020, https://www.ebay.it/sch/i.html?_from=R40&_trksid=p2380057.m570.l1313&_nkw=Varese+Ligure+Castello&_sacat=0.
Eboué, G., 'Report, Dossier "Félix Eboué"', *Archives de l'Ordre de la Libération* (Paris).
Eisenberg, N., 'The Development of Empathy-Related Responding', in *Moral Motivation through the Life Span*, ed. G. Carlo and C. P. Edwards (Lincoln: University of Nebraska Press, 2005), 73–117.
Elce, E. B., 'Cornwall and Kamtschatka: Domesticating Cornwall through Pedestrian Travel in Wilkie Collins's *Rambles beyond Railways* (1851)', *Wilkie Collins Journal* 14 (2017).
Ellen, R., 'The Contribution of H. O. Forbes to Indonesian Ethnography: A Biographical and Bibliographical Note', *Archipel* 16, 1 (1978): 135–59.
Ervine, St J., 'Some Impressions of My Elders: Arnold Bennett', *North American Review* 214 (1921): 371–85.
Esdaile, C., *Napoleon's Wars: An International History, 1803–1815* (London: Penguin, 2008).
Fagge, R., 'J. B. Priestley, the "Modern", and America', *Cultural and Social History* 4, 4 (2007): 481–94.
Fahey, D. M., 'Lees Frederic Richard', *Oxford Dictionary of National Biography* (Oxford University Press, 2004), https://doi.org/10.1093/ref:odnb/39154.
Fairbanks, E., 'A House Divided', *Slate*, 24 June 2013, https://slate.com/news-and-politics/2013/06/university-of-the-free-state-in-bloemfonteins-segregation-how-the-legacy-of-racism-lingers-in-post-apartheid-south-africa.html.

Falkof, N., '"Satan Has Come to Rietfontein": Race in South Africa's Satanic Panic', *Journal of Southern African Studies* 38, 4 (2012): 753–67.
Fang, F., *Wuhan Diary: Dispatches from a Quarantined City*, trans. M. Berry (London: HarperCollins, 2020).
'Farnese Aviaries', *World Monuments Fund*, accessed 7 October 2020, https://www.wmf.org/project/farnese-aviaries.
Fell, A. S., and N. Wardleworth, 'The Colour of War Memory: Cultural Representations of Tirailleurs Sénégalais', *Journal of War & Culture Studies* 9, 4 (2016): 319–34.
Fithian, E., '1897 Vintage Illustration by Edith Fithian of the Actress Sarah Bernhardt in *La Dame Aux Camelias*', *Alamy*, accessed 16 October 2020, https://www.alamy.com/1897-vintage-illustration-by-edith-fithian-of-the-actress-sarah-bernhardt-in-la-dame-aux-camelias-image240663466.html.
Fleming, F., *Killing Dragons: The Conquest of the Alps* (London: Granta Books, 2000).
Fogarty, R. S., *Race & War in France: Colonial Subjects in the French Army, 1914–1918* (Baltimore: Johns Hopkins University Press, 2008).
Forbes, A., *Insulinde: Experiences of a Naturalist's Wife in the Eastern Archipelago* (Edinburgh: William Blackwood and Sons, 1887).
Forbes, H. O., *A Naturalist's Wanderings in the Eastern Archipelago: A Narrative of Travel and Exploration from 1878 to 1883* (New York: Harper and Brothers, 1885).
Forsdick, C., 'French Representations of Niagra: From Hennepin to Butor', in *American Travel and Empire*, ed. S. Castillo and D. Seed (Liverpool: Liverpool University Press, 2009), 56–77.
Foster, G., *New York by Gas–Light and Other Urban Sketches* (New York: DeWitt and Davenport, 1850).
———, *New York in Slices: By an Experienced Carver* (New York: W. F. Burgess, 1849).
Frank, S., *Hostages of Empire and Vichy France* (Lincoln: University of Nebraska Press, forthcoming).
Fromm, G. G., 'Remythologizing Arnold Bennett', *NOVEL: A Forum on Fiction* 16 (1982): 19–34.
Garson, J. G., 'On the Cranial Characters of the Natives of Timor-Laut', *Journal of the Anthropological Institute of Grea Britain and Ireland* 13 (1884): 386–402.
*Generale missiven van gouverneurs-generaal en raden aan heren XVII der Verenigde Oostindische Compagnie*, vol. 4 (1675–1683, GS 134).
*Generale missiven van gouverneurs-generaal en raden aan heren XVII der Verenigde Oostindische Compagnie*, vol. 5 (1686–1697, GS 150).
Geyl, P., *Napoleon: For and Against*, trans. O. Renier (New Haven: Yale University Press, 1949).
———, *Napoleon: voor en tegen in de Franse geschiedschrijving* (Utrecht: Oosthoeck's Uitgevers Mij, 1946).
Giblin, J. D., 'Post-Conflict Heritage: Symbolic Healing and Cultural Renewal', *International Journal of Heritage Studies* 20, 5 (2014): 500–518.
Gilbert, S., *A Club without a Home* (Brighton: Pitch, 2016).
Gill, R., and C. Muller, 'The Limits of Agency: Emily Hobhouse's International Activism and the Politics of Suffering', *Safundi* 19, 1 (2018): 16–35.
Glazebrook, P., 'European Overtures: Rome Revisited: Same City, Changing Perceptions', *Washington Post*, 19 March 1989.
'Glen Coe, Scotland, United Kingdom – Sunrise, Sunset, and Daylength, September 1803', *TimeandDate*, accessed 10 October 2020, https://www.timeanddate.com/sun/@2652652?month=9&year=1803.
Grant, H. B., 'Covering Covid-19: How Headlines Evolved as the Virus Spread', *Journalism Institute: National Press Club*, 5 May 2020, https://www.pressclubinstitute.org/coronavirus-coverage-timeline/.
Gray, J., 'Why This Crisis Is a Turning Point in History', *New Statesman*, 1 April 2020, https://www.newstatesman.com/international/2020/04/why-crisis-turning-point-history.
Grove, A. T., and O. Rackham, *The Nature of Mediterranean Europe. An Ecological History* (New Haven: Yale University Press, 2001).
Grover, M., 'Geography Field Trip to Varese Ligure 2014', *YouTube*, accessed 16 October 2020, https://www.youtube.com/watch?v=8exQqr-xPms.

Grundlingh, A., 'The National Women's Monument: The Making and Mutation of Meaning in Afrikaner Memory of the South African War', in *Writing a Wider War: Rethinking Gender, Race, and Identity in the South African War, 1899–1902*, ed. G. Cuthbertson, A. Grundlingh and M.-L. Suttie (Ohio: Ohio University Press, 2002), 18–36.

Habermas, J., *The Structural Transformation of the Public Sphere: An Inquiry into a Category of Bourgeois Society* (Cambridge: Polity Press, 1989).

Hall, T., '(Re)placing the City: Cultural Relocation and the City as Centre', in *Imagining Cities: Scripts, Signs, Memory*, ed. S. Westwood and J. M. Williams (London: Taylor and Francis, 1997), 201–18.

Halliday, F., 'Orientalism and Its Critics', *British Journal of Middle Eastern Studies* 20, 2 (1993): 145–63.

Hannigan, T., 'The Shepherd's Life: A Challenge to Travel Writers', *Tim Hannigan*, 22 August 2016, https://timhannigan.com/2016/08/22/the-shepherds-life-a-challenge-to-travel-writers/.

Hare, A. J. C., *Last Will and Testament of Augustus Hare* (1903), accessed 16 September 2020, https://en.wikisource.org/wiki/Last_Will_and_Testament_of_Augustus_Hare.

———, *Peculiar People the Story of My Life*, ed. A. Miller and J. Papp (Chicago: Academy Chicago, 2007).

———, 'Pictures of Italian life', *Good words* 14 (1873): 242–45.

———, *Story of My Life* (London: George Allen, 1896).

———, *Walks in Rome* (New York: British Library, 2011).

'Hare's Days Near Rome', *Saturday Review of Politics, Literature, Science, and Art* 39, 17 (April 1875): 510–11.

Harvey, E., and M. Umbach, 'Introduction: Photography and Twentieth-Century German History', *Central European History* 48, 3 (2015): 290–91.

Hasset, D., *Mobilizing Memory: The Great War and the Language of Politics in Colonial Algeria, 1918–39* (Oxford: Oxford University Press, 2019).

Hazeldine, T., *The Northern Question: A History of a Divided Country* (London: Verso, 2020).

Higgs, J., *Watling Street: Travels through Britain and Its Ever Present Past* (London: Weidenfeld and Nicolson, 2017).

Hobhouse, E., *The Brunt of the War and Where It Fell* (Essex: Methuen, 1902).

———, *Report of a Visit to the Camps of Women and Children in the Cape and Orange River Colonies to the Committee of the South African Distress Fund* (London: Friars Printing Association, 1901).

Hobhouse-Balme, J., *Living the Love: Emily Hobhouse Post-War (1918–1926)* (British Columbia: Friesen Press 2016).

Hodes, R., 'Questioning "Fees Must Fall"', *African Affairs* 116, 462 (2017): 140–50.

Hoffler, B., 'Quotes and Proverbs', *Go Tell It on the Mountain*, accessed 20 September 2020, http://gotellitonthemountain.net/quotes-proverbs.

Hoggart, R., *The Uses of Literacy* (Harmondsworth: Penguin, 1958).

Holden, K., '"Showing Them How": The Cultural Reproduction of Ideas about Spinsterhood in Interwar England', *Women's History Review* 20, 4 (2011): 663–72.

'The Holiday Maker in Paris. Sights to See in the French Capital', *Pall Mall Gazette* 48 (September 1911): 397–402.

Holmes, C. E., and M. Loehwing, 'Icons of the Old Regime: Challenging South African Public Memory Strategies in #RhodesMustFall', *Journal of Southern African Studies* 42, 6 (2016): 1207–23.

Hooper, G., and T. Youngs, *Perspectives on Travel Writing* (Aldershot: Ashgate, 2004).

Hoskins, W. G., *The Making of the English Landscape* (London: Hodder and Stoughton, 1955).

Howe, N., 'Deserts, Lost History, Travel Stories', *Southwest Review* 85, 4 (2000): 526–39.

Hudson, B. J., 'Arnold Bennett, Transport and Urban Development', *Geography* 101 (2016): 85–92.

———, 'The Geographical Imagination of Arnold Bennett', *Transactions of the Institute of British Geographers* 7 (1982): 365–79.

Hulme, P., and T. Young, *The Cambridge Companion to Travel Writing* (Cambridge: Cambridge University Press, 2002).

———, 'Introduction', in *The Cambridge Companion to Travel Writing*, ed. P. Hulme and T. Youngs (Cambridge: Cambridge University Press, 2002), 1–14.
Hynes, S., 'The Whole Contention between Mr. Bennett and Mrs. Woolf', *NOVEL: A Forum on Fiction* 1 (1967): 34–44.
Inden, R., *Imagining India* (Oxford: Oxford University Press, 1990).
'Integrated Transformation Plan', *University of the Free State*, 13, accessed 21 September 2020, https://www.ufs.ac.za/docs/default-source/all-documents/the-ufs-integrated-transformation-plan.
Irvine, E. E., 'The Clayhangers: Father and son', *British Journal of Social Work* 12 (1982): 365–79.
'Is Stoke-on-Trent's "Six Towns Mentality" Holding It back?', *BBC News*, 25 July 2013, https://www.bbc.co.uk/news/uk-england-stoke-staffordshire-23163683#:~:text=The%20protesters%20have%20been%20accused,the%20city%20as%20a%20whole.&text=%22It's%20been%20levelled%20at%20us,helped%20organise%20the%20protest%20march.
Jackson, B., *Equality and the British Left* (Manchester: Manchester University Press, 2007).
Jacobs, J., *The Death and Life of Great American Cities* (New York: Random House, 1961).
Jacobs, S., 'South Africa's Ugly Present', *The Guardian*, 28 February 2008, https://www.theguardian.com/commentisfree/2008/feb/28/southafricasuglypresent.
Jamie, K., 'A Lone Enraptured Male', *London Review of Books*, 6 March 2008, https://www.lrb.co.uk/the-paper/v30/n05/kathleen-jamie/a-lone-enraptured-male.
Jansen, J. D., *Leading for Change: Race, Intimacy and Leadership on Divided University Campuses* (London: Routledge, 2015).
———, 'Why We're Withdrawing Charges against Reitz Four', *Politicsweb*, 18 October 2009, https://www.politicsweb.co.za/news-and-analysis/why-were-withdrawing-charges-against-reitz-four--j.
Jeffrey, F., 'Corinne, ou L'Italie', *Edinburgh Review* 11 (October 1807): 183–94.
Jewell, H. M., *The North-South Divide: The Origins of Northern Consciousness in England* (Manchester: Manchester University Press, 1994).
Joseph-Gabriel, A. K., *Reimagining Liberation: How Black Women Transformed Citizenship in the French Empire* (Chicago: University of Illinois Press, 2020).
'Kelly's Post Office Directory of Cornwall 1856, Morvah', *West Penwith Resources*, accessed 17 September 2020, https://west-penwith.org.uk/morvah56.htm.
Kohlmann, B., and M. Taunton, 'Introduction: The Long 1930s', in *A History of 1930s British Literature*, ed. B. Kohlmann and M. Taunton (Cambridge: Cambridge University Press, 2019), 1–14.
Kowaleski, M., 'Introduction: The Modern Literature of Travel', in *Temperamental Journeys: Essays on the Modern Literature of Travel*, ed. M. Koweleski (Athens: University of Georgia Press, 1992), 1–16.
Kramer, M., *Ivory Towers on Sand: The Failure of Middle Eastern Studies in America* (Washington: Washington Institute for Near East Policy, 2001).
Kuehn, J., and P. Smethurst, *Travel Writing, Form, and Empire: The Poetics and Politics of Mobility* (London: Routledge, 2009).
Kynaston, D., *Austerity Britain, 1945–1951* (London: Bloomsbury, 2008).
Labaume, E., *Histoire abrégée de la république de Venise* (Paris: Le Normant, 1811).
———, *Histoire de la chute de Napoléon* (Paris: Anselin & Pochard, 1820).
———, *Relation circonstanciée de la campagne de Russie* (Paris: Panckoucke, 1814).
Lacy, J. W., and C. E. L. Stark, 'The Neuroscience of Memory: Implications for the Courtroom', *Nature Reviews Neuroscience* 14, 9 (2013): 649–58.
Lagomarsini, S., 'Arte religiosa e iconografia in Val di Vara', in *Arte e devozione in Val di Vara*, ed. M. Ratti (Genoa: Sagep Editrice, 1989), 21–32.
———, 'Urban Exploitation of Common Rights: Two Models of Land Use in the Val di Vara', in *Ligurian Landscapes*, ed. R. Balzaretti, M. Pearce and C. Watkins (London: Accordia, 2004), 179–88.

Larkin, P., 'I Remember, I Remember (1954)', in *Phillip Larkin: The Complete Poems*, ed. A. Burnett (London: Faber and Faber, 2012).
Laven, D., 'The British Idea of Italy in the Age of Turner', in *J. M. W. Turner: Sketchbooks, Drawings and watercolours*, ed. D. B. Brown (London: Tate Research, 2015), https://www.tate.org.uk/art/research-publications/jmw-turner/david-laven-the-british-idea-of-italy-in-the-age-of-turner-r1176439.
Lawler, N. E., *Soldiers of Misfortune, Ivoirian Tirailleurs of World War II* (Ohio: Ohio University Press, 1992).
Lawrence, T. E., *Seven Pillars of Wisdom: A Triumph* (London: Jonathan Cape, 1946), 36–37.
Leavenworth, M. L., 'Footsteps', in *The Routledge Research Companion to Travel Writing*, ed. A. Pettinger and T. Youngs (Abingdon: Routledge, 2019).
———, *The Second Journey: Travelling in Literary Footsteps* (Umeå: Umeå Press, 2010).
Lees, F., *Dr. Frederic Richard Lees. A Biography* (London: H. J. Osborn, 1904).
———, *A Summer in Touraine* (London: Methuen, 1909).
———, *Wanderings on the Italian Riviera. The Record of a Leisurely Tour in Liguria* (London: Isaac Pitman and Sons, 1912).
Lees, F. A., *The Flora of West Yorkshire, with a Sketch of the Climatology and Lithology in Connection Therewith* (London: Lovell Reeve, 1888).
Lehola, P., *Census 2011: Census in Brief* (Pretoria: Statistics South Africa, 2012), report no. 03-01-41.
Lentz, T., *Le Grand Consulat (1799–1804)* (Paris: Fayard, 1999).
———, *Napoléon* (Paris: Le Cavalier bleu, 2001).
———, *Napoléon* (Paris: Presses universitaires de France, 2003).
———, *Nouvelle histoire du Premier Empire* (Paris: Fayard, 2002–10).
Leslie, S., *Men Were Different* (London: M. Joseph, 1937).
Levine, B., and K. M. Jensen, *Around the World: The Grand Tour in Photo Albums* (Princeton: Princeton Architectural Press, 2007).
*Ligúria, Toscana settentrionale, Emília. Guida d'Italia* (Milan: Touring Club Italiano, 1916).
Lindner, C., *Imagining New York City: Literature, Urbanism, and the Visual Arts, 1890–1940* (Oxford: Oxford University Press, 2015).
Lisle, D., *The Global Politics of Contemporary Travel Writing* (Cambridge: Cambridge University Press, 2006).
Litherland, J., 'Why Hitler Sent Bombs to Coventry', *The Guardian*, 9 October 2009, https://www.theguardian.com/world/2009/oct/09/coventry-blitz-hitler-munich.
Logan, W., 'Sent to Coventry: Larkin's "I Remember, I Remember"', *New Criterion* 36, 8 (2018): 8–16.
Longman, G., *The Herkomer Art School 1883–1900* (Bushey: Bushey Museum and Art Gallery, 1976), https://busheymuseum.org/bushey-artists/.
Lothrop, E. S., 'The Brownie Camera', *History of Photography* 2, 1 (1978): 1–10.
Lynch, B., *The Italian Riviera. Its Scenery, Customs and Food with Notes upon the Maritime Alps* (London: George G. Harrap, 1927).
Lyon, I. S., *Recollections of an Old Cartman* (Newark: Daily Journal Office, 1872).
Macaulay, T. B., *History of England from the Accession of James II* (London: J. M. Dent, 1953).
MacFarlane, R., *Mountains of the Mind* (London: Granta Books, 2003).
MacKinnon, S. R., *Wuhan, 1938: War, Refugees, and the Making of Modern China* (Berkeley: University of California Press, 2008).
MacLeod, A., and E. Baigent, 'Cultural Perceptions of the Scottish Highlands in Eighteenth-Century Maps', *Imago Mundi* 59 (2007): 126–28.
Maconie, S., *Long Road from Jarrow: A Journey through Britain Then and Now* (London: Ebury Press, 2017).
Macoy, R., *How to See New York and Its Environs, 1776–1876: A Complete Guide and Hand-Book of Useful Information, Collected from the Latest Reliable Sources* (New York: R. Macoy, 1875).

Malan, Y., 'Reconciliation Means Never Having to Say You're Sorry', *Huffington Post*, 3 March 2010, https://www.huffpost.com/entry/reconciliation-means-neve_b_365323?guccounter =1&guce_referrer=aHR0cHM6Ly93d3cuYmVsZmVyY2VudGVyLm9yZy9wdWJsaW NhdGlvbi9yZWNvbmNpbGlhdGlvbi1tZWFucy1uZXZlci1oYXZpbmctdG8tc2F5LXlvdXJl LXNvcnJ5J5&guce_referrer_sig=AQAAAETIjmBT9QxsWgAOLzfRKmR_1zKU7PnU-0hRIqwFyGPZBTuGn92KR74XNfQgKdLZOA9_lE4KFBc7cRlX57c5eCgFPz3B3G0ogArwDl_ v5Pflf5yXRNlEPAOGquBhcYrVOE6_SsGxqolevLXE5fzJdvRtLFqYiFvDGoO0j6D1tLHT.
Malila, V., and A. Garman, 'Listening to the "Born Frees": Politics and Disillusionment in South Africa', *African Journalism Studies* 37, 1 (2016): 64–80.
Mandela, N. R., 'Address by President Nelson Mandela before Free State Leaders, 17 September 1994', accessed 23 September 2020, http://www.mandela.gov.za/mandela_speeches/1994/ 940917_freestate.htm.
———, 'I Am Prepared to Die', 20 April 1964, http://db.nelsonmandela.org/speeches/pub_ view.asp?pg=item&ItemID=NMS010&txtstr=prepared%20to%20die.
———, 'Nelson Mandela's Address to Rally in Bloemfontein', 25 February 1990, http://webcache. googleusercontent.com/search?q=cache:I1ex_qlkJ5YJ:https://archive.nelsonmandela.org/ index.php/za-com-mr-s-21&client=firefox-b-d&hl=en&gl=uk&strip=1&vwsrc=0.
Mangcu, X., 'The State of Race Relations in Post-Apartheid South Africa', in *State of the Nation: South Africa 2003–2004*, ed. J. Daniel, A. Habib and R. Southall (Cape Town: HSRC Press, 2003), 105–17.
'Mardi Gras 2020 Photos', *New Orleans Advocate*, 25 February 2020.
Marrus, M. R., and R. O. Paxton, *Vichy France and the Jews* (Redwood: Stanford University Press, 1995).
Marschall, S., 'Commemorating "Struggle Heroes": Constructing a Genealogy for the New South Africa', *International Journal of Heritage Studies* 12, 2 (2006): 176–93.
———, 'The Long Shadow of Apartheid: A Critical Assessment of Heritage Transformation in South Africa 25 Years On', *International Journal of Heritage Studies* 25, 10 (2019): 1088–102.
———, 'Transforming the Landscape of Memory: The South African Commemorative Effort in International Perspective', *South African Historical Journal* 55, 1 (2006): 165–85.
Martin, E. W., *The Secrets of the Great City: A Work Descriptive of the Virtues and the Vices, the Mysteries, Miseries and Crimes of New York City* (Philadelphia: National Publishing, 1868).
Matson, J., 'Staffordshire and the American Trade', *Metropolitan Museum of Art Bulletin, New Series* 4 (1945): 81–83.
McCabe, J. D., *Lights and Shadows of New York Life* (Philadelphia: National Publishing, 1872).
———, *New York by Sunlight and Gaslight* (Philadelphia: Douglass Brothers, 1882).
McCarron, L., *The Land Beyond* (London: I.B. Tauris, 2017).
———, 'Subterfuge', *BBC*, 25 May 2019, https://www.bbc.co.uk/sounds/play/p07bb836.
McClarence, S., 'That's Enough Larkin About', *The Guardian*, 2 September 2001, https://www. theguardian.com/travel/2001/sep/02/walkingholidays.poetry.observerescapesection.
McClintock, A., '"No Longer in a Future Heaven": Women and Nationalism in South Africa', *Transition* 51 (1991): 104–23.
McCullagh, M., and M. Pearce, 'Surveying the Prehistoric Copper Mine at Libiola (Sestri Levante – GE), Italy', in *Ligurian Landscapes*, ed. R. Balzaretti, M. Pearce and C. Watkins (London: Accordia, 2004), 83–95.
McKinnon, S., *From a Shattered Sun: Hierarchy, Gender and Alliance in the Tanimbar Islands* (Madison: University of Wisconsin Press, 1991).
Merwe, N. J. v. d., *The National Women's Monument* (n.p., 1926).
'The MESA Debate: The Scholars, the Media, and the Middle East', *Journal of Palestinian Studies* 16 (1987): 85–104.
Michel, M., *Les Africains et la grande guerre, l'appel à l'Afrique 1914–1918* (Paris: Karthala, 2003).

Miles, N., '"To Tell the Truth": Locating Authenticity in J.B. Priestley's *English Journey*', *Literature & History* 25, 1 (2016): 41–55.
Miller, D., 'The Importance of China's Nomads', *Rangelands* 24, 1 (2002): 22–24.
Mitchell, R., *Vénus Noire: Black Women and Colonial Fantasies in Nineteenth-Century France* (Athens: University of Georgia Press, 2020).
Mitter, R., *China's War with Japan, 1937–1945: The Struggle for Survival* (London: Penguin, 2013).
Modisane, L., 'Mandela in Film and Television', in *The Cambridge Companion to Nelson Mandela*, ed. R. Barnard (Cambridge: Cambridge University Press, 2014), 224–43.
Moggach, D., 'Arnold Bennett', *Great Lives*, 29 April 2014, https://www.bbc.co.uk/sounds/play/b041xdgm.
Morand, B., *Pierre Daru, 1767–1829. Intendant général de la Grande Armée* (Villargoix: M.-F. Royer-Daru, 1993).
Moreno, D., *Dal documento al terreno. Storia e archeologia dei sistemi agro-silvo-pastorali. Attualità di una proposta storica* (Genoa: Genova University Press, 2019).
———, 'Escaping from "Landscape". The Historical and Environmental Identification of Local Land-Management Practices in the Post-Medieval Ligurian Mountains', in *Ligurian Landscapes*, ed. R. Balzaretti, M. Pearce and C. Watkins (London: Accordia, 2004), 129–40.
Morgan, T., *Maugham* (New York: Simon and Schuster, 1980).
Morris, D., 'Towards a New Knowledge Economy', in *Revival of a City: Coventry in a Globalising World*, ed. J. Begley, T. Donnelly, D. Jarvis and P. Sissons (London: Palgrave Macmillan, 2019), 229–54.
Morton, H. V., *In Search of England* (London: Marshalsea Press, 1927).
'Morvah Documents', *West Penwith Resources*, accessed 17 September 2020, https://west-penwith.org.uk/morvah.htm.
'Mr. Augustus Hare as a Gossip', *The Sketch* 16, 206 (1897): 438.
Muir, E., 'Leopold von Ranke, His Library, and the Shaping of Historical Evidence', *Syracuse University Library Associates Courier* 22, 1 (1987): 3–10.
Mullen, R., and R. Munsen, *'The Smell of the Continent': The British Discover Europe 1814–1914* (London: Pan Macmillan, 2009).
Murray, B. H., and M. Hughes, *Travel Writing, Visual Culture, and Form, 1760–1900* (Basingstoke: Palgrave Macmillan, 2016).
Murray, W., *City of the Soul: A Walk in Rome* (New York: Crown Journeys, 2003).
de Nanteuil, H. d. L. B., *Le Comte Daru ou l'Administration militaire sous la Revolution et l'Empire* (Paris: J. Peyronnet and Cie, 1966).
Nash, G., 'Politics, Aesthetics and Quest in British Travel Writing on the Middle East', in *Travel Writing in the Nineteenth Century*, ed. T. Youngs (London: Anthem Press, 2006), 55–70.
Nasson, B., 'Warriors without Spears: Africans in the South African War, 1899–1902', *Social Dynamics* 9, 1 (1983): 91–95.
Ndaba, B., and M. Moloto, 'Biggest Statue Ever of Madiba on Naval Hill', *The Star*, 13 December 2012, https://www.iol.co.za/the-star.
Ndletyana, M., and D. A. Webb, 'Social Divisions Carved in Stone or Cenotaphs to a New Identity? Policy for Memorials, Monuments and Statues in a Democratic South Africa', *International Journal of Heritage Studies* 23, 2 (2017): 97–110.
Ndlovu, M. W., *#FeesMustFall and Youth Mobilisation in South Africa: Reform or Revolution?* (London: Routledge, 2017).
*Nelson's Guide to the City of New York and Its Neighbourhood* (London: T. Nelson, 1858).
Nevi, P. d., *Viaggio senza ritorno. Documenti, volti e testimonianze d'emigrazione in Val Di Vara* (Val di Vara: Centro Studi Val di Vara, 1989).
*New York Times Book Review*, 20 April 1930, 7.
News24, 'Mandela Statue a "Symbol of Tolerance"', 13 December 2012, https://www.news24.com/News24/Mandela-statue-a-symbol-of-tolerance-20121213.

Niang, M.-F., *Identités françaises: banlieues, féminités et universalisme* (London: Brill, 2019).
Nicholas, S., '"Sly Demagogues" and Wartime Radio: J. B. Priestley and the BBC', *Twentieth Century British History* 6, 3 (1995): 247–66.
Nochlin, L., 'The Imaginary Orient', *Art in America* (May 1983): 118–31, 187–91.
North, J., *Literary Criticism: A Concise Political History* (Cambridge: Harvard University Press, 2017).
Norwich, J. J., *Paradise of Cities. Nineteenth-Century Venice Seen through Foreign Eyes* (London: Viking, 2003).
'Nous sommes en guerre: le verbatim du discours d'Emmanuel Macron', *Le Monde*, 16 March 2020, https://www.lemonde.fr/politique/article/2020/03/16/nous-sommes-en-guerre-retrouvez-le-discours-de-macron-pour-lutter-contre-le-coronavirus_6033314_823448.html.
Nussbaum, M. C., *Love's Knowledge: Essays on Philosophy and Literature* (Oxford: Oxford University Press, 1990).
Oliphant, L., *Narrative of the Earl of Elgin's Mission to China and Japan in the Years 1857, '58, '59*, vol. 2 (Edinburgh: William Blackwood and Sons, 1859).
Ordnance Survey, 'Cornwall LXVII.7 (Morvah; St Just in Penwith)', OS 25 Inch England and Wales, *National Library of Scotland*, https://maps.nls.uk/view/105995917.
Orwell, G., *Inside the Whale, a Selection of Essays also Containing 'Charles Dickens' and 'Boys' Weeklies'* (London: Victor Gollancz, 1940), https://www.orwellfoundation.com/the-orwell-foundation/orwell/essays-and-other-works/inside-the-whale/.
———, 'Review: J. B. Priestley, *Angel Pavement* (1930)', in *Seeing Things as They Are: Selected Journalism and Other Writings*, ed. P. Davison (London: Harvill Secker, 2014).
———, *The Road to Wigan Pier* (London: Penguin Classics, 2001).
Overy, R., *The Morbid Age: Britain Between the Wars* (London: Penguin, 2009).
*Pall Mall Gazette* 35 (June 1905).
Pannell, S., 'Travelling to Other Worlds: Narratives of Headhunting, Appropriation and the Other in the "Eastern Archipelago"', *Oceania* 62 (1992): 162–78.
Pantsov, A. V., and S. I. Levine, *Mao: The Real Story* (New York: Simon and Schuster, 2012).
Paxton, R. O., *Vichy France: Old Guard and New Order 1940–1944* (New York: Columbia University Press, 2001).
Peabody, S., and T. Stovall, *The Color of Liberty, Histories of Race in France* (Durham: Duke University Press 2003).
Pemble, J., *The Mediterranean Passion: Victorians and Edwardians in the South* (Oxford: Oxford University Press, 1988).
Piana, P., C. Watkins and R. Balzaretti, 'Art and Landscape History: British Artists in Nineteenth-Century Val d'Aosta (NW Italy)', *Landscape History* 39, 2 (2018): 91–108.
———, 'The Palm Landscapes of the Italian Riviera', *Landscapes* 19, 1 (2018): 43–65.
———, '"Saved from the Sordid Axe": Representation and Understanding of Pine Trees by English Visitors to Italy in the Eighteenth and Nineteenth Century', *Landscape History* 37, 2 (2016): 35–56.
———, 'Transport, Modernity and Rural Landscapes in Nineteenth Century Liguria', *Rural History* 29, 2 (2018): 167–93.
Piette, A., 'Childhood Wiped Out: Larkin, His Father, and the Bombing of Coventry', *English* 62, 238 (2013): 230–47.
Polgreen, L., and M. Mabry, 'In Nation Remade by Mandela, Social Equality Remains Elusive', *New York Times*, 7 December 2013.
Posel, D., '"Madiba Magic": Politics as Enchantment', in *The Cambridge Companion to Nelson Mandela*, ed. R. Barnard (Cambridge: Cambridge University Press, 2014), 70–91.
Potter, J., 'H. L. Mencken and Arnold Bennett', *Menckenmania* 130 (1994): 1–5.
Pozzi, L., and D. R. Fariñas, 'The Heat-Wave of 1911. A Largely Ignored Trend Reversal in the Italian and Spanish Transition?', *Annales de démographie historique* 2, 120 (2010): 147–78.
Pratchett, T., *A Hat Full of Sky* (New York: HarperCollins, 2004).

Pratt, M. L., *Imperial Eyes: Travel Writing and Transculturation* (Abingdon: Routledge, 2008).
Priestley, J. B., *The Good Companions* (London: Harper and Brothers, 1929).
———, 'Modern English Novelists: Arnold Bennett', *English Journal* 14 (1925): 261–68.
Pryce, L., *Revolutionary Ride: On the Road in Search of the Real Iran* (London: Nicholas Brealey, 2017).
Raggio, O., 'Social Relations and Control of Resources in an Area of Transit: Eastern Liguria, Sixteenth to Seventeenth Centuries', in *Domestic Strategies: Work and Family in France and Italy 1600–1800*, ed. S. Woolf (Cambridge: Cambridge University Press, 1991), 20–42.
Raiteri, R., *Trasformazioni dell'ambiente costruito. La diffusione della sostenibilità* (Rome: Gangemi editore, 2003).
'Review: *Clayhanger*', *North American Review* 192 (1910): 849–51.
'Review: *The Zenana*', *Oriental Herald and Journal of General Literature* 13 (1827): 499–510.
Riedi, E., 'The Women Pro-Boers: Gender, Peace and the Critique of Empire in the South African War', *Historical Research* 86, 231 (2013): 92–115.
Rigby, E., 'Lady Travellers', *Quarterly Review* 76 (1845): 98–137.
Riis, J., *How the Other Half Lives* (New York: Charles Scribner's Sons, 1890).
Roberts, A., *Napoleon the Great* (London: Penguin, 2015).
Robinson, J., *Wayward Women: A Guide to Women Travellers* (Oxford: Oxford University Press, 1991).
———, *Unsuitable for Ladies: An Anthology of Women Travellers* (Oxford: Oxford University Press, 2001).
Romanin, S., *Storia documentata di Venezia* (Venice: Naratovich, 1853–64).
Roque, R., *Headhunting and Colonialism: Anthropology and the Circulation of Human Skulls in the Portuguese Empire, 1870–1930* (London: Palgrave, 2010).
Rossouw, T., 'This Is Why Steyn Must Fall', *Mail & Guardian*, 23 March 2018, https://mg.co.za/article/2018-03-23-00-this-is-why-steyn-must-fall/.
Rowe, W. T., *Hankow: Commerce and Society in a Chinese City, 1796–1889* (Stanford: Stanford University Press, 1984).
*The Royal Academy Summer Exhibition: A Chronicle, 1769–2018* (London: William Clowes and Sons, 1894), https://chronicle250.com/1894#catalogue=~.%20Edith%20Fithian.
Said, E., *Orientalism* (New York: Vintage Books, 1979).
Saloman, R., 'Arnold Bennett's Hotels', *Twentieth Century Literature* 58 (2012): 1–25.
Schapper, A., 'Build the Wall: Village Fortification, Its Timing and Triggers in Southern Maluku, Indonesia', *Indonesia and the Malay World* 47, 138 (2019): 220–51.
Schlick, Y., *Feminism and the Politics of Travel after the Enlightenment* (Lewisburg: Bucknell University Press, 2012).
Schweizer, B., *Radicals on the Road: The Politics of English Travel Writing in the 1930s* (London: University of Virginia Press, 2001).
Scott, W., *The Riviera* (London: A. and C. Black, 1907).
Serekoane, M., and F. Petersen, 'As Statues Fall Globally, the University of the Free State Chose a Different Path', *Daily Maverick*, 9 July 2020.
Sharpley-Whiting, T. D., *Negritude Women* (Minneapolis: University of Minnesota Press, 2002).
Sharrock, D., 'The Road to Wigan Pier, 75 Years On', *The Guardian*, 20 February 2011, www.theguardian.com/books/2011/feb/20/orwell-wigan-pier-75-years.
Sigfriend, A., *Du IIIe au Ve Republique* (Paris: Editions Grasset, 1956).
Simon, T., *Jupiter's Travels* (London: Penguin Books, 1980).
Sismondi, J. C. L. S. d., *Histoire des français* (18 vols; Paris: Treuttel et Würtz, 1821–44).
———, *Histoire des républiques italiennes du moyen âge* (8 vols; Zurich: Henri Gessner, 1807–1809; 16 vols, Paris – vols 1–8, Henri Nicolle, 1809; vols 9–16, Treuttel et Würtz, 1809–16).
Smethurst, P., *Travel Writing and the Natural World, 1768–1840* (Basingstoke: Palgrave Macmillan, 2012).
Smith, A., 'Under the War on Terror Egypt Is Ethnically Cleansing the Sinai Bedouin', *Middle East Monitor*, 7 August 2019, https://www.middleeastmonitor.com/20190807-under-the-war-on-terror-egypt-is-ethnically-cleansing-the-sinai-bedouin/.

Smith, J., 'Vexed Varsity's New Broom', *Saturday Star*, 17 October 2009.
Smith, M. H., *Sunshine and Shadow in New York* (Hartford: J. B. Burr, 1868).
*Società Ligure di Storia Patria*, accessed 18 October 2020, https://www.storiapatriagenova.it/Default.aspx.
'A Sonnet by Browning', *Century Magazine* 27, 4 (1884): 640.
Soudien, C., 'Who Takes Responsibility for the "Reitz Four"? Puzzling Our Way through Higher Education Transformation in South Africa', *South African Journal of Science* 106, 9–10 (2010): 1–4.
Spivak, G., 'Three Women's Texts and a Critique of Imperialism', in *'Race,' Writing, and Difference*, ed. H. L. Gates (Chicago: University of Chicago Press, 1985), 262–81.
Staël, A.-G.-L.d., *Corinne, or Italy* (London: M. Peltier, 1807).
Stark, F., *Baghdad Sketches* (London: John Murray, 1939).
Stasio, C. d., 'Arnold Bennett and Late-Victorian "Woman"', *Victorian Periodicals Review* 28 (1999): 40–53.
Stewart, S., *The Ruins Lesson: Meaning and Material in Western Culture* (Chicago: Chicago University Press, 2020).
Stobart, J., 'Identity, Competition and Place Promotion in the Five Towns', *Urban History* 30 (2003): 163–82.
Stoler, A. L., and F. Cooper, 'Between Metropole and Colony: Rethinking a Research Agenda', in *Tensions of Empire: Colonial Cultures in a Bourgeois World*, ed. F. Cooper and A. L. Stoler (Berkeley: University of California Press, 1997), 1–58.
*The Strand Magazine* 42 (July–December 1911): 323–30.
Straver, J. A. M., *Vaders en dochters. Molukse historie in de Nederlandse literatuur van de negentiende eeuw en haar weerklank in Indonesië* (Leiden University, doctoral thesis, 2018).
Stroh, S., *Gaelic Scotland in the Colonial Imagination: Anglophone Writing from 1600 to 1900* (Evanston: Northwestern University Press, 2017).
Sweetser, M. F., and S. Ford, *How to Know New York City: A Serviceable and Trustworthy Guide, Having Its Starting Point at the Grand Union Hotel, Just across the Street from the Grand Central Depot* (New York: Press of J. J. Little, 1900).
Symons, A., *Cities of Italy* (London: Dent, 1907).
Tabet, X., 'La "Venise nouvelle" de Pierre Daru', *Histoire de la République de Venise*, ed. P. Daru (Paris: Robert Laffont, 2004), ix–xliv.
Taylor, F., *Coventry: Thursday, 14 November 1940* (London: Bloomsbury, 2015).
Taylor, J., 'A Qualitative Exploration of the Reitz Reconciliation Process as an Exercise in Restorative Justice' (University of the Free State, MA dissertation, 2014).
Thesinger, W., *The Marsh Arabs* (London: Penguin Books, 1967).
Thomas, M., *The French Empire at War 1940–1945* (Manchester: Manchester University Press, 1998).
Thompson, C., 'Journeys to Authority: Reassessing Women's Travel Writing, 1763–1862', *Women's Writing* 24 (2017): 131–50.
———, 'Nineteenth-Century Travel Writing', in *The Cambridge History of Travel Writing*, ed. N. Das and T. Youngs (Cambridge: Cambridge University Press, 2019), 108–24.
———, *Travel Writing* (Abingdon: Routledge, 2011).
———, *Women's Travel Writings in India, 1777–1845*, vol. 1 (Abingdon: Routledge, 2020).
Tidrick, K., *Heart Beguiling Araby: The English Romance with Arabia* (London: I.B.Tauris, 1989).
Tiratsoo, N., 'Coventry', in *Urban Reconstruction in Britain and Japan, 1945–1955*, ed. N. Tiratsoo, J. Hasegawa, T. Mason and T. Matsumura (Luton: University of Luton Press, 2002), 24–25.
Tisdall, S., 'Public Discontent Rises as Jacob Zuma's Ship Sinks in South Africa', *The Guardian*, 5 April 2016.
Tomaini, P., *Varese Ligure. Insigne borgo ed antica pieve* (Città di Castello: A. c. Grafiche, 1978).
Trevelyan, G. M., 'Walking', in *Clio, a Muse, and Other Essays Literary and Pedestrian* (London: Longmans, Green, 1913).

Tucci, U., 'Ranke and the Venetian Document Market', *Syracuse University Library Associates Courier* 22, 1 (1987): 27–38.
Tyndale, W., *An Artist in the Riviera* (London: Hutchinson, 1914).
Urry, J., *The Tourist Gaze 3.0* (London: Sage, 2011).
Varisco, D., *Reading Orientalism: Said and the Unsaid* (Seattle: University of Washington Press, 2007).
Verwey, C., and M. Quayle, 'Whiteness, Racism and Afrikaner Identity in Post-Apartheid South Africa', *African Affairs* 111, 445 (2012): 551–75.
Walchester, K., *Our Own Fair Italy* (Bern: Verlag Peter Lang, 2007).
Ware, V., 'All the Rage: Decolonizing the History of the British Women's Suffrage Movement', *Cultural Studies* 34, 4 (2020): 521–45.
Warner, R., *A Tour through Cornwall in the Autumn of 1808* (Bath: Richard Cruttwell, 1809).
Warraq, I., *Defending the West: A Critique of Edward Said's Orientalism* (Amherst: Prometheus Books, 2007).
Warwick, P., *Black People and the South African War 1899–1902* (Cambridge: Cambridge University Press, 1983).
Waters, C., 'J. B. Priestley (1894–1984): Englishness and the Politics of Nostalgia', in *After the Victorians: Private Conscience and Public Duty in Modern Britain*, ed. S. Pedersen and P. Mandler (London: Routledge, 1994), 211–30.
Watkin, D., *The Roman Forum* (Cambridge: Harvard University Press, 2009).
Watkins, C., 'The Management History and Conservation of Terraces in the Val di Vara, Liguria', in *Ligurian Landscapes. Studies in Archaeology, Geography and History in Memory of Edoardo Grendi*, ed. R. Balzaretti, M. Pearce and C. Watkins (London: Accordia, 2004), 141–54.
Watkins, C., and R. Balzaretti, 'Experiences of Historical Ecology in Val di Vara', in *Dal documento al terreno. Storia e archeologia dei sistemi agro-silvo-pastorali. Attualità di una proposta storica*, ed. D. Moreno (Genoa: Genova University Press, 2019), 305–9.
W. B. H., 'Review: *The Flora of West Yorkshire*', *Nature* 38, 972 (1888): 147–48.
Westland, E., 'The Passionate Periphery: Cornwall and Romantic Fiction', in *Peripheral Visions: Images of Nationhood in Contemporary British Fiction*, ed. I. A. Bell (Cardiff: University of Wales Press, 1995), 153–72.
Wilkinson, E., *The Town That Was Murdered: The Life-Story of Jarrow* (London: V. Gollancz, 1939).
Winter, J., *Sites of Memory, Sites of Mourning: The Great War in European Cultural History* (Cambridge: Cambridge University Press, 1995).
Wordsworth, D., *Recollections of a Tour Made in Scotland – A. D. 1803* (Edinburgh, 1875).
———, *Recollections of a Tour Made in Scotland – A. D. 1803*, ed. C. K. Walker (Yale: Yale University Press, 1997).
Young, P., 'Rambles beyond Railways: Gothicised Place and Globalised Space in Victorian Cornwall', *Gothic Studies* 13, 1 (2011): 55–74.
Young, R., *Postcolonialism: An Historical Introduction* (Oxford: Wiley-Blackwell, 2001).
Youngs, T., *The Cambridge Introduction to Travel Writing* (Cambridge: Cambridge University Press, 2013).
———, *Travel Writing in the Nineteenth Century: Filling in the Blank Spaces* (London: Anthem Press, 2006).
Youngs, T., and C. Forsdick, *Travel Writing* (Oxford: Routledge, 2012).
Yusha, Z., and L. Caiyu, 'China's Commendation of Role Models Who Fought Covid-19 Signals the Country's Phased Victory in Virus Battle: Chief Epidemiologist', *Global Times*, 6 September 2020, https://www.globaltimes.cn/content/1200067.shtml.
Ziff, L., *Return Passages: Great American Travel Writing, 1780–1910* (New Haven: Yale University Press, 2000).

www.ingramcontent.com/pod-product-compliance
Lightning Source LLC
Chambersburg PA
CBHW021829300426
44114CB00009BA/376